Modeling and Optimization of Complex Engineering Systems under Uncertainties

Modeling and Optimization of Complex Engineering Systems under Uncertainties

Guest Editors

Debiao Meng
Shui Yu

MDPI

Basel • Beijing • Wuhan • Barcelona • Belgrade • Novi Sad • Cluj • Manchester

Guest Editors
Debiao Meng
School of Mechanical and Electrical Engineering
University of Electronic Science and Technology of China
Chengdu
China

Shui Yu
Shenzhen Institute for Advanced Study
University of Electronic Science and Technology of China
Shenzhen
China

Editorial Office
MDPI AG
Grosspeteranlage 5
4052 Basel, Switzerland

This is a reprint of the Special Issue, published open access by the journal *Mathematics* (ISSN 2227-7390), freely accessible at: https://www.mdpi.com/journal/mathematics/special_issues/Modeling_Optim_Complex_Eng_Syst.

For citation purposes, cite each article independently as indicated on the article page online and as indicated below:

Lastname, A.A.; Lastname, B.B. Article Title. *Journal Name* **Year**, *Volume Number*, Page Range.

ISBN 978-3-7258-7146-9 (Hbk)
ISBN 978-3-7258-7147-6 (PDF)
https://doi.org/10.3390/books978-3-7258-7147-6

Contents

About the Editors

Debiao Meng

Debiao Meng is currently a Professor in the School of Mechanical and Electrical Engineering, University of Electronic Science and Technology of China (UESTC), China. He obtained a BSc (2007) in Mechanical Engineering from Northwest A&F University and a Ph.D. degree from the School of Mechanical and Electrical Engineering, UESTC, with a major in Mechanical Engineering (2014). From 2013 to 2014, he was a joint Ph.D. student in the Department of Civil and Environmental Engineering at Vanderbilt University in the USA. Also, from 2014 to 2015, he was a visiting professor in Civil Engineering at the University of Bologna in Italy. His main research fields are structural integrity and uncertainty-based design optimization. He has published more than 90 journal and proceedings papers on system reliability analysis, multidisciplinary design optimization, surrogate modeling, and uncertainty quantification and propagation. He serves as the Editor-in-Chief of the *International Journal of Ocean Systems Management* and a member of the Early Career Editorial Board of the *International Journal of Structural Integrity* (JCR Q1).

Shui Yu

Shui Yu is currently an Associate Researcher in Shenzhen Institute for Advanced Study, University of Electronic Science and Technology of China. His research focuses on AI-powered automated design, reliability analysis, and optimization of electromechanical products, and surrogate modeling integrating knowledge and data. He has led 9 provincial/ministerial-level or above vertical projects, directed 3 horizontal projects funded by institutions such as the China Aerospace Innovation Institute, and has participated in more than 10 research initiatives, including projects under China's National Key R&D Program. As first author or corresponding author, he has published 20 papers in leading international journals in the fields of artificial intelligence, mechanical design, and reliability. One of his publications has been designated as an ESI Highly Cited Paper. Dr. Yu serves as a Guest Editor for *Mathematics* and *Complex Engineering Systems* and as a Youth Editorial Board Member of the *Journal of Electronic Mechanical Engineering*. He holds five national invention patents and two software copyrights.

mathematics

Editorial

Editorial for the Special Issue "Modeling and Optimization of Complex Engineering Systems Under Uncertainties"

Debiao Meng [1,*] and Shui Yu [2]

1 School of Mechanical and Electrical Engineering, University of Electronic Science and Technology of China, Chengdu 611731, China
2 Shenzhen Institute for Advanced Study, University of Electronic Science and Technology of China, Shenzhen 518110, China; yushui@uestc.edu.cn
* Correspondence: dbmeng@uestc.edu.cn

1. Introduction to This Special Issue

The contemporary engineering frontier is defined by a paradigm shift toward hyper-integrated systems operating within increasingly volatile environments, ranging from precision micro-electronics to critical large-scale infrastructure and sustainable energy ecosystems [1,2]. A pivotal challenge in this domain is the ubiquity of uncertainty—spanning inherent physical stochasticity to epistemic modeling deficits—which poses severe risks to structural integrity and operational continuity [3]. As traditional deterministic approaches struggle to cope with these complexities, often leading to over-conservative designs or catastrophic vulnerabilities, the development of robust modeling and optimization strategies has become paramount [4]. This Special Issue underscores the critical need to transition from static safety margins to dynamic uncertainty management, thereby guaranteeing the long-term resilience, cost-effectiveness, and sustainability of complex engineering systems facing real-world unpredictability.

This Special Issue, titled "*Modeling and Optimization of Complex Engineering Systems under Uncertainties*", was curated to address this critical gap by assembling a collection of high-quality research that bridges advanced mathematical theories with practical engineering applications. The primary objective of this volume is to explore novel methodologies that can quantify, manage, and optimize systems despite the presence of stochastic variables, material degradation, and environmental fluctuations. The contributions selected for this issue demonstrate a convergence of disciplines, merging reliability-based design optimization, scientific machine learning, swarm intelligence, and rigorous mechanical analysis to solve problems that were previously intractable. By integrating probabilistic methods with deep learning and heuristic algorithms, the researchers featured herein provide a roadmap for the next generation of resilient engineering systems. This editorial synthesizes the significant findings of the eight published papers, categorizing them into design strategies, control methodologies, and practical applications, thereby highlighting the multidisciplinary nature of the solutions required to navigate the complexities of modern engineering under uncertainty.

2. Designs Proposed in This Special Issue

The establishment of robust design frameworks is the foundational step in mitigating the risks associated with engineering uncertainties [5–8]. Two significant contributions to this Special Issue address the fundamental challenge of design optimization and threshold determination under conditions where parameters are not fixed but fluctuate within probabilistic or interval bounds.

 https://doi.org/10.3390/math14020371

The work by Yang et al. (Contribution 1) introduces a sophisticated Reliability-Based Design Optimization strategy capable of handling hybrid uncertainties. Their research confronts the computational inefficiency often plaguing traditional double-loop reliability methods by constructing a decoupled framework that integrates an improved particle swarm optimization algorithm with a simulated annealing algorithm. This hybrid approach allows for the efficient identification of the most probable point of failure without the prohibitive computational cost usually associated with high-dimensional nonlinear problems. By validating their method on complex mechanical components such as gear reducers and composite cylinders, they demonstrate that decoupling the reliability analysis from the optimization loop can significantly enhance both solution speed and design accuracy. Complementing this algorithmic approach to design, the study by Hao et al. (Contribution 2) focuses on the material-to-mechanical analysis required to establish safety thresholds for critical infrastructure. Their investigation into the GINA gaskets used in immersed tunnels provides a rigorous method for determining warning thresholds for deformation. By analyzing the hyperelastic constitutive models of rubber materials and considering the uneven settlement patterns of tunnel elements, they derive a graded warning mechanism. This design-centric research connects the material properties of the gasket, specifically its hardness and cross-sectional shape, to the macroscopic mechanical behavior of the tunnel joint under shear and bending loads.

These two papers collectively illustrate that effective design under uncertainty requires a dual approach that encompasses both the algorithmic efficiency of optimization solvers and the rigorous mechanical definition of safety limits for physical components.

3. Control Methods Discussed in This Special Issue

Beyond the initial design phase, the operational phase of complex systems requires advanced control methods and algorithmic tools to manage uncertainties that arise during real-time performance. The contributions in this section highlight the growing role of artificial intelligence and deep learning in creating control mechanisms that are robust to noise and data imperfections. Erbet et al. (Contribution 3) propose a comprehensive methodology for uncertainty-aware Scientific Machine Learning. Their work addresses a critical gap in the application of neural networks to physical systems by integrating Bayesian inference via Markov Chain Monte Carlo methods with the training of soft sensors. By rigorously quantifying the epistemic and aleatory uncertainties in the model identification process, they provide a framework that ensures machine learning models remain reliable even when trained on synthetic or limited data, as demonstrated in their polymerization reactor case study. In a similar vein of enhancing algorithmic performance, Yang et al. (Contribution 4) presents a method for the parameter optimization of analog circuits. Their approach couples a bidirectional Long Short-Term Memory network with an enhanced whale optimization algorithm. This combination allows for the precise tuning of circuit parameters by leveraging the sequence processing capabilities of the neural network to model complex dependencies, while the swarm intelligence algorithm efficiently navigates the hyperparameter space. This method proves particularly effective in handling the nonlinearities inherent in analog circuit design. Furthermore, the work by Ander et al. (Contribution 5) addresses the specific control challenge of simultaneous object localization and classification in robotic systems. They introduce a novel loss function within a custom training loop for Convolutional Neural Networks. By balancing the cross-entropy loss for classification with the mean squared error for regression, their method improves the ability of robotic vision systems to accurately locate objects in unstructured environments. This contribution is vital for the development of collaborative robots that must operate safely alongside humans in manufacturing settings where visual data is

 https://doi.org/10.3390/math14020371

often noisy or ambiguous. Together, these papers underscore the necessity of embedding uncertainty quantification and robust optimization directly into the control algorithms that govern modern engineering systems [9–11].

4. Applications Discussed in This Special Issue

The theoretical models and control strategies discussed above find their ultimate validation when applied to specific, high-stakes engineering problems ranging from renewable energy to civil infrastructure and anomaly detection. The Special Issue features several papers that demonstrate the practical utility of these advanced methods in diagnosing faults and ensuring operational continuity. Olivier and Jung (Contribution 6) tackle the challenge of structural health monitoring in laminated composite plates, materials that are critical to the aerospace and automotive industries. They propose an unsupervised anomaly detection framework that combines a self-attention autoencoder with a Gaussian mixture model. This architecture is designed to learn the latent representations of healthy Lamb wave signals and identify damages as statistical outliers. By utilizing a generative adversarial network to augment their training data, they successfully address the common issue of data scarcity in damage scenarios, proving that deep learning can effectively detect delamination and cracks without extensive labeled datasets. In the renewable energy sector, Gao et al. (Contribution 7) investigate the reliability of wind turbine gears under multistage random loadings. Their research develops a residual strength degradation model that accounts for the interaction between loads and the sequence of loading events. By integrating the rain flow counting method with the Goodman correction, they map the seasonal variations in wind load to the fatigue life of the gear, providing a dynamic reliability assessment that is crucial for the preventive maintenance of wind farms. Finally, Eric et al. (Contribution 8) applies swarm intelligence to the construction industry, a sector rife with uncertainties related to human logistics and safety. Their study utilizes an Artificial Bee Colony algorithm to optimize the movement paths of workers on construction sites to maintain safe physical distancing. This application demonstrates that mathematical optimization tools can be effectively deployed to solve logistical challenges in real time, ensuring worker safety during complex operations such as those necessitated by the COVID-19 pandemic. These diverse applications highlight the versatility of the proposed mathematical frameworks, showing that whether the system is a composite plate, a wind turbine gearbox, or a construction crew, the core principles of modeling uncertainty remain applicable and effective.

5. Conclusions

The collection of articles presented in this Special Issue *"Modeling and Optimization of Complex Engineering Systems under Uncertainties"* offers a comprehensive overview of the current state of the art in reliability engineering and applied mathematics. The research highlights a fundamental transition in engineering design and control, moving away from static safety factors toward dynamic, probabilistic, and data-driven frameworks. We have observed that hybrid optimization algorithms, such as the coupled Simulated Annealing and Particle Swarm Optimization, offer superior efficiency in navigating high-dimensional design spaces. We have seen that Scientific Machine Learning can be made robust to uncertainty through Bayesian inference, ensuring that soft sensors and control models remain trustworthy in critical applications. Furthermore, the successful application of these methods to diverse fields, including tunnel engineering, wind energy, structural health monitoring, and construction safety, confirms the universal relevance of uncertainty quantification. However, challenges remain, particularly in the computational cost of uncertainty propagation for large-scale systems and the interpretability of deep learning models

https://doi.org/10.3390/math14020371

in safety-critical contexts. Future research must continue to refine these methodologies, perhaps by exploring physics-informed neural networks that enforce physical laws to reduce the data requirements for uncertainty quantification. We hope that the methodologies and findings presented in this volume will serve as a foundation for future inquiries and inspire researchers to further explore the intricate dynamics of complex engineering systems. We express our sincere gratitude to all the authors for their valuable contributions and to the reviewers for their rigorous assessment, which ensured the high scientific quality of this Special Issue.

Author Contributions: Writing—original draft preparation, D.M.; writing—review and editing, D.M. and S.Y. All authors have read and agreed to the published version of the manuscript.

Funding: This research was funded by Guangdong Basic and Applied Basic Research Foundation, grant number No. 2024A1515240025.

Data Availability Statement: Some data are available from the corresponding authors upon request.

Acknowledgments: The authors are very grateful to the *Mathematics* editorial office for their guidance, assistance, and help that led to the success of this Special Issue.

Conflicts of Interest: The authors declare that they have no conflict of interest.

List of Contributions:

1. Yang, S.; Wang, H.; Xu, Y.; Guo, Y.; Pan, L.; Zhang, J.; Guo, X.; Meng, D.; Wang, J. A Coupled Simulated Annealing and Particle Swarm Optimization Reliability-Based Design Optimization Strategy under Hybrid Uncertainties. *Mathematics* **2023**, *11*, 4790.
2. Ding, H.; Huang, J.; Jiang, X.; Yan, Y.; Du, S.; Chen, J.; Ai, Q. Investigation of Warning Thresholds for the Deformation of GINA Gasket of Immersed Tunnel Based on a Material-to-Mechanical Analysis. *Mathematics* **2023**, *11*, 1010.
3. Costa, E.A.; Rebello, C.M.; Fontana, M.; Schnitman, L.; Nogueira, I.B.R. A Robust Learning Methodology for Uncertain-ty-Aware Scientific Machine Learning Models. *Mathematics* **2023**, *11*, 74.
4. Yang, H.; Yang, S.; Meng, D.; Hu, C.; Wu, C.; Yang, B.; Nie, P.; Si, Y.; Su, X. Optimization of Analog Circuit Parameters Using Bidirectional Long Short-Term Memory Coupled with an Enhanced Whale Optimization Algorithm. *Mathematics* **2025**, *13*, 121.
5. Sanchez-Chica, A.; Ugartemendia-Telleria, B.; Zulueta, E.; Fernandez-Gamiz, U.; Gomez-Hidalgo, J.M. A New Loss Function for Simultaneous Object Localization and Classification. *Mathematics* **2023**, *11*, 1205.
6. Munyaneza, O.; Sohn, J.W. Anomaly Detection on Laminated Composite Plate Using Self-Attention Autoencoder and Gaussian Mixture Model. *Mathematics* **2025**, *13*, 2445.
7. Gao, J.; Liu, Y.; Yuan, Y.; Heng, F. Residual Strength Modeling and Reliability Analysis of Wind Turbine Gear under Different Random Loadings. *Mathematics* **2023**, *11*, 4013.
8. Forcael, E.; Carriel, I.; Opazo-Vega, A.; Moreno, F.; Orozco, F.; Romo, R.; Agdas, D. Artificial Bee Colony Algorithm to Optimize the Safety Distance of Workers in Construction Projects. *Mathematics* **2024**, *12*, 2087.

References

1. Pereira, J.; Di Meo, G.A.; Van Den Einden, B.; Sacré, P. Flexible Multimode Avionics Enabled by Hyper Integrated Software Defined Radio Solutions. In Proceedings of the 2025 Integrated Communications, Navigation and Surveillance Conference (ICNS), Brussels, Belgium, 8–10 April 2025; pp. 1–12.
2. Wu, Z.; Zhang, H. Review on Autonomous and Sustainable Urban Mobility Systems: Challenges and Future Directions. *TechRxiv* **2025**. [CrossRef] [PubMed]
3. Billah, M.M.; Elleithy, M.; Khan, W.; Yıldız, S.; Eğer, Z.E.; Liu, S.; Acar, P. Uncertainty quantification of microstructures: A perspective on forward and inverse problems for mechanical properties of aerospace materials. *Adv. Eng. Mater.* **2025**, *27*, 2401299. [CrossRef]

https://doi.org/10.3390/math14020371

4. Jia, X.; Hou, W.; Papadimitriou, C. Hierarchical Bayesian modeling for uncertainty quantification and reliability updating using data. *J. Reliab. Sci. Eng.* **2025**, *1*, 025002. [CrossRef]
5. Meng, D.; Yang, S.; De Jesus, A.M.P.; Fazeres-Ferradosa, T.; Zhu, S.-P. A novel hybrid adaptive Kriging and water cycle algorithm for reliability-based design and optimization strategy: Application in offshore wind turbine monopile. *Comput. Methods Appl. Mech. Eng.* **2023**, *412*, 116083. [CrossRef]
6. Yang, C.; Yu, Q. Multi-objective optimization-inspired set theory-based regularization approach for force reconstruction with bounded uncertainties. *Comput. Methods Appl. Mech. Eng.* **2025**, *438*, 117814. [CrossRef]
7. Meng, D.; Yang, S.; De Jesus, A.M.P.; Zhu, S.-P. A novel Kriging-model-assisted reliability-based multidisciplinary design optimization strategy and its application in the offshore wind turbine tower. *Renew. Energy* **2023**, *203*, 407–420.
8. Azarhoosh, Z.; Ghazaan, M.I. A review of recent advances in surrogate models for uncertainty quantification of high-dimensional engineering applications. *Comput. Methods Appl. Mech. Eng.* **2025**, *433*, 117508. [CrossRef]
9. Wang, K.; Shen, C.; Li, X.; Lu, J. Uncertainty quantification for safe and reliable autonomous vehicles: A review of methods and applications. *IEEE Trans. Intell. Transp. Syst.* **2025**, *26*, 2880–2896. [CrossRef]
10. Wang, T.; Wang, Y.; Zhou, J.; Peng, B.; Song, X.; Zhang, C.; Sun, X.; Niu, Q.; Liu, J.; Chen, S.; et al. From aleatoric to epistemic: Exploring uncertainty quantification techniques in artificial intelligence. *arXiv* **2025**, arXiv:2501.03282. [CrossRef]
11. Shi, Y.; Wei, P.; Feng, K.; Feng, D.C.; Beer, M. A survey on machine learning approaches for uncertainty quantification of engineering systems. *Mach. Learn. Comput. Sci. Eng.* **2025**, *1*, 11. [CrossRef]

https://doi.org/10.3390/math14020371

mathematics

MDPI

Article

A Coupled Simulated Annealing and Particle Swarm Optimization Reliability-Based Design Optimization Strategy under Hybrid Uncertainties

Shiyuan Yang [1,2], Hongtao Wang [1,2], Yihe Xu [3], Yongqiang Guo [4], Lidong Pan [4], Jiaming Zhang [4], Xinkai Guo [2], Debiao Meng [1,2,*] and Jiapeng Wang [1]

1 School of Mechanical and Electrical Engineering, University of Electronic Science and Technology of China, Chengdu 611731, China
2 Institute of Electronic and Information Engineering of UESTC in Guangdong, Dongguan 523808, China
3 Glasgow College, University of Electronic Science and Technology of China, Chengdu 611731, China
4 Beijing Research Institute of Mechanical & Electrical Technology Ltd., Beijing 100083, China
* Correspondence: dbmeng@uestc.edu.cn

Abstract: As engineering systems become increasingly complex, reliability-based design optimization (RBDO) has been extensively studied in recent years and has made great progress. In order to achieve better optimization results, the mathematical model used needs to consider a large number of uncertain factors. Especially when considering mixed uncertainty factors, the contradiction between the large computational cost and the efficiency of the optimization algorithm becomes increasingly fierce. How to quickly find the optimal most probable point (MPP) will be an important research direction of RBDO. To solve this problem, this paper constructs a new RBDO method framework by combining an improved particle swarm algorithm (PSO) with excellent global optimization capabilities and a decoupling strategy using a simulated annealing algorithm (SA). This study improves the efficiency of the RBDO solution by quickly solving MPP points and decoupling optimization strategies. At the same time, the accuracy of RBDO results is ensured by enhancing global optimization capabilities. Finally, this article illustrates the superiority and feasibility of this method through three calculation examples.

Keywords: reliability-based design and optimization; particle swarm optimization algorithm; simulated annealing algorithm; most probable point

MSC: 60C05; 65Y04; 65Y20; 62D05

1. Introduction

The construction of engineering systems will inevitably be affected by complex uncertain factors [1–3]. Especially with the increasing complexity of engineering systems, various uncertainties will be mixed and difficult to distinguish [4]. If these factors cannot be analyzed accurately, the reliability and security of the engineering system cannot be guaranteed [5–8]. At present, the Reliability-Based Design Optimization (RBDO) method has been widely used to improve the reliability and safety of complex mechanical systems [9]. However, with the growth of social demand, new technology should be introduced constantly to improve the development level of reliability optimization design and meet the needs of economic development for engineering [10].

RBDO takes into account the inevitable random factors in engineering systems [11–14]. It ensures that the reliability of the object system is within an acceptable range by optimizing the objective function [15]. It is an extension of deterministic optimization methods and is used to solve complex uncertain engineering system optimization problems [16,17]. In recent years, RBDO has been discussed and studied by a large number of scholars. Many algorithms and models have been developed to solve the RBDO problem. Liao et al. [18] adopted an improved double-loop calculation method to improve the computational efficiency of the RBDO model. In this method, RBDO is divided into two layers and is calculated step by step through reliability analysis (RA) and deterministic optimization (DO). The optimization strategy of this double-loop method usually has a low optimization rate. Wang et al. [19] proposed an improved Modified Conjugate Gradient Approach (MCGA) to improve the RBDO efficiency of nonlinear function functions. This method uses the improved conjugate gradient method (CGA) to search the most probable point (MPP) point direction, which improves the efficiency of RBDO. At the same time, unlike gradient algorithms, metaheuristic algorithms are widely used in RBDO methods. Safaeian et al. used the particle swarm algorithm (PSO) [20] combined with a weighted simulation-based design method for design optimization, which improved the accuracy of the RBDO method and the ability to solve general RBDO problems. However, this method uses a double-loop method to solve the problem, which is less efficient. Zhong et al. used a Harris Hawks Optimization algorithm [21], which has a higher efficiency in solving the global optimal solution. Since the derivative of the limit state function is not required, this method has a higher calculation speed, but its accuracy still has room for improvement. Jafar et al. [22] improved the previous Harris Hawks Optimization algorithm and transformed the problem of solving unit vectors with a highly nonlinear performance function into a constrained optimization problem, which greatly improved the solution efficiency of this method.

The above algorithm does not consider mixed uncertainties. However, studies have long found that mixed uncertainty also has a great impact on the analysis of engineering systems [23]. In recent years, engineering problems considering mixed uncertainties have been extensively studied. Such problems containing multiple uncertainties pose challenges to the optimization efficiency and difficulty of RBDO. Zhang et al. [24] proposed a hybrid uncertainty analysis method based on probability and evidence theory, which improved the efficiency of RBDO analysis. Wang et al. [25] proposed an RBDO solution strategy that relies on conditioning processing and convexity theorem. This method uses an improved genetic algorithm and has a relatively good application effect on optimization tasks that consider time-varying and time-invariant mixed variables. However, this method is only suitable for time-related RBDO problems. Thu et al. [26] used the PSO algorithm combined with the Gaussian process to propose a new reliability design optimization method. This method utilizes the excellent global optimization capabilities of the PSO method, but its optimization capabilities for engineering problems that consider uncertainty are yet to be discussed. As shown in Figure 1, the methods used in past studies are demonstrated. Due to space limitations, only typical algorithm strategies are selected to demonstrate the development process.

After the literature research, it was found that the PSO method can better solve the problem of local convergence in the analysis process than other heuristic algorithms. Compared with the double-loop method with huge computational cost and the single-loop method optimization algorithm with difficulty in ensuring the optimization accuracy of high-dimensional nonlinear problems, the decoupled optimization strategy combined with the computationally efficient simulated annealing (SA) algorithm has a higher solution speed. This study combines these two optimization algorithms and proposes a new RBDO method. It is used to solve the RBDO problem of high-dimensional nonlinear engineering structures considering mixed uncertainties. This method is dedicated to solving the purpose of improving the accuracy and computational efficiency of optimization results during the optimization process.

The rest of the parts of this paper include: Section 2 summarizes the PSO algorithm and SA algorithm; Section 3 illustrates the idea of combining the two algorithms. Section 4 verifies and compares with other methods through examples; Section 5 provides a summary and future work.

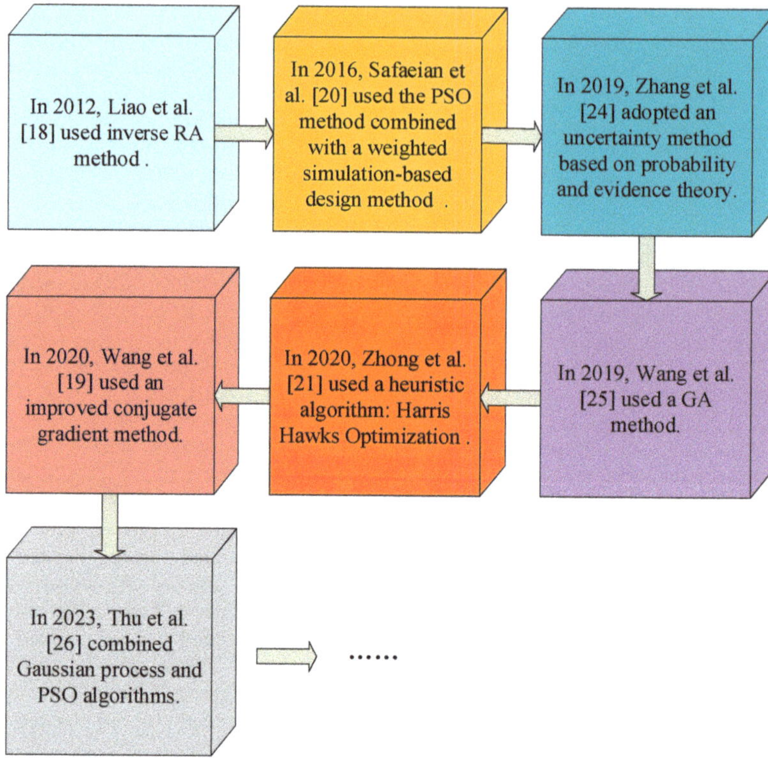

Figure 1. Development history of algorithm strategies in engineering structure analysis and optimization.

2. Two Algorithms for Optimizing the Problem

2.1. Particle Swarm Optimization

2.1.1. Definition of Particle Swarm Optimization

PSO also known as the foraging algorithm, is a widely used meta-heuristic algorithm, which is derived from the study of bird predation behavior [27,28]. The algorithm is originally a simplified model based on swarm intelligence inspired by the regularity of bird swarm activity. Based on the observation of the activity behavior of animal clusters, the PSO algorithm makes use of the information sharing of each individual in the group, so that the movement of the whole group can evolve from disorder to order in the problem-solving space [29,30]. Finally, it can obtain the optimal solution successfully.

In PSO, the optimal solution is generated by reducing the distance between each search individual and the target point [31]. Under this goal, the position of the particle varies depending on two factors: the velocity of the particle and the current position of the particle. During the search for the optimal solution, the velocity of the particle and the current position of the particle are constantly changing. The value of velocity is determined by the particle with the optimal current position and the particle with the optimal global position. Its mathematical expression is

$$\begin{cases} V_{k+1} = wV_k + c_1 r_1 (p_{best} - X_k) + c_2 r_2 (g_{best} - X_k) \\ X_{k+1} = X_k + V_{k+1} \end{cases} \tag{1}$$

where V_k represents the particle velocity of k iterations; X_k represents the particle position of k iterations; w represents inertia weight; p_{best} represents the optimal value of the particle at its current position; g_{best} represents the global optimal value; c_1, c_2, respectively represent individual learning coefficient and global learning coefficient; r is a random value between 0 and 1, called the learning rate.

In the process of iteration, speed boundary detection should be carried out after each speed update, that is, whether the maximum speed limit is exceeded. Generally, adopting $v(v > v_{\max}) = v_{\max}$, so as the location. The common termination conditions are reaching the set number of iterations and keeping the fitness for n times without changing [32].

2.1.2. Optimization of PSO Algorithm

Equation (1), w describes the "inertia" of particles. In the early stage of iteration, the value of w should be larger to ensure the independent flight of each particle and to search the space as fully as possible. In the later stage of iteration, the value of w should be smaller and more "learned" from other particles. Similarly, c_1 and c_2 are the maximum flight steps toward individual and global extremes, respectively. c_1 should be larger in the early stage, while c_2 should be larger in the late stage, to balance the local search ability and global search ability of particles. In the PSO algorithm, the parameters w, c, and r jointly affect the search direction of particles. So even if other particles find a better solution, the inertia of the current particles is too large to fly to a better position quickly.

Against the deficiency of standard particle swarm algorithm, through the introduction of new mechanism and parameter optimization of adaptive changes of PSO algorithm [33]. Firstly, the parameter optimization of the PSO algorithm. As mentioned above, the inertia weight w should be larger in the early stage of search and smaller in the late stage, so that particles can search the entire design space as much as possible in the early stage and more carefully in the late stage. For this optimization strategy, the inertia weight w is adjusted as follows [30]:

$$w_k = w_{\min} + \frac{ger - k}{ger}(w_{\max} - w_{\min}), \tag{2}$$

where w_k represents the inertia weight at each iteration; $w_{\min}$ and $w_{\max}$, respectively, denote the lower and upper bounds of the inertia weight; k represents the number of current iterations; ger represents the total number of iterations; as can be seen from the expression of w_k, the value of inertia weight w_k decreases monotonically, realizing the function of decreasing gradually with the process of search. Similarly, the same optimization strategy is adopted for the learning coefficient c. The expression of the optimized c_1 and c_2 is shown as follows:

$$\begin{cases} c_{k1} = c_{\min} + \frac{ger-k}{ger}(c_{\max} - c_{\min}) \\ c_{k2} = c_{\max} - \frac{ger-k}{ger}(c_{\max} - c_{\min}) \end{cases}, \tag{3}$$

where c_{k1} represents the individual learning coefficient in each iteration; c_{k2} represents the global learning coefficient of each iteration. In addition, the learning rate r is no longer a random value between 0 and 1, but a random variable subject to the standard normal distribution, namely $r \sim (0,1)$.

Secondly, to make the search process avoid falling into local optima and focus more on global optima, an additional method of updating particle position X and velocity V are used for reference here. The method is as follows:

$$\begin{cases} X_{k+1} = X_k + V_{k+1}^E \\ V_{k+1}^E = r_3(g_{best} - X_k) + Normrand(0,1) \times \gamma_k \\ \gamma_k = \sqrt{1 - k/ger} \end{cases}, \tag{4}$$

where the new position is calculated by the global optimal value and the random number obeying the normal distribution. r_3 is a random number between 0 and 1; $Normrand(0,1)$ is a randomly generated vector conforming to the standard normal distribution; γ_k is an adaptively variable step that changes the size of the random value.

As can be seen from the expression of V_{k+1}^E, since a random value is introduced, the probability of falling into a local optimal when updating the position can be reduced.

However, the efficiency of the search will decrease accordingly in the meantime. In order to balance the two results, a new decision mechanism is introduced here:

$$X_{k+1} = \begin{cases} X_k + V_{k+1}^E, r \leq P_k \\ X_k + V_{k+1}, r > P_k \end{cases}, \tag{5}$$

where r is a random number between 0 and 1; P_k represents the probability of the particle choosing two position updating modes. The expression is

$$P_k = 0.2 + 0.8\sqrt{k/ger}. \tag{6}$$

As can be seen from the expression of P_k, with the progress of iteration, the value of P_k keeps increasing, which makes the probability of using V_{k+1}^E to update the speed of V correspondingly increase.

This mechanism for updating particle positions ensures that the particle is more focused on the global optimal value later in the search process. This improves the efficiency to some extent and reduces the probability of falling into local optimal.

2.2. Simulated Annealing Algorithm

2.2.1. Definition of Simulated Annealing Algorithm

The annealing process of a metal involves heating the metal to a sufficiently high temperature and then letting it slowly cool down to give the metal some properties it did not have before [34–36]. When the temperature increases, the particles inside the solid become disordered as the temperature increases. An increase in internal energy then occurs and the particles become unstable. The particles gradually become orderly when slowly cooled. As the energy decreases, the particles become stable [37]. The simulated annealing algorithm starts from a higher initial temperature. With the continuous decline of temperature parameters, the algorithm combines the probability jump characteristics to randomly find the global optimal solution of the objective function in the solution space.

2.2.2. Simulated Annealing Algorithm

The SA mechanism can avoid falling into local optimum to some extent. Different from many intelligent optimization algorithms, the SA algorithm will jump to the solution with a certain probability. Even if it finds a worse solution than the current solution in the process of local search, it can avoid falling into the local optimal [38]. This way of updating solutions requires an important judgment criterion called the Metropolis criterion:

$$P = \begin{cases} 1, E_{t+1} < E_t \\ e^{\frac{-(E_{t+1}-E_t)}{kT}}, E_{t+1} \geq E_t \end{cases} \tag{7}$$

where P is the probability of accepting the new solution; E_t is the system energy corresponding to the current solution X_t (objective function); k is the temperature drop coefficient, which is a value between 0 and 1. T indicates the initial temperature. Based on this criterion, it can be concluded that (here is to find the minimum value):

(1) When the objective function corresponding to the new solution is less than the objective function value of the current solution, it will accept the new solution. That is, the probability of accepting the new solution is 1;

(2) When the corresponding objective function of the new solution is greater than the objective function value of the current solution, the new solution will be accepted with a certain probability. When other variables are certain, the more the value of the objective function corresponding to the new solution exceeds the value of the objective function of the current solution, the smaller the probability of accepting the new solution.

The steps of the SA algorithm are as follows:

Step 1: Set the initial temperature T; The initial solution X_0 is generated randomly and the objective function $E(X_0)$ is calculated;
Step 2: Make $T = kT, k \in (0, 1)$;
Step 3: Make random perturbation to the current solution X_t, generate a new solution X_{t+1} in its field, and calculate its corresponding function value $E(X_{t+1})$. Meanwhile, judge whether to accept the new solution according to the Metropolis criterion above;
Step 4: At temperature T, iterate the disturbance and acceptance process for L times;
Step 5: Determine whether the terminal temperature is reached. If so, terminate; otherwise, return to step 2.

3. The Combination of Intelligent Algorithms

3.1. First-Order Reliability Method

3.1.1. First-Order Reliability Method

The basic idea of the First-order reliability method (FORM) is to simplify the joint probability density function $f_x(x)$ and the approximate limit state function $g(x)$, primarily by performing a first-order Taylor approximation expansion at MPP [39–42]. The process of using FORM to calculate reliability includes coordinate space conversion and integral boundary approximation [43,44].

Coordinate space conversion refers to converting random variables subject to various probability distributions into variables subject to a standard normal distribution by the Rosenblatt method [45]. Suppose the random variable follows the normal distribution with mean value and standard deviation value, then the random variable transformed by the Rosenblatt method is

$$u = \frac{x - \mu}{\sigma}. \tag{8}$$

The approximation of the integral boundary is an important part of FORM. Its main idea is to perform first-order Taylor expansion of the integral boundary $g(u) = 0$ to make the integral solution of failure probability easier. The first-order Taylor expansion of $g(u)$ can be expressed as

$$g(u) = g(u^*) + \nabla g(u^*)(u - u^*)^T, \tag{9}$$

where u^* represents the expansion point; $\nabla g(u^*)$ represents the gradient of the expansion point. To reduce the precision loss caused by Taylor expansion, the MPP point on the fundamental boundary $g(u) = 0$ is expanded. Search for MPP points on integral boundary $g(u) = 0$, that is, maximize the joint probability density:

$$\begin{cases} \max & \prod\limits_{i=1}^{n} \frac{1}{\sqrt{2\pi}} e^{-\frac{u_i^2}{2}} \\ \text{s.t.} & g(u) = 0 \end{cases}. \tag{10}$$

By observing Equation (10), it can be seen that the above process is a constrained optimization problem. The deformation of Equation (10) is carried out:

$$\prod_{i=1}^{n} \frac{1}{\sqrt{2\pi}} e^{-\frac{u_i^2}{2}} = \frac{1}{\sqrt{2\pi}} e^{-\frac{1}{2}\sum\limits_{i=1}^{n} u_i^2}. \tag{11}$$

And,

$$\max \prod_{i=1}^{n} \frac{1}{\sqrt{2\pi}} e^{-\frac{u_i^2}{2}} \sim \min \sum_{i=1}^{n} u_i^2. \tag{12}$$

Therefore, the search model of MPP points can be expressed as:

$$\begin{cases} \min & \|u\| \\ \text{s.t.} & g(u) = 0' \end{cases} \tag{13}$$

where $\|u\| = \sqrt{u_1{}^2 + \cdots + u_n{}^2}$ represents the magnitude of the vector u. The above formula is solved to obtain $u = u^*$, which is the MPP point. Let $\beta = \|u^*\|$, from the perspective of two-dimensional geometry, the MPP point can be viewed as the point $g(u) = 0$ tangent to a circle centered at the origin and with radius β. According to literature, the calculation formula of reliability can be expressed as:

$$R = \phi(\beta), \tag{14}$$

where $\phi(\cdot)$ represents the cumulative distribution function obeying normal distribution.

The above are the general steps of the First-order reliability analysis method. According to different solving methods, FORM can be divided into the Reliability Index Approach (RIA) [40] and the Performance Measure Approach (PMA) [46].

3.1.2. Reliability Index Method

RIA uses a reliability index instead of failure probability constraints, the mathematical model is the MPP point search model [47–50]. It can be seen that the mathematical model is an optimization problem. A variety of optimization algorithms, such as Sequential Quadratic Programming (SQP), can be used to solve the optimization model.

3.1.3. Performance Measure Approach

When the failure probability is 0 or 1, the corresponding reliability index will approach infinity or infinitesimal, resulting in RIA failure. At this time, PMA can be used to solve the problem. Its mathematical model is [51]:

$$\begin{cases} \min & g(u) \\ \text{s.t.} & \|u\| = \beta_t \end{cases}{}', \tag{15}$$

where β_t represents the target reliability index. The above model indicates that under the given reliability, if $g(u) > 0$, it means that the solution can meet the given reliability requirements.

Through the mathematical model of RIA and PMA, it can be seen that the solution of the two ways is a reciprocal inverse process. The difference is that the feasible region of PMA is a sphere, while that of RIA is a hypersurface. In terms of computational efficiency, PMA has more advantages than RIA.

3.1.4. Reliability Analysis Method Considering Stochastic and Interval Uncertainties

In the above introduction to FORM, design variables are random variables that obey a normal distribution. However, in many practical engineering applications, the distribution of some random variables may not be clear [52–54]. The possible values of these uncertain variables are usually only in the specified interval without accurate distribution information. That is, there is interval uncertainty. When dealing with such mixed uncertainty RBDO problems, the computational complexity will be greatly increased. A simple method is to treat the interval variables as random variables to approximate the calculation. Although this method can simplify the reliability analysis, it cannot guarantee the accuracy of the results [55]. To solve such problems, Du et al. [23] proposed a kind of mixed uncertainty analysis method.

Compared with the reliability analysis considering random and interval uncertainty, some changes should be made based on the original calculation model. The transformed RIA model is directly presented here:

$$\begin{cases} \min & \|u_{MPP}(y)\| \\ \text{s.t.} & g(u, y) = 0 \\ & y^L \le y \le y^U \end{cases}, \tag{16}$$

where y represents interval variable; y^L represents the lower bound of the interval; y^U is the upper bound of the interval. Similarly, the PMA mathematical model considering stochastic and interval uncertainty is:

$$\begin{cases} \min & g(d,u,y) \\ s.t. & \|u\| = \beta_t \\ & y^L \le y \le y^U \end{cases} . \tag{17}$$

It can be seen that reliability analysis considering random and interval uncertainty is equivalent to adding a set of interval variables and changing the failure boundary based on reliability analysis considering random uncertainty. The rest parts are the same exactly. Therefore, when there is interval uncertainty, reliability analysis using the above method will not bring about redundant calculation steps, so it will not significantly reduce the calculation efficiency.

3.1.5. Method of Solving MPP Points by Improving PSO

For FORM, the main task is to solve the MPP points. According to the mathematical models of RIA and PMA, the solution of MPP points is an optimization problem with constraints. When solving optimization problems, intelligent optimization algorithms, including PSO, do not need gradient information [56–60]. They can deal with discrete variable optimization problems since they have strong global search ability [61,62]. The detailed steps of MPP point solving using the improved PSO algorithm are as follows.

When an intelligent optimization algorithm is used to solve MPP points, the probability constraint model in first-order reliability analysis can be processed by penalty function in general [63], as shown below:

$$\min f = \|U\| + \eta \max\{0, g(X)\}, \tag{18}$$

where f represents fitness; η represents the penalty factor, whose expression is:

$$\eta = \frac{100}{|g(\mu)|} \tag{19}$$

Taking fitness f as the optimization objective, the general steps of solving MPP points by using the improved PSO algorithm are shown as follows:

Step 1: Set the initial conditions for searching MPP points, including the limit state function $g(X)$, the probability distribution function of the design variable X (a normal distribution with mean value μ and standard deviation σ), parameters of PSO algorithm, namely: population number N, the total number of iterations ger, inertia coefficient w, and flight step length c;
Step 2: Set the boundary conditions, including the lower bound $X^L = \mu - 5\sigma$ and upper bound $X^U = \mu + 5\sigma$ of the design variable; the maximum value $v_{\max} = X^U - X^L/100$ and minimum value $v_{\min} = -v_{\max}$ of the speed;
Step 3: Generate the initial population. The initial position $X_0 = X^L + r \times (X^U - X^L)$ and initial velocity $V_0 = v_{\min} + r \times (v_{\max} - v_{\min})$ of the population should be calculated. The penalty factor η should be set;
Step 4: Update local optimal value p_{best} and global optimal value g_{best}. Firstly, the design variable U was converted into the random variable X, which obeyed the standard normal distribution. Then, fitness $f = \|U\| + \eta \max\{0, g(X)\}$ was calculated. Finally, p_{best} and g_{best} were screened out;
Step 5: Update the population location. The population location updating method mentioned above was used to update all the particles;
Step 6: Check whether convergence occurs. The convergence condition can be $g(g_{best}) < 0.001$ or $k = ger$. If either condition is satisfied, the iteration can be stopped and $X_{MPP} = g_{best}$ is output. Otherwise, do $k = k + 1$ and return to step (4) to continue the iteration.

The above is the method of solving MPP points by using the improved PSO.

3.2. The Used PSO Algorithm

By using the enhanced PSO algorithm, each constraint function is considered separately. During the algorithm process, the best fitness of each individual particle is updated through the constraint function, and then the best position of the particle is obtained by comparing the fitness of each individual. Through the optimal position of each particle in the population, the optimal population position for the current constraint function is finally obtained. Finally, by comparing the calculation results of each constraint function, the optimal MPP point is obtained. The calculation steps of the used PSO algorithm are shown in the Table 1.

Table 1. The calculation steps of the used PSO algorithm.

	The PSO Algorithm
Step 1	Firstly, PSO is used to generate a set of initial solutions;
Step 2	For each particle, the value of its objective function is calculated and the current optimal solution is recorded;
Step 3	Calculate the speed of each particle, according to the speed of updating the positions of the particles in the solution space;
Step 4	Using the Metropolis criterion to decide whether to accept the new position;
Step 5	The particles are updated in a certain order to make the local optimal particle position move to the global optimal, which improves the global search performance of the algorithm
Step 6	Repeat Steps 2 through 5 until the termination condition is reached

By using this method, the advantages of a simple and efficient PSO algorithm can be brought into play. The SA algorithm can keep the original performance without expending the energy to adjust the parameters.

3.3. RBDO Decoupling Method

RBDO solution strategies can be divided into double-loop method, single-loop method, and decoupling method [64]. The double-loop method is the most basic and direct solution strategy [65]. Its flow is a double-layer nested cycle optimization flow. What is more, its solving efficiency is the lowest. The single-loop method is the most efficient solution strategy. However, it has problems such as low precision and difficult convergence [66]. Compared with the other two methods, the decoupling strategy is a very important RBDO method, which can give consideration to both solving accuracy and solving efficiency.

Sequence Optimization and Reliability Assessment (SORA) method is an efficient decoupling method for solving RBDO problems [67]. Based on the decoupling idea, SORA serializes the traditional two-layer nested cycle optimization process. Forming a sequential deterministic design optimization and controllability analysis process [68]. The main idea of SORA is to approximate the solution of the RBDO problem. The main method is to make the constraint gradually shift to the direction of the probability constraint, so as to quickly get the optimal solution. Its mathematical expression is

$$\begin{cases} \text{find}: & \mu_X \\ \min: & C(\mu_X) \\ s.t. & g_i(\mu_X - s_i) \geq 0 (i = 1, 2, \cdots, m) \\ & \mu_X^L \leq \mu_X \leq \mu_X^U \end{cases}, \tag{20}$$

where $s_i = \mu_X^{(k-1)} - x_i^*(i = 1, 2, \cdots, m)$ is the offset vector of the ith probability constraint; 3 was the design point of the last iteration. In SORA, each iteration cycle will construct an offset vector based on the reliability analysis results of the previous iteration to move the boundary of the probability constraint. According to the constraint boundary after moving, the DO is constructed to update the optimal design scheme. The nested RBDO is decomposed into a series of reliability analyses and DO problems.

3.4. The Proposed RBDO Method Based on the PSO and SA Algorithm

The analysis optimization method proposed in this paper is a fusion of the meta-heuristic algorithm RBDO method. Its main idea is that: the SA algorithm and enhanced PSO algorithm are, respectively, used to perform reliability optimization and reliability analysis after decoupling. The purpose of improving the efficiency of analysis and optimization is achieved.

The overall process is as follows:

Step 1: Set the probability distribution of random variables and the reliability index of the target β_t;
Step 2: Set parameters of the PSO algorithm and SA algorithm;
Step 3: Enter the optimization cycle of the SA algorithm. Select the design variable set in step (1) as the initial point to calculate the value of the objective function;
Step 4: Reliability analysis is carried out on the results obtained in step (3). The improved PSO algorithm is used to solve the MPP points, calculate the reliability index, and judge its reliability. If the reliability requirements are met, this solution is output as the optimal solution. Otherwise, calculate the offset vector, update the probability constraint function, and return to step (3) for a new round of reliability optimization.

The pseudocode is shown below:

```
Set initial variables
While1 Reliability index not met
  %%Obtain the optimal solution space through annealing method
      Using simulated annealing method to generate initial solution space
      Random number generator initialization
      While2 Does not meet Metropolis criterion Equation (7)
          For From 1 to the set number of annealing times
               Generate random perturbations to obtain new solutions
               Check whether the Metropolis criterion Equation (7) is met, if so, exit the
current annealing
               Perform annealing and save the optimal solution during the annealing process.
          End for loop
          Update random number generator
      End the while2 loop and obtain the optimal design variable solution space
  %%Using PSO algorithm to find MPP points
  %%Perform the following operations for each limit state function
     Initialize the population position and velocity according to the optimal solution space
obtained by the annealing algorithm
     While3 The current iteration is less than the maximum number of iterations
         Update the population position and velocity according to the objective function value of
each population particle
         Dealing with boundary issues
     End the current while3 loop
     Translational failure boundary
     Solve to obtain the optimal MPP point
     Use this point as the initial solution space for the next cycle.
End the while1 loop
```

The flowchart of this method is shown in Figure 2:

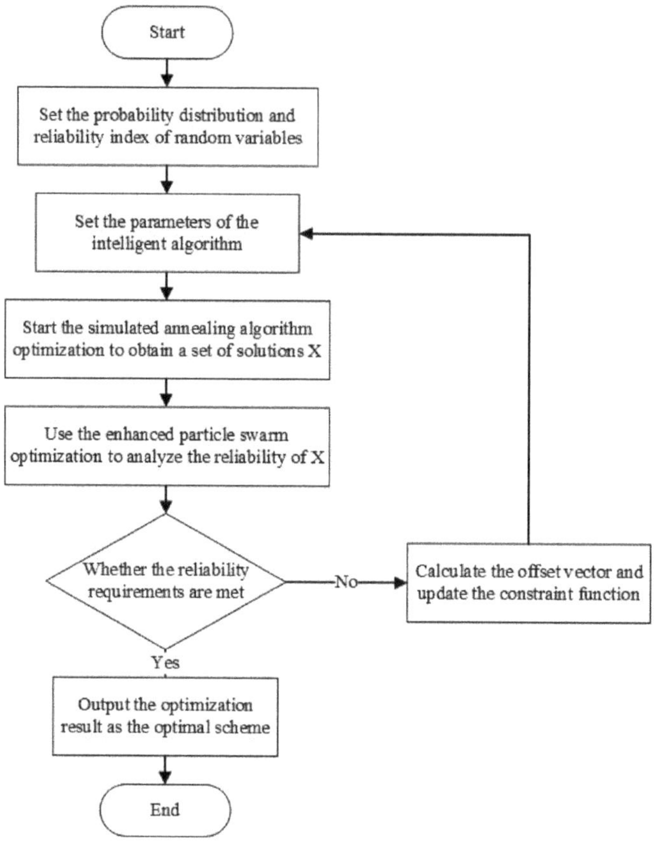

Figure 2. Flow chart of RBDO algorithm incorporating meta-heuristic algorithm.

4. Experimental Results and Discussion

4.1. Example Verification

In order to obtain the performance of reliability analysis by using the PSO algorithm, two mathematical examples are selected in this section for verification. The SQP method and Monte Carlo Simulation (MCS) are selected as a comparison. The MCS is considered an approximate solution. Therefore, its calculation error is considered to be 0. In this article, it is represented by the symbol "$--$". The two examples are a convex function and a concave function, respectively. The variables of the convex function only have random uncertainty, while those of the concave function have both random uncertainty and interval uncertainty.

4.1.1. Convex Limit State Function

The expression of the limit state function of this example is:

$$g = -e^{x_1 - 7} - x_2 + 10, \tag{21}$$

where both x_1 and x_2 have random uncertainty; $x_1 \sim N(6.0, 0.8), x_2 \sim N(6, 0.8)$. The limit state function is solved. Its convergence process is shown in Figure 3. Different colors in the figure represent contour distribution. The red dot represents the optimization solution process. The comparison of results is shown in Table 2 below:

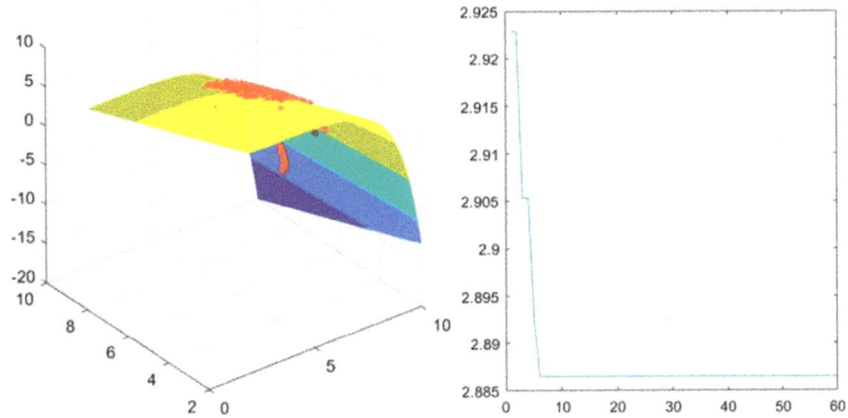

(a) (b)

Figure 3. Convex function iterative solution procedure. (**a**) State position change—Number of iterations: 60 (**b**) Optimal fitness evolution process.

Table 2. Reliability index of the convex function.

Method	Reliability Index	Error	Solution Time (Milliseconds)
MCS	2.8445	--	1,948,731.39
SQP	2.8782	1.2%	988.71
Improved PSO	2.8865	1.5%	47.67

It can be seen from the calculation results that the improved PSO algorithm is equivalent to the SQP algorithm in solving accuracy. However, about 50% faster than the SQP algorithm. It can be seen that the PSO algorithm has better performance in reliability analysis under stochastic uncertainty.

4.1.2. Concave Limit State Function

In this example, the limit state function can be expressed as:

$$g = \frac{e^{0.8x_1-1.2} + e^{0.7x_2-0.6} - 7}{10}, \tag{22}$$

where variable x_1 has random uncertainty, $x_1 \sim N(4.0, 0.8)$; variable x_2 has interval uncertainty, $x_2 \in [3.2, 4.2]$. To solve this concave limit state function, the convergence process is shown in Figure 4. Different colors in the figure represent contour distribution. The red dot represents the optimization solution process. The comparison of results is shown in Table 3.

It can be seen from the table that the accuracy of PSO is about 24% higher than that of SQP when solving the concave limit state function considering random and interval uncertainty. It can be seen that the sequential quadratic programming algorithm is not suitable for dealing with the reliability analysis problem of concave functions under mixed uncertainty. The improved PSO algorithm has good fitness when dealing with the mixed uncertainty analysis problems of convex function type and concave function type, which proves that the performance of the PSO algorithm is good enough to solve MPP points in first-order reliability analysis.

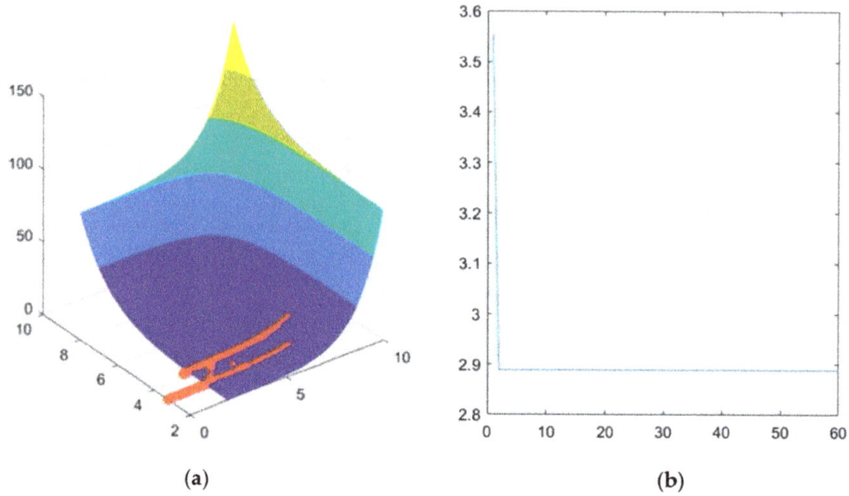

Figure 4. Concave function iterative solution procedure. (**a**) State position change-Number of iterations: 60 (**b**) Optimal fitness evolution process.

Table 3. Concave function reliability index.

Method	Reliability Index	Error	Solution Time (Milliseconds)
MCS	2.9906	−−	1,851,997.89
SQP	2.1681	27.5%	80.32
Improved PSO	2.8891	3.4%	228.12

4.2. Mathematical Example

In this section, a nonlinear mathematical example is used to verify the RBDO method of the proposed fusion meta-heuristic algorithm. The objective function of this mathematical example is the sum of two normally distributed design variables x_1 and x_2. The constraint function consists of three nonlinear functions. The mathematical model of the optimization problem is as follows:

$$\begin{cases} \text{find} \quad \mu_X = [\mu_{x_1}, \mu_{x_2}] \\ \min \quad f(\mu_x) = \mu_{x_1} + \mu_{x_2} \\ s.t. \quad Prob(g_i(X) \geq 0) \geq \varphi(\beta^t), i = 1,2,3 \end{cases}, \tag{23}$$

where β^t represents the target reliability index. Its value here is $\beta^t = 3.0$; μ_{x_1} and μ_{x_2} are the mean values of design variables x_1 and x_2, respectively. Their standard deviation σ is 0.3. The mean values range between 0 and 10, i.e.,:

$$\begin{cases} X \sim N(\mu_X, 0.3^2) \\ 0 \leq \mu_X \leq 10 \end{cases} \tag{24}$$

The limiting equation of state is

$$\begin{cases} g_1(X) = {x_1}^2 x_2/20 - 1 \\ g_2(X) = (x_1 + x_2 - 5)^2/30 + (x_1 - x_2 - 12)^2/120 - 1 \\ g_3(X) = 80/({x_1}^2 + 8x_2 + 5) - 1 \end{cases}. \tag{25}$$

The solution space formed by the limit state equation is shown in Figure 5.

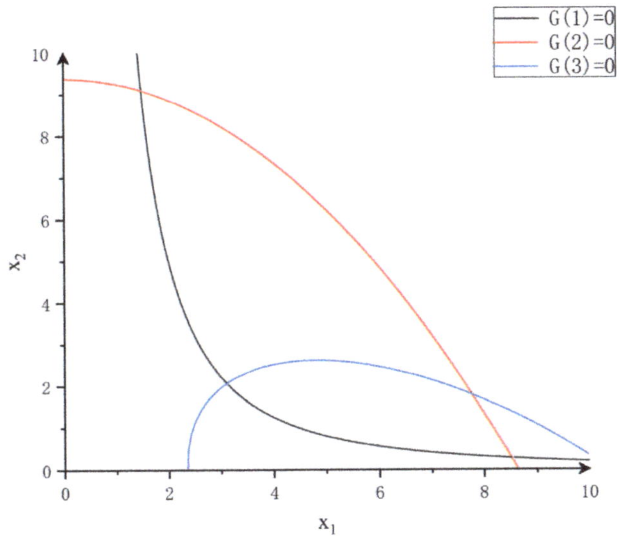

Figure 5. Design variable feasible domain.

In order to test the performance of the RBDO method of the fusion meta-heuristic algorithm proposed in this paper, the proposed method is compared with the results obtained by using the optimization algorithm SQP, GA, and the theoretical solution in the literature [69]. The results are shown in Table 4. "——" means there is no relevant information in Table 4.

Table 4. Optimization result.

Method	Optimal Solution	Error	Solution Time (Milliseconds)
Theoretical method	6.7318	——	——
SQP	7.4195	10.2%	320.5
GA	6.9754	3.6%	6975.4
The proposed method	7.0988	5.5%	211.9

As shown in Table 4, the method proposed in this study is identical to the results obtained using two other heuristic algorithms SQP and Genetic algorithm (GA). Compared with SQP method, the method proposed in this study is closer to the exact solution. Compared with GA method, the time used in this study is greatly reduced, and the solving speed is increased by 32 times. It can be seen that the method proposed in this study has reliable accuracy and superior solving efficiency.

4.3. *Volume Optimization of Gear Reducer*

In the engineering example of this section, a classic case of the gear reducer is selected to optimize the reliability design. In order to verify the method presented in this paper [70,71], the original example is modified to make it a single-discipline design optimization problem considering stochastic and interval uncertainty.

The structure diagram of the gear reducer is shown in Figure 6. The optimization model has seven design variables that determine the component size of the reducer. When only random uncertainty analysis is considered, all seven variables are set as random variables and have a normal distribution, as shown in Table 5. At the same time, this study also considers mixed random variables to improve the accuracy of calculation results. As shown in Table 6, change the diameter of the axis to an interval variable. In this example, the target reliability index is set as $\beta_t = 2.4$. The corresponding reliability is $R = 99.18\%$.

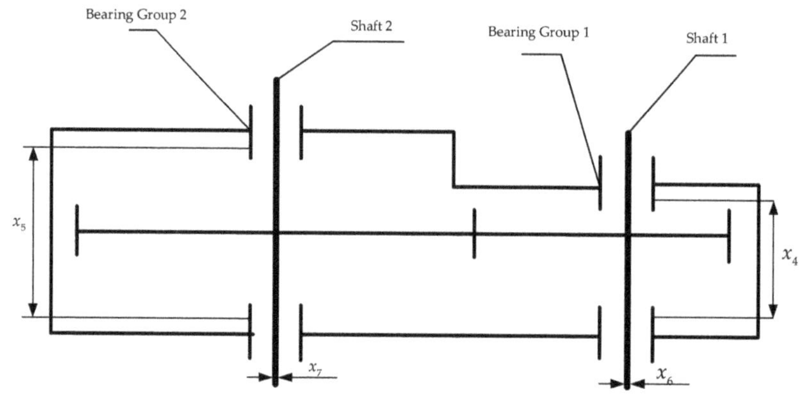

Figure 6. Structure diagram of gear reducer.

Table 5. Random uncertainty description.

Design Variable	Mean Value	Standard Deviation	Distribution Type	Lower Bound of Mean	Upper Bound of Mean
Tooth width factor x_1	x_1^M	$0.01x_1^M$	Orthographic distribution	2.63	3.57
Module of gear teeth x_2	x_2^M	$0.01x_2^M$	Orthographic distribution	0.71	0.81
Number of teeth of gear 1 x_3	x_3^M	$0.01x_3^M$	Orthographic distribution	17	23
Length of shaft 1 x_4	x_4^M	$0.01x_4^M$	Orthographic distribution	7.31	8.29
Length of shaft 2 x_5	x_5^M	$0.01x_5^M$	Orthographic distribution	7.31	8.29
Shaft 1 diameter x_6	x_6^M	$0.01x_6^M$	Orthographic distribution	2.93	3.87
Shaft 2 diameter x_7	x_7^M	$0.01x_7^M$	Orthographic distribution	5.03	5.47

Table 6. Interval uncertainty description.

Design Variable	Upper Bound of Interval	Lower Bound of Interval
Shaft 1 diameter x_6	2.93	3.87
Shaft 1 diameter x_7	5.03	5.47

In this optimization problem, the objective is to minimize the volume V of the gear reducer, whose mathematical expression is

$$V = V_1 + V_2, \tag{26}$$

where V_1 and V_2 represent the volume of the gear and the volume of the bearing, respectively. The volume of the gear can be expressed as

$$V_1 = 0.7854x_1{x_2}^2(3.3333{x_3}^2 + 14.9334x_3 - 43.0934) - 1.508x_1({x_6}^2 + {x_7}^2). \tag{27}$$

The volume of the bearing can be expressed as

$$V_2 = 7.477({x_6}^3 + {x_7}^3) + 0.7854(x_4{x_6}^2 + x_5{x_7}^2). \tag{28}$$

The constraint function is the related performance index of the gear reducer, including stress, size, displacement, etc., 11 in total.

The optimization model of this problem is

$$\begin{cases} \text{find} \quad X = [x_1, x_2, x_3, x_4, x_5, x_6, x_7] \\ \text{min} \qquad\quad f = V_1 + V_2 \\ s.t. \quad Prob(g_i(X) \geq 0) \geq \varphi(\beta^t), i = 1, 2, \cdots, 11 \end{cases} . \tag{29}$$

The stress constraint function of the gear reducer performance is

$$\begin{cases} g_1 = 1 - 27/(x_1 x_2{}^2 x_3) \\ g_2 = 1 - 397.5/(x_1 x_2{}^2 x_3{}^2) \\ g_3 = 12 - x_1/x_2 \\ g_4 = x_1/x_2 - 5 \end{cases} . \tag{30}$$

The dimension constraint function is

$$\begin{cases} g_5 = 1 - 1.93 x_4{}^3/(x_2 x_3 x_6{}^4) \\ g_6 = 1 - 1.93 x_5{}^3/(x_2 x_3 x_7{}^4) \\ g_7 = 1100 - A_1/B_1 \\ g_8 = 1 - (1.5x_6 + 1.9)/x_4 \\ g_9 = 1 - (1.1x_7 + 1.9)/x_5 \end{cases} . \tag{31}$$

where $A_1 = \sqrt{[745x_4/(x_2x_3)]^2 + 16.9 \times 10^6}$; $B_1 = 0.1x_6{}^3$.

The displacement constraint function is

$$\begin{cases} g_{10} = 850 - A_2/B_2 \\ g_{11} = 40 - x_2 x_3 \end{cases} , \tag{32}$$

where $A_2 = \sqrt{[745x_5/(x_2x_3)]^2 + 157.5 \times 10^6}$, $B_2 = 0.1x_7{}^3$.

For this optimization model, the RBDO method of fusion meta-heuristic algorithm proposed in this paper is used to solve it. Meanwhile, the case where only random uncertainty is considered is calculated. The calculation results of the two uncertain cases are shown in Table 7 below.

Table 7. Optimization result.

Uncertainty Description	Optimal Solution	Error
Comparison method(MCS)	2753.8	
SQP	2851.2653	3.54%
GA	2891.1236	4.99%
The proposed method 1	2773.0126	0.69%
The proposed method 2	2814.9546	2.22%

For this algorithm, this study uses the results obtained by MCS to be approximately regarded as the exact solution to compare other solutions. Judging from the calculation results in Table 7, it is found that when using the optimization results (The proposed method 1) that do not consider mixed variables, the optimization results of this article are very close to the exact solution. Considering the complex influencing factors in engineering, this paper also adopts complex optimization conditions that consider multiple variables. Although the result is worse than the proposed method 1, it has higher stability. In addition, this article also compared it with two other heuristic algorithms, SQP and GA algorithms, and found that the results of this algorithm are basically consistent with the other two results. This proves the feasibility of this method.

4.4. Composite Cylinder Size Optimization

This section further illustrates the effectiveness of the proposed method by combining cylinder size optimization cases [72]. The composite cylinder is composed of an inner cylinder and an outer cylinder. The inner diameter of the inner cylinder is a, the outer diameter is b, the inner diameter of the outer cylinder is b, and the outer diameter is c. The height of the composite cylinder is 50 mm. The cylinder body is subjected to a pressure of size p. The structure and initial size of the composite cylinder are shown in Figure 7.

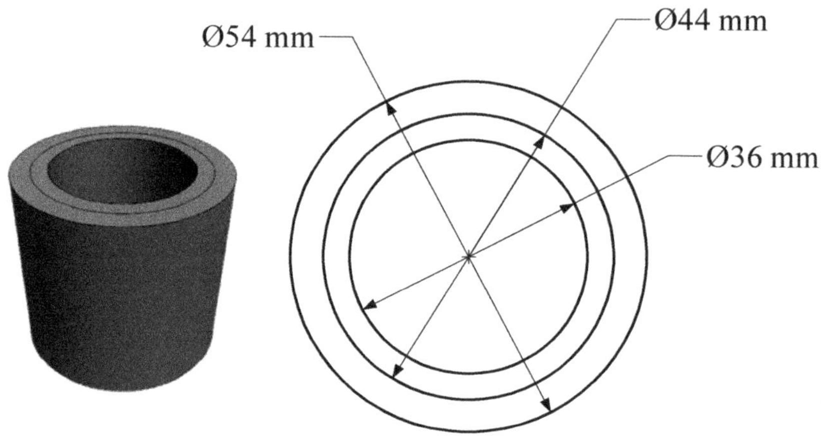

Figure 7. Composite cylinder structure diagram.

The optimization goal of the composite cylinder is to minimize the volume of the composite cylinder while satisfying the allowable equivalent stress and tangential stress of the inner and outer cylinders. The optimization problem includes three design variables: x_1, x_2, and x_3, corresponding to the inner diameter a and outer diameter b of the inner cylinder and the outer diameter c of the outer cylinder, respectively. There are 8 constraint conditions, among which the equivalent stress and tangential stress are all implicit expressions. The approximate mathematical expressions need to be established by finite element analysis. The optimization model of the composite cylinder is as follows:

$$\begin{cases} \text{find} \quad x = (x_1, x_2, x_3) \\ \max \quad f = V = 12.5\pi {x_1}^2 \\ \text{s.t.} \quad Prob(g_i(X) \geq 0) \geq \varphi(\beta^t), i = 1, 2, \cdots, 8 \end{cases}, \tag{33}$$

where β^t is the target reliability index. Here, $\beta^t = 2.4$.

The stress constraint and geometric constraint of the inner cylinder are

$$\begin{cases} g_1 = S - S_1 \\ g_2 = \tau - \tau_1^a \\ g_3 = \tau - \tau_1^b \\ g_4 = b - 1.2a \end{cases}. \tag{34}$$

The stress constraint and geometric constraint of the outer cylinder are

$$\begin{cases} g_5 = S - S_2 \\ g_6 = \tau - \tau_2^b \\ g_7 = \tau - \tau_2^c \\ g_8 = c - 1.2b \end{cases}. \tag{35}$$

The value range of the design variable of the composite cylinder is as follows:

$$\begin{cases} 31.496 \le a \le 40.64 \\ 38.1 \le b \le 50.8 \\ 30.48 \le c \le 60.96 \end{cases}, \tag{36}$$

where S and τ represent allowable equivalent stress and tangential stress, respectively; S_1 and S_2 represent the maximum equivalent stress of inner cylinder and outer cylinder, respectively; τ_1^a and τ_1^b represent the maximum tangential stress on inside diameter a and outside diameter b of the inner cylinder; τ_2^b and τ_2^c represent the maximum tangential stresses on inside diameters b and outside diameters c of the outer cylinder. Ansys Workbench software was used for finite element analysis. The relevant parameters of the composite cylinder are shown in Table 8.

Table 8. Composite cylinder-related parameters.

Name	Symbol	Value
Modulus of elasticity/GPa	E	210
Poisson's ratio	ρ	0.3
Internal pressure/MPa	p	139.7
Allowable stress/MPa	S	607.7
Allowable shear stress/MPa	τ	244.5

Three-dimensional modeling was carried out in Ansys Workbench. The inner diameter a of the inner cylinder, outer diameter b of the inner cylinder, and outer diameter c of the outer cylinder were set as input parameters, which were used to solve the subsequent response surface. Tetrahedral elements are used to divide the grid. To ensure the number of elements and nodes on the composite cylinder wall, the cell size is set as 1 mm. The displacement constraints in the direction of X, Y, and Z are, respectively applied to the cylinder end face of the composite cylinder. Meanwhile, the stress loading p is applied to the inner cylinder of the inner cylinder. The contact between the inner cylinder and the inner cylinder is selected as "no separation" in the "connection" option. The equivalent stress and maximum shear stress were solved, respectively. The results are shown in Figure 8. The equivalent stress and maximum shear stress were set as output parameters.

According to the results of finite element analysis, the stress of the inner cylinder exceeds the maximum allowable value, so it cannot meet the use requirements at present. Its size parameters need to be further optimized. In this example, the expressions of the equivalent stress and tangential stress are approximated by polynomials. Quadratic polynomials with cross terms are selected here. The form is that the finite element analysis results show that the stress of the inner cylinder exceeds the maximum allowable value, so it cannot meet the use requirements at present. Its size parameters need to be further optimized. In this example, the expressions of equivalent stress and tangential stress are approximated by polynomials. Here, the quadratic polynomial with cross terms is selected. Its form is

$$\widetilde{F}(x) = a_0 + \sum_{i=1}^{3} b_i x_i + \sum_{i=1}^{3} c_i {x_i}^2 + \sum_{i=1}^{2} \sum_{j=i+1}^{3} d_{ij} x_i x_j + e_{123} x_1 x_2 x_3. \tag{37}$$

The response surface module in Ansys Workbench software is used to generate design points and calculate corresponding output values. The results are shown in Table 9.

The coefficients of the quadratic polynomial are solved in Matlab by using the above 10 groups of design points. The obtained values of each system are shown in Table 10.

By the above method, the limit state function is expressed explicitly instead of implicitly. In this problem, which has random uncertainty, their probability distribution is normal. Their standard deviation is 1% of their mean. c has interval uncertainty. Its value range is shown in Equation (36). The results are shown in Table 11 below. It can be seen from the optimization results that the method proposed in this article can obtain a smaller objective function value. This shows that the optimization results obtained by this method are more superior. In order to verify the feasibility of this method, the optimization results of this method are modeled and analyzed through finite element analysis.

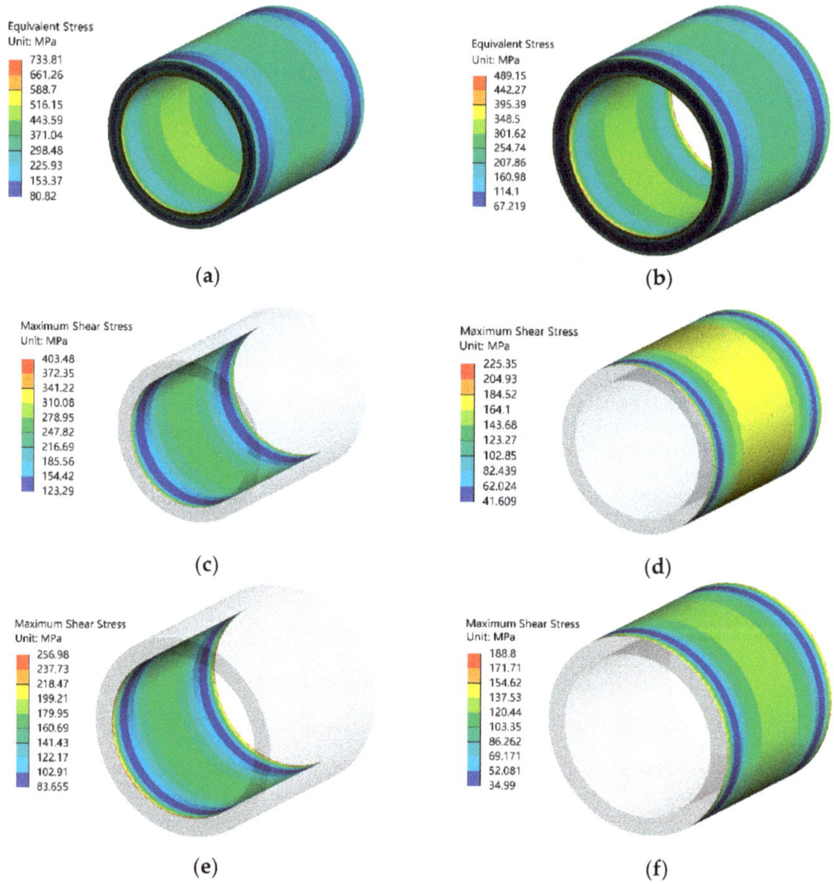

Figure 8. Stress nephogram of the composite cylinder. (**a**) Equivalent stress of inner cylinder, (**b**) Equivalent stress of outer cylinder, (**c**) Tangential stress on inner diameter of the inner cylinder, (**d**) Tangential stress on outer diameter of the inner cylinder, (**e**) Tangential stress on inner diameter of the outer cylinder, and (**f**) Tangential stress on the outer diameter of the outer cylinder.

Table 9. Design point.

	a	b	c	S_1	S_2	τ_1^a	τ_1^b	τ_2^b	τ_2^c
1	38.5	39.9	49.7	889.90	997.82	483.00	400.66	526.84	346.94
2	39.2	49.6	53.1	1069.30	518.25	578.87	273.39	273.69	180.97
3	33.0	49.5	55.5	589.82	252.57	324.35	130.22	133.18	89.94
4	39.3	43.8	58.0	792.55	528.81	441.83	281.42	279.47	186.87
5	37.1	47.6	50.4	751.12	438.64	414.24	234.62	230.51	177.81
6	32.8	39.7	52.7	605.15	391.49	337.28	195.88	207.00	135.23
7	34.2	43.1	52.3	811.37	436.74	442.53	218.96	231.57	170.05
8	36.4	49.0	56.8	881.32	430.42	483.57	201.98	226.71	155.63

Table 9. *Cont.*

	a	b	c	S_1	S_2	τ_1^a	τ_1^b	τ_2^b	τ_2^c
9	39.7	47.5	49.7	1256.80	565.43	675.41	353.23	308.07	260.49
10	39.7	49.5	55.1	990.28	564.01	536.79	274.83	297.29	199.18

Table 10. Polynomial coefficient.

	S_1	S_2	τ_1^a	τ_1^b	τ_2^b	τ_2^c
a_0	1,306,319	41,973.2	685,669.2	116,143.7	34,266.6	−23,063.3
b_1	−34,404	−644.3	−18,032.3	−2974.9	−663.4	748.8
b_2	−28,761.7	−1219.7	−15,093.5	−2522.8	−894.6	502.7
b_3	−24,292.4	−753.5	−12,764.2	−2184.7	−628.1	367.9
c_1	−5	−1.7	−3	0.8	−0.7	0.6
c_2	−10.9	0.5	−5.5	−1.1	0.01	−1.7
c_3	−9.4	−3.1	−4.7	−0.4	−1.5	0.3
d_{12}	761.1	18.5	399.3	65.2	16.7	−14
d_{13}	645.8	18.3	339	55.2	15.2	−14.6
d_{23}	550.9	23.7	288.7	48.9	17.5	−6.8
e_{123}	−14.1	−0.4	−7.4	−1.2	−0.3	0.3

Table 11. Optimization result.

Variable	a	b	c	V
GA	37.65	38.10	59.58	55,662.18
SQP	38.47	38.10	59.26	57,190.73
Result	37.40	45.72	60.96	54,929.13

In order to verify the accuracy of the results, modeling and finite element analysis were conducted on the optimized composite cylinder again. The results are shown in Figure 9. It can be seen from the stress program that the maximum equivalent stress and maximum shear stress of the composite cylinder do not exceed the allowable value, which proves that the optimization scheme is feasible.

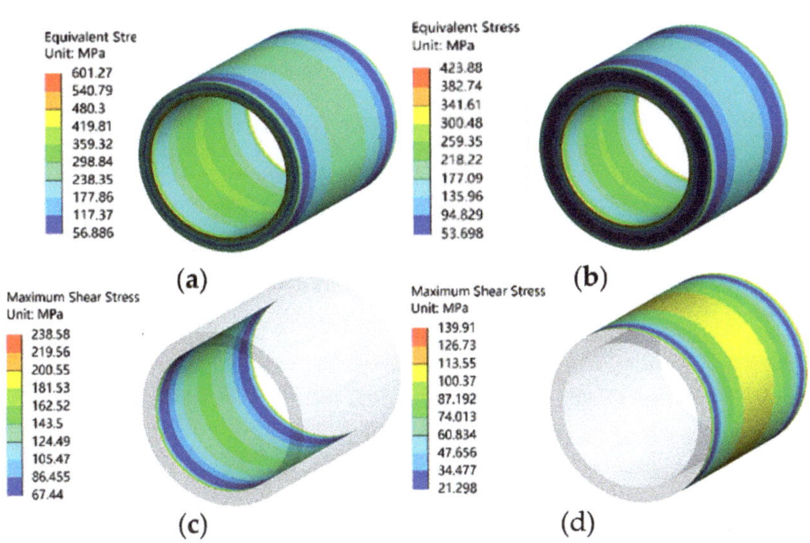

Figure 9. *Cont.*

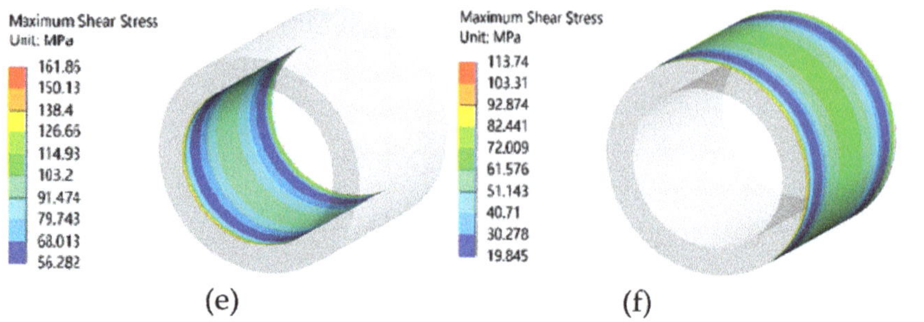

Figure 9. Stress nephogram of the composite cylinder after optimization. (**a**) Equivalent stress of inner cylinder, (**b**) Equivalent stress of outer cylinder, (**c**) Tangential stress on inner diameter of the inner cylinder, (**d**) Tangential stress on outer diameter of the inner cylinder, (**e**) Tangential stress on inner diameter of the outer cylinder, and (**f**) Tangential stress on the outer diameter of the outer cylinder.

5. Conclusions

This study constructs a RBDO method framework for RBDO considering mixed uncertainties, combined with a metaheuristic algorithm with superior performance. The research contents include: (1). Through the enhanced PSO algorithm, give full play to the global optimization ability of the algorithm to obtain better MPP points for the update optimization of the SA algorithm; (2). Through the decoupling method, the enhanced PSO of the algorithm is combined with the SA algorithm and put into an optimization framework. Realize the construction of a complete reliability-based design optimization algorithm; (3). Adopt a decoupling optimization strategy based on the SA algorithm, taking advantage of the faster convergence characteristics of SA. Compared with the ordinary double-loop method and single-loop method, this optimization method has faster solution efficiency and solution accuracy. The method proposed in this paper is dedicated to solving the RBDO problem considering mixed uncertainties. By applying the metaheuristic algorithm to the reliability analysis and optimization process of engineering structures, it provides new ideas to solve the problems of high computational cost and slow solution efficiency during the design optimization of increasingly complex engineering structures. Through the improved PSO algorithm and the decoupled convergence process combined with the SA algorithm, on the basis of ensuring the accuracy of the convergence results, the optimization efficiency is improved and the problem of easily falling into local convergence is solved. At the end of the article, the feasibility and superiority of this method are verified through a mathematical example and two complex engineering examples. It can be seen from the optimization results that compared with the double-loop RBDO method using the SQP method and the ordinary reliability optimization based on the first-order Taylor formula, the results of this method are better and the calculation efficiency is higher. Through the finite element analysis of the results and combined with the constraint conditions, it was found that under the same load conditions, the results of this method have smaller deformation amounts and stress and strain values. The reliability and feasibility of this method are proved.

In order to synthesize the role of each constraint function and obtain the optimal MPP point, this study performed equal calculations on each constraint function. However, in actual engineering, different constraint functions play different roles for each engineering situation, and sometimes there are even situations where the function does not play a constraining role. Therefore, in future work, by reducing the calculation of ineffective constraint functions in RBDO, the efficiency of optimization calculations can be further greatly improved.

This study uses the improved PSO algorithm to solve the global optimal MPP point, although it is compared with the SQP method and the simple FORM method. However, heuristic algorithms include more, such as multi-objective flower pollination algorithm, multi-objective bat algorithm, multi-objective multiverse optimization, and multi-objective water cycle optimizer algorithms that are not mentioned in the article. In future work, it will be meaningful to explore and compare the efficiency of various optimization algorithms in solving RBDO problems considering mixed uncertainties.

Author Contributions: Conceptualization, S.Y., H.W., Y.X., Y.G., L.P., J.Z., X.G., D.M. and J.W.; Methodology, S.Y., H.W., Y.X., Y.G., L.P., J.Z., X.G., D.M. and J.W.; Validation, S.Y., H.W., Y.X., Y.G., L.P., J.Z., X.G., D.M. and J.W.; Formal analysis, S.Y., H.W., Y.X., Y.G., L.P., J.Z., X.G., D.M. and J.W.; Resources, S.Y., H.W., Y.X., Y.G., L.P., J.Z., X.G., D.M. and J.W.; Writing—original draft, S.Y., H.W., Y.X., Y.G., L.P., J.Z., X.G., D.M. and J.W.; Writing—review and editing, S.Y., H.W., Y.X., Y.G., L.P., J.Z., X.G., D.M. and J.W.; Funding acquisition, Y.X., Y.G., L.P., J.Z., X.G. and D.M. All authors have read and agreed to the published version of the manuscript.

Funding: This research was funded by the National Natural Science Foundation of China (Grant No. 52175130), the Guangdong Basic and Applied Basic Research Foundation (Grant No. 2022A1515240010), the Sichuan Science and Technology Program (Grants No. 2022YFQ0087 and 2022JDJQ0024), and Students Go Abroad for Scientific Research and Internship Funding Program of University of Electronic Science and Technology of China.

Data Availability Statement: All data that support the findings of this study are included within the article.

Conflicts of Interest: Authors Yongqiang Guo, Lidong Pan, and Jiaming Zhang were employed by the company Beijing Research Institute of Mechanical & Electrical Technology Ltd. The remaining authors declare that the research was conducted in the absence of any commercial or financial relationships that could be construed as a potential conflict of interest.

References

1. Zhong, Y.; Chen, Z.; Zhou, Z.; Hu, H. Uncertainty analysis and resource allocation in construction project management. *Eng. Manag. J.* **2018**, *30*, 293–305. [CrossRef]
2. Zhu, Q. Nonlinear Systems: Dynamics, Control, Optimization and Applications to the Science and Engineering. *Mathematics* **2022**, *10*, 4837. [CrossRef]
3. Meng, D.; Yang, S.; He, C.; Wang, H.; Lv, Z.; Guo, Y.; Nie, P. Multidisciplinary design optimization of engineering systems under uncertainty: A review. *Int. J. Struct. Integr.* **2022**, *13*, 565–593. [CrossRef]
4. Tan, Y.; Zhan, C.; Pi, Y.; Zhang, C.; Song, J.; Chen, Y.; Golmohammadi, A.M. A Hybrid Algorithm Based on Social Engineering and Artificial Neural Network for Fault Warning Detection in Hydraulic Turbines. *Mathematics* **2023**, *11*, 2274. [CrossRef]
5. Xue, Y.; Deng, Y. Extending set measures to orthopair fuzzy sets. *Int. J. Uncertain. Fuzziness Knowl.-Based Syst.* **2022**, *30*, 63–91. [CrossRef]
6. Zhu, S.P.; Keshtegar, B.; Bagheri, M.; Hao, P.; Trung, N.T. Novel hybrid robust method for uncertain reliability analysis using finite conjugate map. *Comput. Methods Appl. Mech. Eng.* **2020**, *371*, 113309. [CrossRef]
7. Bagheri, M.; Zhu, S.P.; Ben Seghier, M.E.A.; Keshtegar, B.; Trung, N.T. Hybrid intelligent method for fuzzy reliability analysis of corroded X100 steel pipelines. *Eng. Comput.* **2021**, *37*, 2559–2573. [CrossRef]
8. Plotnikov, L. Preparation and Analysis of Experimental Findings on the Thermal and Mechanical Characteristics of Pulsating Gas Flows in the Intake System of a Piston Engine for Modelling and Machine Learning. *Mathematics* **2023**, *11*, 1967. [CrossRef]
9. Zhang, D.; Zhang, J.; Yang, M.; Wang, R.; Wu, Z. An enhanced finite step length method for structural reliability analysis and reliability-based design optimization. *Struct. Multidiscip. Optim.* **2022**, *65*, 231. [CrossRef]
10. Meng, D.; Yang, S.; De Jesus, A.M.; Fazeres-Ferradosa, T.; Zhu, S.P. A novel hybrid adaptive Kriging and water cycle algorithm for reliability-based design and optimization strategy: Application in offshore wind turbine monopile. *Comput. Methods Appl. Mech. Eng.* **2023**, *412*, 116083. [CrossRef]
11. Yang, I.T.; Hsieh, Y.H. Reliability-based design optimization with discrete design variables and non-smooth performance functions: AB-PSO algorithm. *Autom. Constr.* **2011**, *20*, 610–619. [CrossRef]
12. Yang, M.; Zhang, D.; Wang, F.; Han, X. Efficient local adaptive Kriging approximation method with single-loop strategy for reliability-based design optimization. *Comput. Methods Appl. Mech. Eng.* **2022**, *390*, 114462. [CrossRef]
13. Meng, Z.; Li, G.; Wang, B.P.; Hao, P. A hybrid chaos control approach of the performance measure functions for reliability-based design optimization. *Comput. Struct.* **2015**, *146*, 32–43. [CrossRef]
14. Wang, Z.; Zhao, D.; Guan, Y. Flexible-constrained time-variant hybrid reliability-based design optimization. *Struct. Multidiscip. Optim.* **2023**, *66*, 89. [CrossRef]
15. Dui, H.; Song, J.; Zhang, Y.A. Reliability and Service Life Analysis of Airbag Systems. *Mathematics* **2023**, *11*, 434. [CrossRef]
16. Zhang, D.; Shen, S.; Jiang, C.; Han, X.; Li, Q. An advanced mixed-degree cubature formula for reliability analysis. *Comput. Methods Appl. Mech. Eng.* **2022**, *400*, 115521. [CrossRef]

17. Meng, Z.; Li, H.; Zeng, R.; Mirjalili, S.; Yıldız, A.R. An efficient two-stage water cycle algorithm for complex reliability-based design optimization problems. *Neural Comput. Appl.* **2022**, *34*, 20993–21013. [CrossRef]
18. Liao, K.W.; Lu, B.C.; Yu, S.P. A Concurrent Approach for a Reliability-Based Optimization Design Problem. *J. Adv. Mech. Des. Syst. Manuf.* **2012**, *6*, 1015–1030. [CrossRef]
19. Wang, Z.; Zhang, Y.; Song, Y. A modified conjugate gradient approach for reliability-based design optimization. *IEEE Access* **2020**, *8*, 16742–16749. [CrossRef]
20. Safaeian Hamzehkolaei, N.; Miri, M.; Rashki, M. An enhanced simulation-based design method coupled with meta-heuristic search algorithm for accurate reliability-based design optimization. *Eng. Comput.* **2016**, *32*, 477–495. [CrossRef]
21. Zhong, C.; Wang, M.; Dang, C.; Ke, W.; Guo, S. First-order reliability method based on Harris Hawks Optimization for high-dimensional reliability analysis. *Struct. Multidiscip. Optim.* **2020**, *62*, 1951–1968. [CrossRef]
22. Jafari-Asl, J.; Seghier, M.E.A.B.; Ohadi, S.; Correia, J.; Barroso, J. Reliability analysis based improved directional simulation using Harris Hawks optimization algorithm for engineering systems. *Eng. Fail. Anal.* **2022**, *135*, 106148. [CrossRef]
23. Du, X.P.; Sudjianto, A.; Huang, B.Q. Reliability-based design with the mixture of random and interval variables. *J. Mech. Des.* **2005**, *127*, 1068–1076. [CrossRef]
24. Zhang, H.; Wang, H.; Wang, Y.; Hong, D. Incremental shifting vector and mixed uncertainty analysis method for reliability-based design optimization. *Struct. Multidiscip. Optim.* **2019**, *59*, 2093–2109. [CrossRef]
25. Wang, L.; Ma, Y.; Yang, Y.; Wang, X. Structural design optimization based on hybrid time-variant reliability measure under non-probabilistic convex uncertainties. *Appl. Math. Model.* **2019**, *69*, 330–354. [CrossRef]
26. Van Huynh, T.; Tangaramvong, S.; Do, B.; Gao, W.; Limkatanyu, S. Sequential most probable point update combining Gaussian process and comprehensive learning PSO for structural reliability-based design optimization. *Reliab. Eng. Syst. Saf.* **2023**, *235*, 109164. [CrossRef]
27. Keshtegar, B.; Chakraborty, S. A hybrid self-adaptive conjugate first order reliability method for robust structural reliability analysis. *Appl. Math. Model.* **2018**, *53*, 319–332. [CrossRef]
28. Bartoccini, U.; Carpi, A.; Poggioni, V.; Santucci, V. Memes evolution in a memetic variant of particle swarm optimization. *Mathematics* **2019**, *7*, 423. [CrossRef]
29. Li, J.; Chen, J. Solving time-variant reliability-based design optimization by PSO-t-IRS: A methodology incorporating a particle swarm optimization algorithm and an enhanced instantaneous response surface. *Reliab. Eng. Syst. Saf.* **2019**, *191*, 106580. [CrossRef]
30. Zhang, Y.; Liu, X.; Li, C. Determining the reasonable state of cable-stayed bridges with twin towers based on multi-objective swarm optimization algorithm. *J. Chang. Univ. Sci. Technol. (Nat. Sci.)* **2019**, *16*, 22–27.
31. Zhu, S.P.; Keshtegar, B.; Seghier, M.E.A.B.; Zio, E.; Taylan, O. Hybrid and enhanced PSO: Novel first order reliability method-based hybrid intelligent approaches. *Comput. Methods Appl. Mech. Eng.* **2022**, *393*, 114730. [CrossRef]
32. Yu, S.; Wang, Z. A general decoupling approach for time-and space-variant system reliability-based design optimization. *Comput. Methods Appl. Mech. Eng.* **2019**, *357*, 112608. [CrossRef]
33. Wang, C.; Matthies, H.G. A comparative study of two interval-random models for hybrid uncertainty propagation analysis. *Mech. Syst. Signal Process.* **2020**, *136*, 106531. [CrossRef]
34. Chopard, B.; Tomassini, M.; Chopard, B.; Tomassini, M. Simulated annealing. In *An Introduction to Metaheuristics for Optimization*; Springer: Berlin/Heidelberg, Germany, 2018; pp. 59–79.
35. Alnowibet, K.A.; Mahdi, S.; El-Alem, M.; Abdelawwad, M.; Mohamed, A.W. Guided hybrid modified simulated annealing algorithm for solving constrained global optimization problems. *Mathematics* **2022**, *10*, 1312. [CrossRef]
36. Liu, X.; Liu, X.; Zhou, Z.; Hu, L. An efficient multi-objective optimization method based on the adaptive approximation model of the radial basis function. *Struct. Multidiscip. Optim.* **2021**, *63*, 1385–1403. [CrossRef]
37. Delahaye, D.; Chaimatanan, S.; Mongeau, M. Simulated annealing: From basics to applications. In *Handbook of Metaheuristics*; Springer: Berlin/Heidelberg, Germany, 2019; pp. 1–35.
38. Franzin, A.; Stützle, T. Revisiting simulated annealing: A component-based analysis. *Comput. Oper. Res.* **2019**, *104*, 191–206. [CrossRef]
39. Liu, X.; Gong, M.; Zhou, Z.; Xie, J.; Wu, W. An improved first order approximate reliability analysis method for uncertain structures based on evidence theory. *Mech. Based Des. Struct. Mach.* **2023**, *51*, 4137–4154. [CrossRef]
40. Wang, Q.; Huang, Z.; Dong, J. Reliability-based design optimization for vehicle body crashworthiness based on copula functions. *Eng. Optim.* **2020**, *52*, 1362–1381. [CrossRef]
41. Ai, Q.; Yuan, Y.; Jiang, X.; Wang, H.; Han, C.; Huang, X.; Wang, K. Pathological diagnosis of the seepage of a mountain tunnel. *Tunn. Undergr. Space Technol.* **2022**, *128*, 104657. [CrossRef]
42. Li, W.; Li, C.; Gao, L.; Xiao, M. Risk-based design optimization under hybrid uncertainties. *Eng. Comput.* **2020**, *38*, 2037–2049. [CrossRef]
43. Liu, X.; Li, T.; Zhou, Z.; Hu, L. An efficient multi-objective reliability-based design optimization method for structure based on probability and interval hybrid model. *Comput. Methods Appl. Mech. Eng.* **2022**, *392*, 114682. [CrossRef]
44. Luo, C.; Keshtegar, B.; Zhu, S.P.; Taylan, O.; Niu, X.P. Hybrid enhanced Monte Carlo simulation coupled with advanced machine learning approach for accurate and efficient structural reliability analysis. *Comput. Methods Appl. Mech. Eng.* **2022**, *388*, 114218. [CrossRef]

45. Liu, X.; Lai, H.; Wang, X.; Song, X.; Liu, K.; Wu, S.; Li, Q.; Wang, F.; Zhou, Z. Aerospace Structural Reliability Analysis Method Based on Regular Vine Copula Model with the Asymmetric Tail Correlation. *Aerosp. Sci. Technol.* **2023**, *142*, 108670. [CrossRef]
46. Thakkar, A.; Lohiya, R. A survey on intrusion detection system: Feature selection, model, performance measures, application perspective, challenges, and future research directions. *Artif. Intell. Rev.* **2022**, *55*, 453–563. [CrossRef]
47. Wang, Y.H.; Zhang, C.; Su, Y.Q.; Shang, L.Y.; Zhang, T. Structure optimization of the frame based on response surface method. *Int. J. Struct. Integr.* **2019**, *11*, 411–425. [CrossRef]
48. Yang, S.; Meng, D.; Wang, H.; Chen, Z.; Xu, B. A comparative study for adaptive surrogate-model-based reliability evaluation method of automobile components. *Int. J. Struct. Integr.* **2023**, *14*, 498–519. [CrossRef]
49. Meng, D.; Yang, S.; de Jesus, A.M.; Zhu, S.P. A novel Kriging-model-assisted reliability-based multidisciplinary design optimization strategy and its application in the offshore wind turbine tower. *Renew. Energy* **2023**, *203*, 407–420. [CrossRef]
50. Chen, J.; Zhang, X.; Jing, Z. A cooperative PSO-DP approach for the maintenance planning and RBDO of deteriorating structures. *Struct. Multidiscip. Optim.* **2018**, *58*, 95–113. [CrossRef]
51. Lai, X.; Huang, J.; Zhang, Y.; Wang, C.; Zhang, X. A general methodology for reliability-based robust design optimization of computation-intensive engineering problems. *J. Comput. Des. Eng.* **2022**, *9*, 2151–2169. [CrossRef]
52. Qiang, C.; Deng, Y. A new correlation coefficient of mass function in evidence theory and its application in fault diagnosis. *Appl. Intell.* **2022**, *52*, 7832–7842. [CrossRef]
53. Ai, Q.; Yuan, Y.; Shen, S.L.; Wang, H.; Huang, X. Investigation on inspection scheduling for the maintenance of tunnel with different degradation modes. *Tunn. Undergr. Space Technol.* **2020**, *106*, 103589. [CrossRef]
54. Gao, J.W.; Dai, X.; Zhu, S.P.; Zhao, J.W.; Correia, J.A.; Wang, Q. Failure causes and hardening techniques of railway axles—A review from the perspective of structural integrity. *Eng. Fail. Anal.* **2022**, *141*, 106656. [CrossRef]
55. Yang, S.; Meng, D.; Wang, H.; Yang, C. A novel learning function for adaptive surrogate-model-based reliability evaluation. *Philos. Trans. R. Soc. A* **2023**, *382*, 20220395. [CrossRef] [PubMed]
56. Xiong, L.; Su, X.; Qian, H. Conflicting evidence combination from the perspective of networks. *Inf. Sci.* **2021**, *580*, 408–418. [CrossRef]
57. Yu, S.; Li, Y. Active learning kriging model with adaptive uniform design for time-dependent reliability analysis. *IEEE Access* **2021**, *9*, 91625–91634. [CrossRef]
58. Gao, X.; Su, X.; Qian, H.; Pan, X. Dependence assessment in human reliability analysis under uncertain and dynamic situations. *Nucl. Eng. Technol.* **2022**, *54*, 948–958. [CrossRef]
59. Meng, Z.; Keshtegar, B. Adaptive conjugate single-loop method for efficient reliability-based design and topology optimization. *Comput. Methods Appl. Mech. Eng.* **2019**, *344*, 95–119. [CrossRef]
60. Li, W.; Xiao, M.; Garg, A.; Gao, L. A New Approach to Solve Uncertain Multidisciplinary Design Optimization based on Conditional Value at Risk. *IEEE Trans. Autom. Sci. Eng.* **2021**, *18*, 356–368. [CrossRef]
61. Meng, D.; Yang, S.; Lin, T.; Wang, J.; Yang, H.; Lv, Z. RBMDO using gaussian mixture model-based second-order mean-value saddlepoint approximation. *Comput. Model. Eng. Sci.* **2022**, *132*, 553–568. [CrossRef]
62. Li, X.Q.; Song, L.K.; Bai, G.C. Recent advances in reliability analysis of aeroengine rotor system: A review. *Int. J. Struct. Integr.* **2021**, *13*, 1–29. [CrossRef]
63. Yang, S.; Meng, D.; Guo, Y.; Nie, P.; Jesus, A.M.D. A reliability-based design and optimization strategy using a novel MPP searching method for maritime engineering structures. *Int. J. Struct. Integr.* **2023**, *14*, 809–826. [CrossRef]
64. Lu, L.; Wu, Y.; Zhang, Q.; Qiao, P. A Transformation-Based Improved Kriging Method for the Black Box Problem in Reliability-Based Design Optimization. *Mathematics* **2023**, *11*, 218. [CrossRef]
65. Song, L.K.; Bai, G.C.; Li, X.Q.; Wen, J. A unified fatigue reliability-based design optimization framework for aircraft turbine disk. *Int. J. Fatigue* **2021**, *152*, 106422. [CrossRef]
66. Song, X.; Xiao, F. Combining time-series evidence: A complex network model based on a visibility graph and belief entropy. *Appl. Intell.* **2022**, *52*, 10706–10715. [CrossRef]
67. Song, K.; Zhang, Y.; Zhuang, X.; Yu, X.; Song, B. Reliability-based design optimization using adaptive surrogate model and importance sampling-based modified SORA method. *Eng. Comput.* **2021**, *37*, 1295–1314. [CrossRef]
68. Wang, Z.; Xiao, F.; Cao, Z. Uncertainty measurements for Pythagorean fuzzy set and their applications in multiple-criteria decision making. *Soft Comput.* **2022**, *26*, 9937–9952. [CrossRef]
69. Dunn, W.L.; Shultis, J.K. *Exploring Monte Carlo Methods*, 3rd ed.; Elsevier: Burlington, MA, USA, 2012; pp. 154–196.
70. Liang, J.; Mourelatos, Z.P.; Tu, J. A single-Loop method for reliability-based design optimization. *Proc. ASME Des. Eng. Tech. Conf.* **2004**, *1*, 419–430.
71. Azarm, S.; Li, W.C. Multi-level design optimization using global monotonicity analysis. *J. Mech. Transm. Autom. Des.* **1989**, *111*, 259–263. [CrossRef]
72. Gunawan, S.; Azarm, S.; Wu, J.; Boyars, A. Quality-assisted multi-objective multidisciplinary genetic algorithms. *Aiaa J.* **2003**, *41*, 1752–1762. [CrossRef]

mathematics MDPI

Article

Investigation of Warning Thresholds for the Deformation of GINA Gasket of Immersed Tunnel Based on a Material-to-Mechanical Analysis

Hao Ding [1], Jingsong Huang [2], Xinghong Jiang [1,3], Yu Yan [4], Shouji Du [2], Juntao Chen [5] and Qing Ai [2,*]

1 Tunnel and Underground Engineering Branch, China Merchants Chongqing Communications Technology Research & Design Institute Co., Ltd., Chongqing 400067, China
2 School of Naval Architecture, Ocean and Civil Engineering, Shanghai Jiao Tong University, Shanghai 200240, China
3 State Key Laboratory of Coal Mine Dynamics and Control, Chongqing University, Chongqing 400044, China
4 Hong Kong-Zhuhai-Macao Bridge Authority, Zhuhai 519060, China
5 Department of Construction Engineering, Chongqing University of Science & Technology, Chongqing 401331, China
* Correspondence: ai.qing@sjtu.edu.cn; Tel.: +86-021-34206196

Abstract: As the first waterproof component of the immersed tunnel, it is very important to ensure the remaining compression of the GINA gasket to resist external water intrusion. This paper proposed a method for determining warning thresholds for the remaining compression of the GINA gasket based on a material-to-mechanical analysis. In terms of material analysis, two factors that affect the GINA gasket are investigated: rubber hardness and cross-sectional shape, and they are adopted as the basis for subsequent mechanical analysis. In terms of mechanical analysis, uneven settlement during the operation period is considered to be the major cause of joint deformation, which is further divided into four modes: bending, shear, expansion, and torsion, with the computation model of the GINA gasket established to obtain the warning threshold. After that, a graded early warning method is adopted, and corresponding thresholds are given after an investigation of previous studies, which are validated by a three-dimensional finite element analysis. The deformation monitoring data between the E28 and E29 elements of the Hong Kong–Zhuhai–Macao Bridge Immersed Tunnel are used to verify the proposed method. The results show that the GINA gasket of the Hong Kong–Zhuhai–Macao Bridge Immersed Tunnel is currently in a safe state, and its deformation is much lower than the minimum warning level.

Keywords: immersed tunnel; GINA gasket; joint opening; graded warning method

MSC: 37M10

1. Introduction

The operational environment of the immersed tunnel is complex and changeable, such as the underwater soil being soft and the siltation being serious, which easily causes uneven settlement [1]. The uneven settlement will further lead to shear, torsion, and other deformation at the immersed tunnel joint, resulting in the risk of leakage at the joint [2]. As the GINA gasket is the key component to preventing leakage from the immersed tunnel joint, the determination of its warning threshold is critical [3].

Many studies have paid attention to the leakage caused by uneven settlement of immersed tunnel joints at the beginning of the 21st century [4,5]. Ding and Liu [6] investigated the stress-strain property of the deformation for immersed tunnel joints, and the stresses of the GINA gasket and OMEGA gasket were both discussed. The stress-strain curve of the GINA gasket was fitted by experimental data, and the fitting formulas for two stages of compression deformation $\leq$80 mm and >80 mm were given, respectively.

Liu et al. [7] proposed a mechanical model for immersed tunnel joints considering the effect of uneven settlement and identified that there is a positive proportion between the joint stiffness of the immersed tunnel and the compression stiffness of the GINA gasket. Wang et al. [8] divided the uneven longitudinal settlement of immersed tunnel joints into bending deformation and shear deformation; in addition, they discussed the longitudinal uneven settlement development trend of immersed tunnels under periodic tidal loads. However, the remaining compression of the GINA gasket is not considered in this study. To date, many studies have mainly focused on the establishment of a mechanical model for immersed tunnel joints, and there are only a few studies relating to the warning thresholds for the remaining compression of the GINA gasket during operation.

The immersed tunnel joints can be divided into rigid joints and flexible joints according to the stiffness ratio of the joint and element. Most immersed tunnels adopt flexible joints, such as the Ningbo Yongjiang immersed tunnel, the Changhong immersed tunnel, the Honggu immersed tunnel, and the Shanghai Outer-ring immersed tunnel in China [9–12]. For flexible joints, the remaining compression of the GINA gasket determines the water-tightness of the immersed tunnel joint [13]. However, there is no uniformly recognized specification for the monitoring of the GINA gasket during operation, and the establishment of the monitoring system mainly depends on design experience [14]. Therefore, the warning threshold and specification for the GINA gasket need to be further studied.

This paper intends to investigate an early warning method that can be applied to the remaining compression of the GINA gasket during operation. Thus, the warning thresholds of the deformation of immersed tunnel joints can be determined and guarantee that the structural health monitoring of the immersed tunnel plays a key role in ensuring the operational safety of the immersed tunnel.

2. Immersed Tunnel Joint and GINA Gasket

2.1. Overview of Immersed Tunnel Joint

A wide variety of immersed tunnel joints are available to provide different adaptability to differential settlement. These joints are generally classified according to the ratio between the stiffness of the joint itself and the stiffness of the element section: cast-in-place concrete joints are considered rigid, joints that do not contain shear resistance are considered flexible, and those with a stiffness ratio between the above two are considered semi-rigid and semi-flexible to semi-rigid [15,16]. Therefore, the types of immersed tunnel joints can be divided into four categories in detail: rigid joints, flexible joints, semi-rigid joints, and semi-flexible to semi-rigid joints. As the rigid joints formed by cast-in-place concrete are not considered in this study, their cross-section is not given below. The cross-sections of the other three joints are shown in Figure 1.

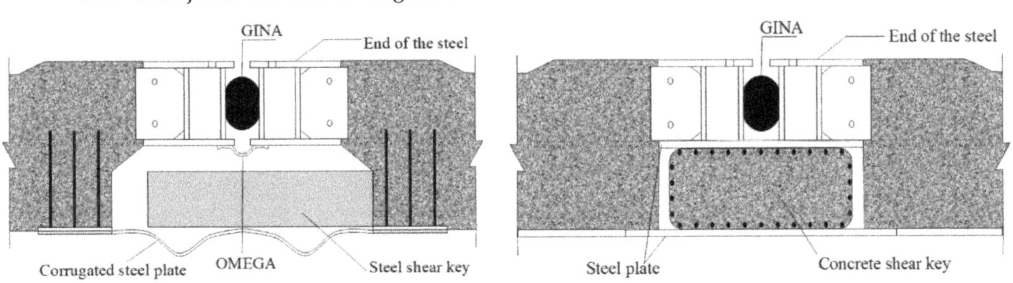

(a) (b)

Figure 1. *Cont.*

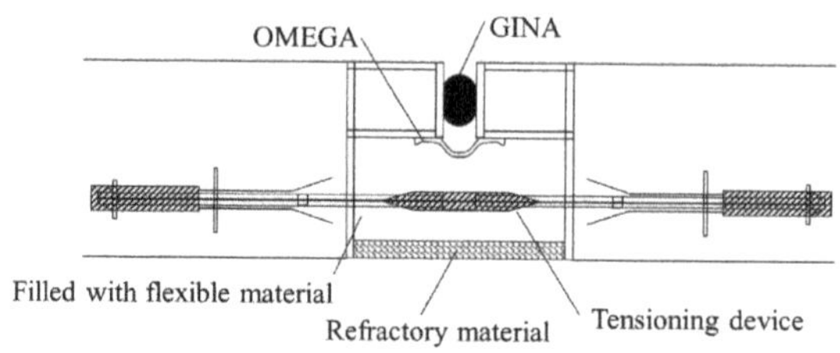

(c)

Figure 1. The different types of immersed tunnel joints (redrawn according to Wei and Lu [17] and Xue [18]). (**a**) Semi-flexible to semi-rigid joint. (**b**) Semi-rigid joint. (**c**) Flexible joint.

As shown in Figure 1, the main components of the first two joints are similar, which are the end of the steel, GINA gasket, OMEGA gasket, steel plate, and shear key. Moreover, all three types of joints adopt the GINA gasket as the first line of defense for joint waterproofing.

2.2. GINA Gasket

Many studies have revealed that the greater the compression of the GINA gasket is, the better the sealing performance, according to the field tests. Two factors mainly affect the compression of the GINA gasket: one is the rubber hardness of the GINA gasket, and the other is the cross-sectional shapes of the GINA gasket.

2.2.1. The Rubber Hardness of the GINA Gasket

The rubber hardness of the GINA gasket is proven to affect the deformation performance of the GINA gasket. Peng et al. [19] identified three GINA gaskets with different rubber hardness to test the deformation capacity of the GINA gasket, and the results are shown in Figure 2.

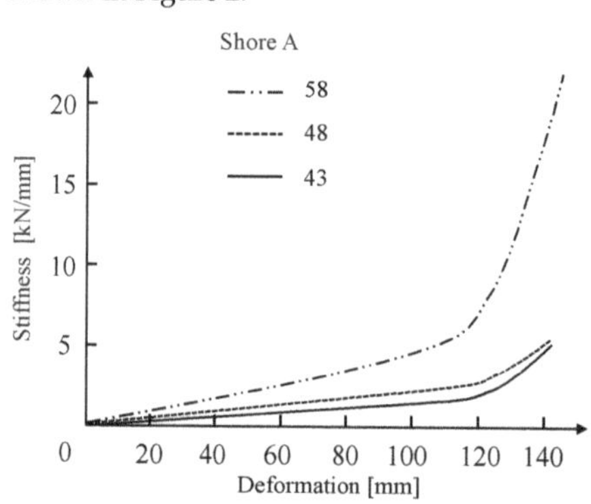

Figure 2. Stiffness–deformation curve of the GINA gasket (redrawn according to the results of Peng et al. [19]).

The two types with the hardness of 43 and 48 Shore A show a small change in stiffness at the same deformation, and the type with the hardness of 58 Shore A shows a large change in stiffness, according to Figure 2. The unit Shore A is a physical measure of a substance's ability to deform under pressure or resist puncture. Shore A is generally used to characterize softer rubber materials with a hardness range of 10 to 90. The higher the value of Shore A is, the higher the hardness [20]. The influence of rubber hardness on the stiffness is not obvious when the compression deformation is less than 90 mm, and the stiffness changes significantly with increasing hardness when the compression deformation is more than 120 mm. The material characteristics of the GINA gasket with an abrupt inflection point provide an important reference for determining the threshold of waterproof failure.

In fact, the mechanical properties of the GINA gasket (made of rubber) are not determined by a single factor, such as hardness, but are also related to a variety of factors, such as the size and the frequency of the load. Its constitutive model cannot be characterized by a simple modulus of elasticity. The constitutive models of GINA gasket are mostly derived from the phenomenology theory, which assumes that rubber is homogeneous and incompressible in its undeformed state [21]. From the above assumptions, the constitutive model of the GINA gasket can be expressed as a strain energy density function, and a common model is the Mooney–Rivlin model, as shown in Equation (1).

$$W = C_{10}(I_1 - 3) + C_{01}(I_2 - 3) \tag{1}$$

where W is the strain energy density, and a greater density represents a greater compression stiffness; C_{10} and C_{01} are Rivlin constants, which depend on the rubber stiffness and are positively related to the rubber stiffness; and I_1 and I_2 represent the first and second Green strain invariants, respectively. Jiang, Bai, and Su [22] adopted Equation (1) to determine the parameters in finite element simulation for obtaining the mechanical performance of the immersed tunnel joints, including the GINA gasket and compared the results of simulation with a 1:10 scale experimental test. The two results are basically the same, which verifies the correctness of the above formula.

Therefore, based on a lot of numerical simulations and field test results, the compression of the GINA gaskets with different hardness is usually designed to be greater than 90 mm to ensure that the GINA gaskets have sufficient waterproof performance.

2.2.2. The Cross-Sectional Shapes of GINA Gasket

As shown in Figure 3, the traditional GINA gasket is made of rubber with a sharp rib, main part, bottom rib, and winged edge [10]. This type of GINA gasket is widely used in the Pearl River Immersed Tunnel and the Hong Kong–Zhuhai–Macao Bridge Immersed Tunnel.

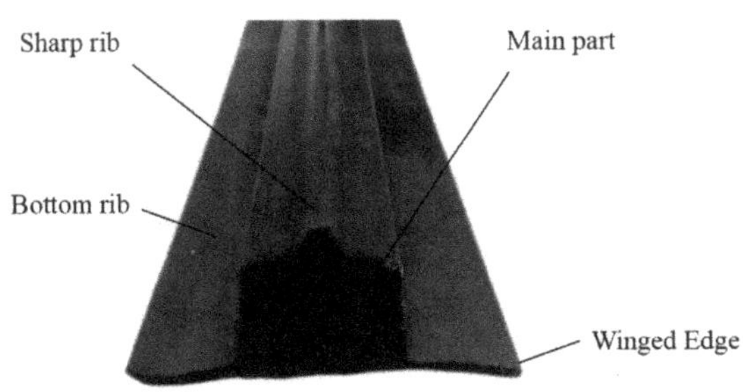

Figure 3. The traditional GINA gasket (redrawn according to Xiao et al. [10]).

The traditional GINA gasket has developed a variety of cross-sectional shapes based on years of practice. The representative ones are the TRELLEBORC type, developed in the Netherlands; the PHOENIX type, developed in Germany; the HORN type, developed in Japan; the STIRN type; and the GINA improved type. Several types of cross-sectional shapes of GINA gaskets are shown in Figure 4.

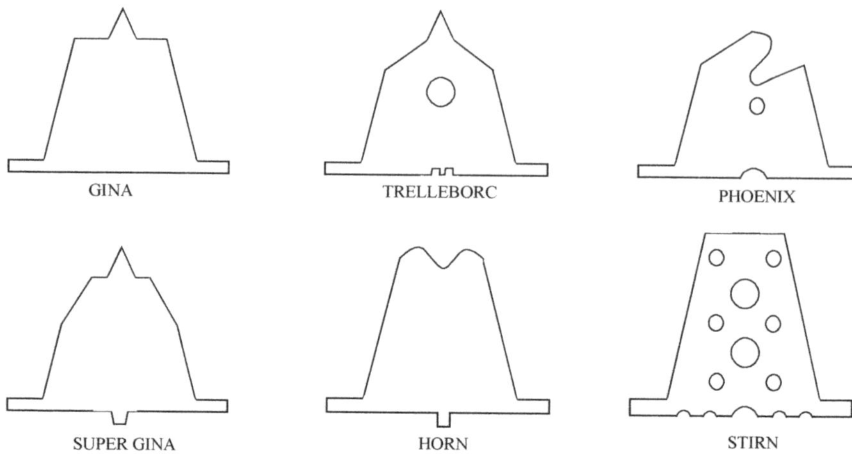

Figure 4. The different cross-sectional shapes of GINA gaskets (redrawn according to Hu et al. [23]).

The abovementioned different cross-sectional shapes of GINA gaskets are divided into four typical types [23], and the four typical types are shown in Figure 5.

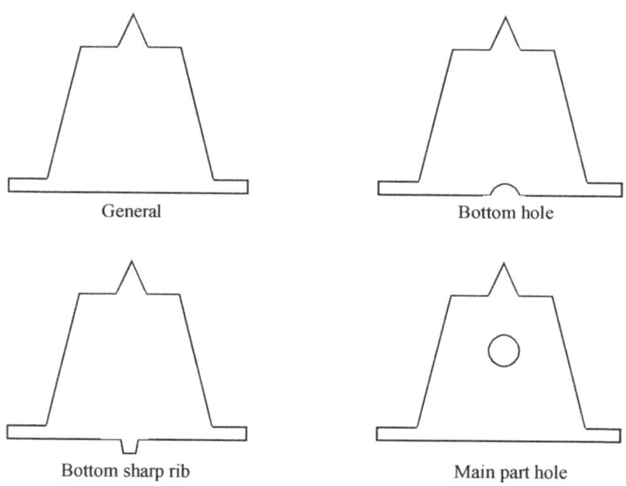

Figure 5. The four typical types of GINA gaskets (redrawn according to Hu et al. [23]).

The conclusions are as follows: the type of bottom hole has the best contact with the bottom plate, so the bottom hole can improve the waterproof performance of the bottom plate. The type of sharp bottom rib is easy to overturn in the prophase of compression of the GINA gasket because of the small action area with the steel plate, which will result in poor waterproofing. The type of main part hole can significantly reduce the stress concentration of the sharp rib, which is more beneficial to the long-term waterproofing of the GINA gasket. The traditional type can better withstand the eccentric load.

3. Deformation of GINA Gasket

3.1. The Compression of GINA Gasket

3.1.1. The Minimum Compression of GINA Gasket

The minimum compression of the GINA gasket is determined by the magnitude of the water pressure, i.e., the higher the groundwater level in the immersed tunnel is, the higher the minimum compression needed, as shown in Figure 6.

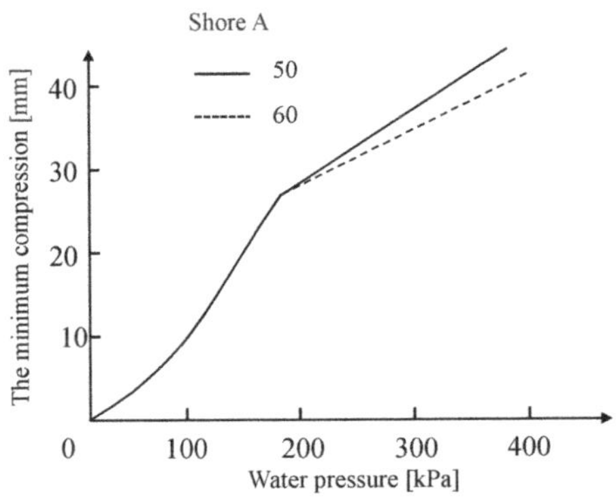

Figure 6. The relationship curve between the minimum compression and water pressure (redrawn according to the results of Tang, Guan and Wan [24]).

The minimum compression of the GINA gasket Δ_m can be determined according to Figure 6. To avoid the risk of errors and uncertainties, the actual remaining compression in practice should exceed the calculated minimum compression by a certain number, e.g., 20 mm, to preserve enough waterproof performance of the immersed tunnel joint during the operation [24].

3.1.2. The Compression Characteristic of GINA Gasket

The design compression is usually not equal to the remaining compression of the GINA gasket because the remaining compression of the GINA gasket will vary due to external loads or deformations, e.g., uneven settlement. The relationship between each compression characteristic is shown in Figure 7. In the design and installation phase, the design compression Δ_d is determined according to Equation (2),

$$F = \frac{\gamma \times H \times S}{C} \quad (2)$$

where F is the pressure of the GINA gasket (kPa); γ is the capacitance of the water overlying the immersed tunnel (N/m^3); H is the water depth to the section of the immersed tunnel joint shape center (m); S is the hydraulic crimp area of the immersed tunnel joint (m^2); and C is the perimeter of the GINA gasket (m).

Δ_r is the remaining compression during operation. As known above, to prevent water leakage from the immersed tunnel joint, the remaining compression of the GINA gasket should be greater than the minimum compression and should have a certain safety reserve. Moreover, the stress relaxation of the GINA gasket will occur under long time stress conditions because the GINA gasket is made of rubber. This is also a nonnegligible factor affecting the warning threshold of the GINA gasket. Hence, the warning threshold of the GINA gasket can be obtained by Equation (3),

$$U_0 = \frac{\Delta_m}{k} + c_1 + c_2 + c_3 + c_4 \quad (3)$$

$$\Delta_r = \Delta_d - d \quad (4)$$

$$g_n \times U_0 \leq \Delta_r < g_{n+1} \times U_0 (n = 1, \cdots, m) \tag{5}$$

where U_0 is the warning threshold; Δ_m is the minimum compression; k is the relaxation coefficient, the range is (0, 1), and the degree of relaxation increases as the relaxation coefficient decreases; c_1 is the safety reserve (the value is generally adopted as 20 mm); c_2 is the unevenness of the surface at the joint (the value is generally 10 mm); c_3 is the longitudinal displacement of the joint caused by the temperature effect (the value is generally 10 mm); c_4 is the installation error (the value is generally 10 mm); d is the change in compression caused by uneven settlement; g_n is the graded warning coefficient, and the graded warning is divided into m levels.

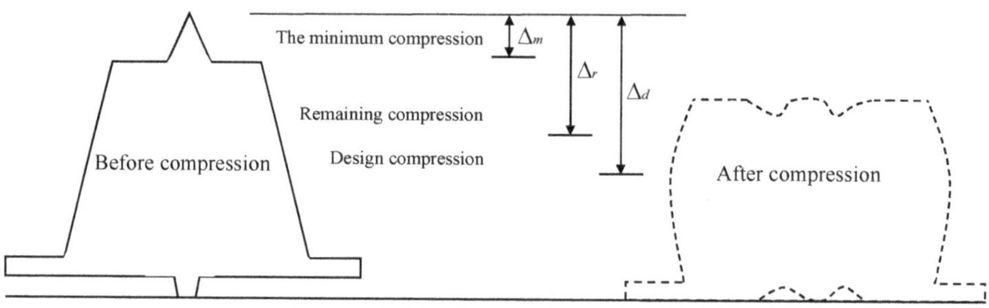

Figure 7. The relationship of compression characteristics of GINA gasket (redrawn according to Liu et al. [25]).

The warning thresholds can be obtained by calculating the minimum compression, relaxation coefficient, and constant term according to Equation (3). The remaining compression is calculated by the change in compression caused by uneven settlement according to Equation (4). The graded warning can be divided into multiple levels according to Equation (5). If the remaining compression falls into the interval of warning thresholds of different levels, corresponding measures will be taken to ensure the safety of the immersed tunnel during operation.

3.2. Deformation Modes and Computation Model

3.2.1. The Four Deformation Modes of Immersed Tunnel Joint

Regarding the change in compression caused by uneven settlement, i.e., d in Equation (4), this term can be estimated by mechanical analysis of the immersed tunnel joint. Generally, the uneven settlement of the immersed tunnel can lead to four deformation modes of the immersed tunnel joint, as shown in Figure 8, which are bending, shear, expansion, and torsion.

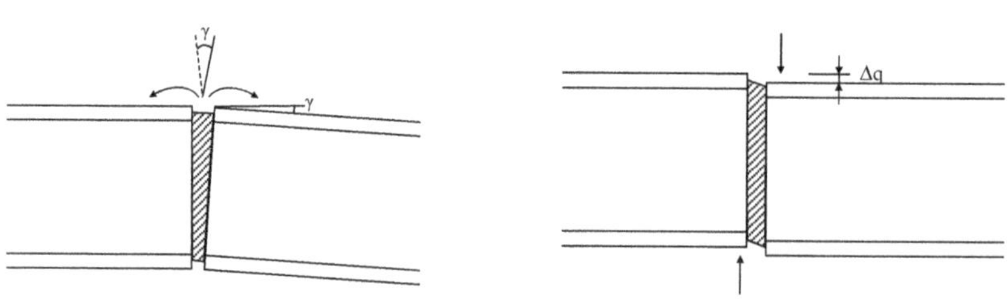

(**a**) (**b**)

Figure 8. *Cont.*

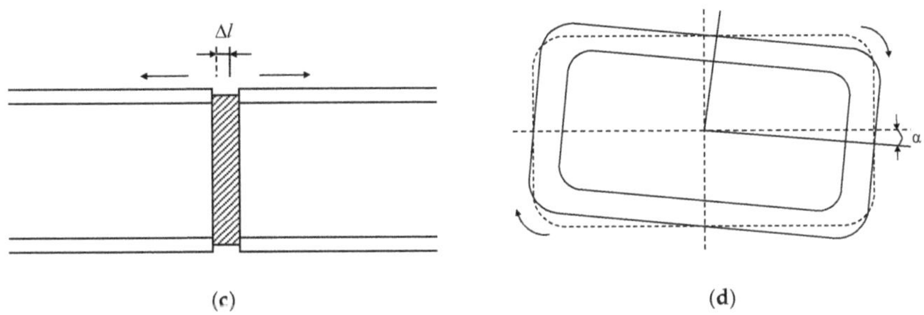

Figure 8. The four deformation modes of immersed tunnel joint (redrawn according to Xie et al. [26]): (**a**) bending; (**b**) shear; (**c**) expansion; (**d**) torsion.

The formulas for calculating the change in compression due to the four deformation modes of the uneven settlement are presented as follows (revised according to HP-CLab [27]).

1. Bending deformation

As shown in Figure 9, the change in compression can be obtained by Equations (6)–(9) in the case of bending deformation,

$$h' = L\cdot \sin(\theta - \gamma) + \Delta s = L\cdot \sin\theta \tag{6}$$

$$d_1 = H' \sin\gamma \tag{7}$$

$$d_1^2 + \frac{H'}{L}\cos\theta(L\cdot \sin\theta - \Delta s)d_1 + \frac{H'^2}{L^2}\left(\Delta s^2 - 2\Delta s\cdot L\cdot \sin\theta\right) = 0 \tag{8}$$

$$d_1 = \frac{H'}{L}\left[\sin\theta\sqrt{L^2 - (L\cdot \sin\theta - \Delta s)^2} - (L\cdot \sin\theta - \Delta s)\cos\theta\right] \tag{9}$$

where Δs is the uneven settlement in the vertical direction; h' is the design height difference at both ends of the elements; γ is the rotation angle caused by the deviation of the elements from the original equilibrium position; L is the length of the element; H is the vertical height of the element; H' is the height difference for the installation centerline of GINA gasket; θ is the fabrication elevation of the element; and d_1 is the change in compression for the GINA gasket due to bending deformation.

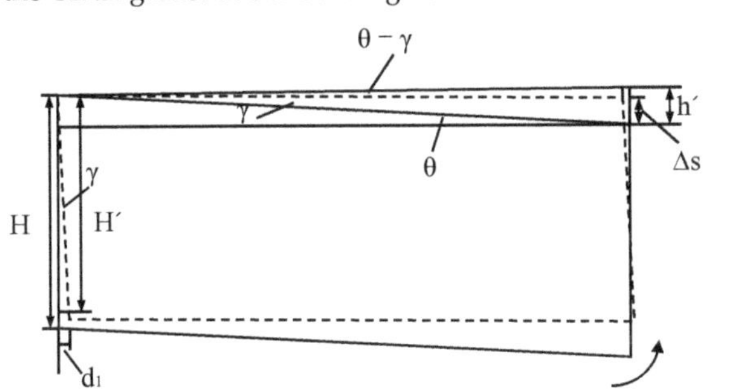

Figure 9. Geometric diagram of bending deformation.

The assumptions in the above geometric calculation are illustrated as follows:

(1) The element is completely rigid, the axis of the element remains straight in the rotation, the axial length is unchanged, and the deformation of the element is negligible.

(2) The amount of rigid body translation displacement for each element is identical, and the element under the effect of uneven settlement only produces the corresponding rotation.

(3) The tensile stiffness of the joint is less than the compressive stiffness, and the center point of rotation is located on the compressive side of the end of the element.
(4) The bending deformation of the joint is small.

The bending direction determines the change in the compression of each part of the GINA gasket. If the bending is counterclockwise, the compression of the GINA gasket at the top of the element increases while the compression at the bottom of the element decreases.

2. Shear deformation

As shown in Figure 10, the change in compression can be obtained by Equation (10) in the case of shear deformation.

$$d_2 = \sqrt{\Delta_q^2 + B^2} - B \tag{10}$$

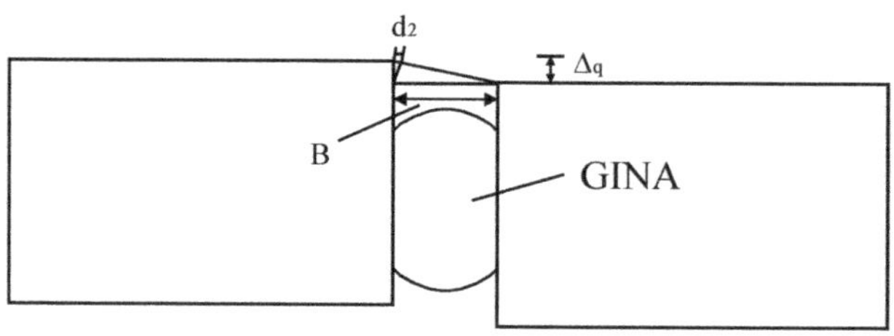

Figure 10. Geometric diagram of shear deformation.

In Figure 10 and Equation (10), B is the initial compression of the GINA gasket; Δ_q is the shear deformation; and d_2 is the change in compression for the GINA gasket due to shear deformation.

The assumptions in the above geometric calculation are illustrated as follows:

(1) The element is completely rigid, and the deformation of the element is negligible.
(2) The element only has rigid translation in the vertical direction, and it does not produce rotation and movement in the horizontal direction.
(3) The relative settlement is small, smaller than the shear displacement limit of the joint. There is sufficient friction between the GINA gasket and the end of the steel.

The change in compression of the GINA gasket caused by shear deformation will reduce the remaining compression. If the dislocation distance is large, the immersed tunnel joint will occur leakage, which may lead to direct damage to the immersed tunnel joint in serious situations.

3. Expansion deformation

As shown in Figure 11, the change in compression can be obtained by Equation (11) in the case of expansion deformation,

$$d_3 = \Delta l \tag{11}$$

where B is the initial compression of the GINA gasket; Δl is the expansion deformation; and d_3 is the change in compression of the GINA gasket due to expansion deformation.

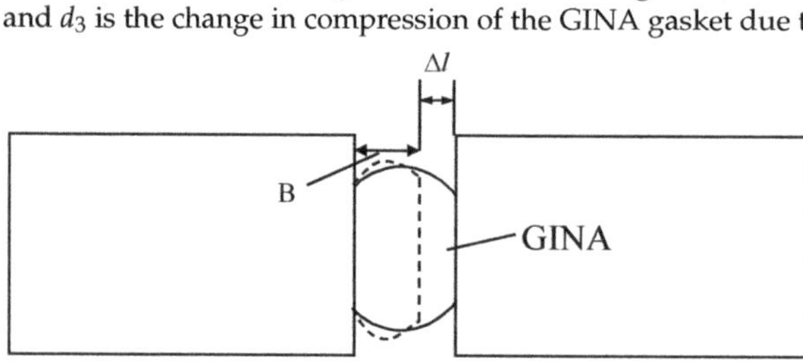

Figure 11. Geometric diagram of expansion deformation.

The assumptions in the above geometric calculation are illustrated as follows:

(1) The element only has rigid body translation along the axial direction, and it does not produce rotation and uneven settlement in the vertical direction;
(2) The deformation along the axis of the end of steel to the end of the joint can be ignored.

4. Torsion deformation

The torsion deformation of the joint is induced by the uneven settlement along the cross-section of the element. Since the torsion deformation only occurs on the plane of the cross-section of the element and does not deform in the perpendicular direction, this minuscule torsion deformation of the joint hardly changes the compression of the GINA gasket, which can be ignored in the calculation.

3.2.2. Formulas of Final Change of Compression

According to the analysis in Section 3.2.1, the final change in compression of the GINA gasket caused by the uneven settlement can be calculated by Equation (12).

$$d = d_1 + d_2 + d_3 \tag{12}$$

Thus, the remaining compression of the GINA gasket can be determined according to Equations (12) and (4). This term is important because excessive change may result in insufficient remaining compression of the GINA gasket and trigger an early warning.

3.3. *Estimation of Relaxation Coefficient*

According to Equation (3), the relaxation coefficient is also involved in determining the warning thresholds of the GINA gasket. This paper reviews the test results related to the stress relaxation of the GINA gasket, and they are summarized in Table 1.

Table 1. Testing results of the stress relaxation rate in previous studies.

Author	Rubber Hardness (Shore A)	Initial Compression (mm)	Accumulated Stress Relaxation (kN/m)	Estimated Stress Relaxation Rate after 100a
Lu et al. [28] (2003)	65	80 100 110	89.4 184.2 317	55%
Huang [29] (2010)	/	30 40 50	approximately 20% of the total stress	52.3%
Hu et al. [30] (2020)	48	50 70 110 125	approximately 35% of the total stress	30.6% 32% 34.3% 43.1%

It can be easily estimated that the relaxation rate of the GINA gasket is positively proportional to its rubber hardness and initial compression, based on the data in Table 1. Furthermore, it is also revealed that the relaxation rate is positively proportional to the service time. The stress relaxation rate of the GINA gasket is nearly 40% after 50 years and more than 50% after 100 years [29]. Therefore, the relaxation coefficient k in Equation (3) can be estimated by Equation (13),

$$k = 1 - s_{(n,\ \Delta_d)} \tag{13}$$

where s is the relaxation rate; n is the service time of immersed tunnel; and Δ_d is the design compression.

4. Warning Method of Immersed Tunnel

4.1. Graded Warning Method

4.1.1. Graded Warning of GINA Gasket

Using monitoring data for early warning is an important measure to ensure the structural safety of the immersed tunnel, and the graded early warning method can pay attention to possible problems in advance and take corresponding measures. Liu et al. [25] gave the graded warning method for the warning threshold of each monitoring index based on the Yongjiang immersed tunnel, as shown in Table 2. Xie et al. [26] investigated the graded warning thresholds of the remaining compression of the GINA gasket, of which the stress relaxation was considered in the minimum compression of the GINA gasket.

Table 2. The graded warning thresholds of Yongjiang immersed tunnel (revised according to the results of Xie et al. [26]).

Alert Level	Graded Warning	Colors
IV	$U < 0.5U_0$	Green
III	$0.5U_0 \leq U < 0.7U_0$	Yellow
II	$0.7U_0 \leq U < 0.9U_0$	Orange
I	$U \geq 0.9U_0$	Red

Notes: U_0 is the warning threshold and U is the monitoring value.

Xu et al. [31,32] established a monitoring system for the Honggu tunnel during operation. In this study, the warning threshold of the GINA gasket was not directly obtained, but the warning threshold of the relative displacement for the immersed tunnel joint was given. The warning thresholds were divided into four grades, A, B, C, and D, where A was the best and D was the worst, as shown in Table 3.

Table 3. The graded warning thresholds of Honggu tunnel (revised according to Hu et al. [31]).

Index	A	B	C	D
Joint opening (mm)	≤21.6	21.6–25	25–28.3	≥28.3
Joint compression (mm)	≤20.5	20.5–23.3	23.3–33.3	≥33.3
Joint horizontal displacement (mm)	≤25	25–30	30–35.3	≥35.3
Uneven settlement (mm)	≤30	30–40	40–50	≥50

4.1.2. The Specification of Graded Warning for GINA Gasket

Currently, there is no specification of graded warning for the structural health monitoring of the GINA gasket, but it is clearly stipulated that the compression of the GINA gasket should be monitored during the operation in the Specifications for Design of Highway Immersed Tunnel (JTG/T 3371-01—2022) [33]. The transportation administration of Jiangsu Province of China also released the latest relevant specification involving the description of the graded warning, which is the Technical Specification of Structure Health Monitoring for Underwater Tunnel (DB32/T 4243–2022) [34]. This specification proposed a unified graded warning threshold method for all monitored components, as shown in Table 4.

Table 4. The unified graded warning thresholds for monitored components of underwater tunnel (revised according to Table 6.6.8 in [34]).

Alert Level	Description	Alert Status	Warning Thresholds
I	Particularly serious	Red warning	$\geq U_0$
II	Serious	Orange warning	[0.75–1) U_0
III	Relatively serious	Yellow warning	[0.5–0.75) U_0
IV	General	Blue warning	[0.25–0.5) U_0
V	Normal	/	<0.25 U_0

Notes: U_0 is the warning threshold.

In the above tables, the graded warning is divided into multiple levels, and the graded warning coefficients are roughly similar to those in other studies. This classification method can be used for reference. Although a general graded warning method has been given, there is still a lack of a unified formulation method for determining the graded warning threshold of the GINA gasket during operation.

4.2. Determining the Warning Thresholds of an Immersed Tunnel

4.2.1. Outlines of the Hong Kong–Zhuhai–Macao Bridge Immersed Tunnel

This study adopts the Hong Kong–Zhuhai–Macao Bridge (HZMB) Immersed Tunnel as an illustrative example. The HZMB is a 55-km-long mega project spanning Lingdingyang Bay. It includes three components: the main project of the bridge, island, and undersea tunnel; the ports of Hong Kong, Zhuhai, and Macao; and the connecting line between the three cities. As a part of the main project, the most challenging task is the 6.7-km-long undersea tunnel [35,36]. As a complex sea-crossing project, the HZMB immersed tunnel has a transition section at the head of the artificial islands where different foundation solutions are adopted: pile foundations in the artificial island and sand compaction pile (SCP) flexible composite foundations in the transition section. More details about the foundation strategy of the HZMB immersed tunnel can be found in Hu et al. [37]. Additionally, the thickness of the placed backfill is uneven [38]. Meanwhile, the deposition of sediments should also be taken into consideration during the operation life of the structure. Load changes in the tunnel's longitudinal direction will also result in a larger internal force in the tunnel [39,40]. All the above situations will make the operational safety of the GINA gasket of the immersed tunnel a great challenge.

The immersed tunnel section has a length of 5.67 km and consists of 33 elements, as shown in Figure 12. Among all the elements, E28–E33 is located on the flat curve with a radius (R) of 5500 m, and the rest are located on the straight section [41]. The closure joint is between E29 and E30, and the water depth at the bottom of the closure joint is 27.9 m. The mechanical properties of soil layers under the HZMB-immersed tunnel were extracted from recent publications [37], as shown in Table 5.

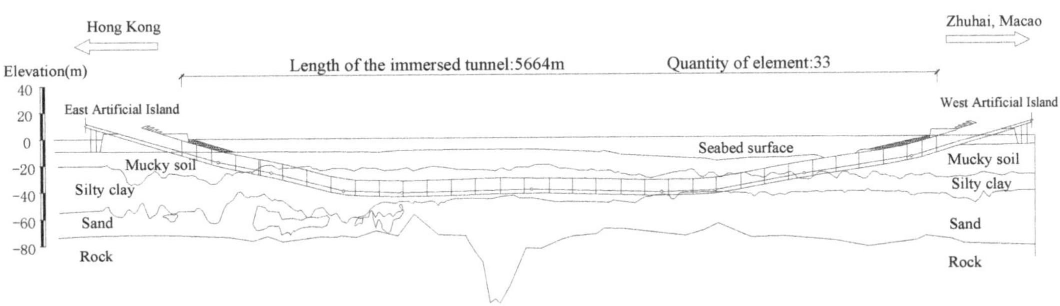

Figure 12. Longitudinal layout of the HZMB immersed tunnel (redrawn according to Lin et al. [41]).

Table 5. Mechanical properties of soil layers under the HZMB immersed tunnel (data extracted from Hu et al. [37]).

Soil Layer	Unit Weight (kN/m^3)	Direct Shear Test			
		Quick Shear		Consolidated Quick Shear	
		c (kPa)	φ (°)	c (kPa)	φ (°)
Mucky soil	17.6	8.0	7.0	10.0	16.0
Silt clay	19.3	20.0	20.0	25.0	25.0
Sand	21.4	/	/	/	/

The standard tunnel element is 180 m long, consisting of eight segments, each of which stretches 22.5 m. The immersed tunnel provides a dual three-lane carriageway with a width of 2 × 14.55 m and a vertical clearance of 8.4 m, as shown in Figure 13. The GINA gasket between E28 and E29 is selected for analysis. The central elevation of the E29 element is −25.5 m. The total length of the GINA gasket of each section is 92 m.

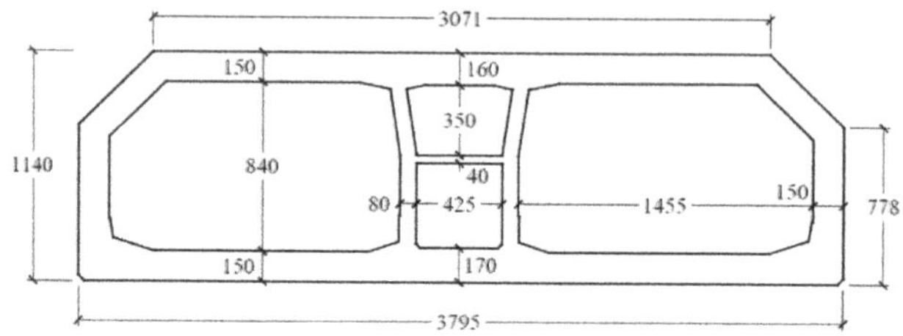

Figure 13. Cross-sectional geometry of the HZMB immersed tunnel (unit: cm).

4.2.2. Estimated Values of Thresholds and Safety Assessment

According to Equation (2) and the compressive stress–deformation curve of the GINA gasket (Figure 14), it can be estimated that the design compression of the GINA gasket of the E29 element is approximately 140 mm.

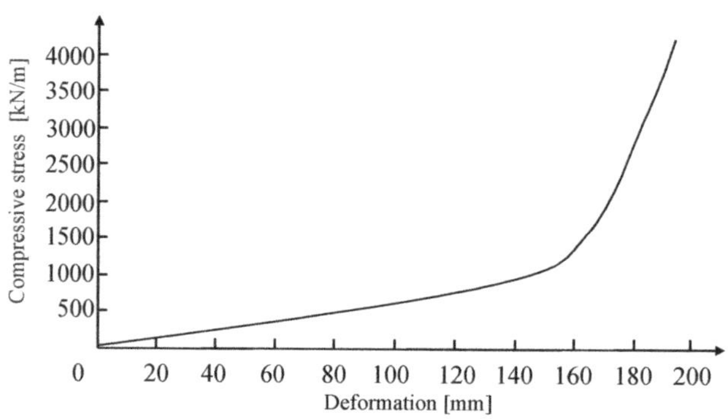

Figure 14. The compressive stress–deformation curve of the GINA gasket (redrawn according to Lin and Liu [42]).

According to the elevation of the E29 element and the curve of the relationship between the minimum compression and water pressure (Figure 6), the minimum compression is approximately 35 mm. According to Section 3.3, the stress relaxation rate of the GINA gasket is estimated at 40%. Thus, the relaxation coefficient is 0.6, according to Equation (13), and the warning threshold U_0 of the GINA gasket is 108 mm, according to Equation (3).

The graded warning method is a risk management tool that is related to the risk acceptance level of managers. The HZMB is a mega-project with a low level of risk acceptance. In order to guarantee that no leakage occurs in the immersed tunnel under all warning grades, it is assumed that the contact pressure of the GINA gasket under the highest level of warning still guarantees 1–2 times the water pressure. Therefore, the warning level coefficients are initially set to 1, 0.9, 0.8, and 0.7, corresponding to blue (lowest), yellow, orange, and red (highest) warning levels, respectively. The graded warning thresholds of the remaining compression of the GINA gasket can be established, as shown in Table 6. The GINA gasket's ability to resist water pressure at the deformations corresponding to these warning levels was verified by finite element analysis in Section 4.3.

Table 6. The graded warning thresholds of the remaining compression of GINA gasket for the HZMB Immersed Tunnel.

Alert Level	Description	Alert Status	Remaining Compression (mm)	Change of Compression (mm)
I	Particularly serious	Red warning	<86.4	>53.6
II	Serious	Orange warning	[86.4–97.2)	(42.8–53.6]
III	Relatively serious	Yellow warning	[97.2–108)	(32–42.8]
IV	General	Blue warning	≥108	≤32

4.3. Illustrative Example of the Proposed Graded Warning Method

4.3.1. Results Identified by Simplified Formulations

Based on the uneven settlement data of E28 and E29 of the HZMB Immersed Tunnel during the first half of 2020, the total change in compression of the GINA gasket can be calculated by Equation (12). The mechanical decomposition of the deformation modes of immersed tunnel joint is presented in Figure 15.

(1) The uneven settlement of the head and tail for E28 is 6.3 mm, and the uneven settlement of the head and tail for E29 is 1.2 mm. According to Equation (9), d_1 of the E28 and E29 elements can be calculated as 0.16 mm.

(2) The differential post-construction settlement between the tail of E28 and the head of E29 is only 0.1 mm. According to Equation (10), d_2 of the E28 and E29 elements can be calculated as 3.6×10^{-5} mm, which can be ignored.

(3) At the same time, there is also a compression change d_3 caused by expansion deformation. Based on the monitoring data, the maximum value of d_3 is recorded as 4.2 mm.

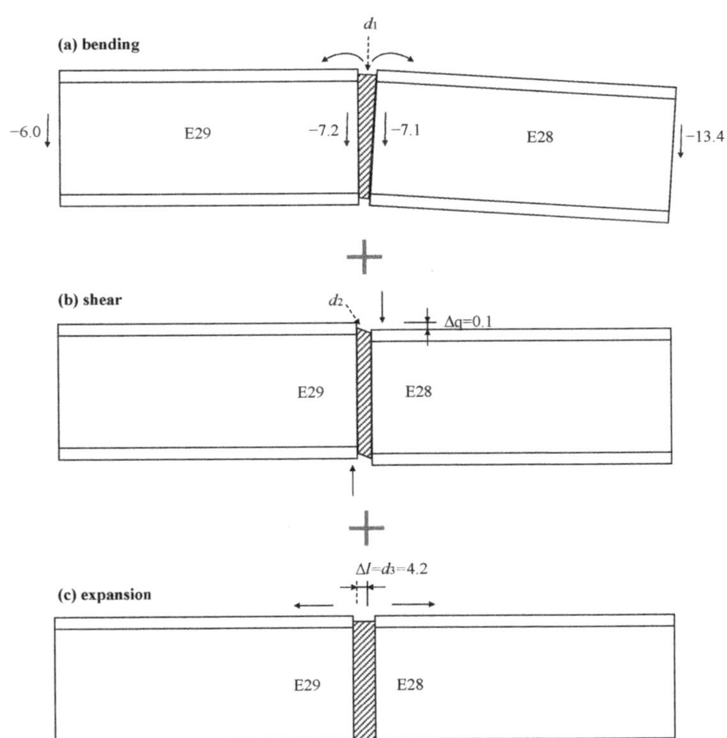

Figure 15. Mechanical decomposition of the deformation modes of immersed tunnel joint between E28 and E29 elements.

The summation of $(d_1 + d_2 + d_3)$ is assumed to be equal to the total change of the GINA gasket d. Then, the total change of the GINA gasket d varying with time is calculated by the monitoring data, which is shown in Figure 16.

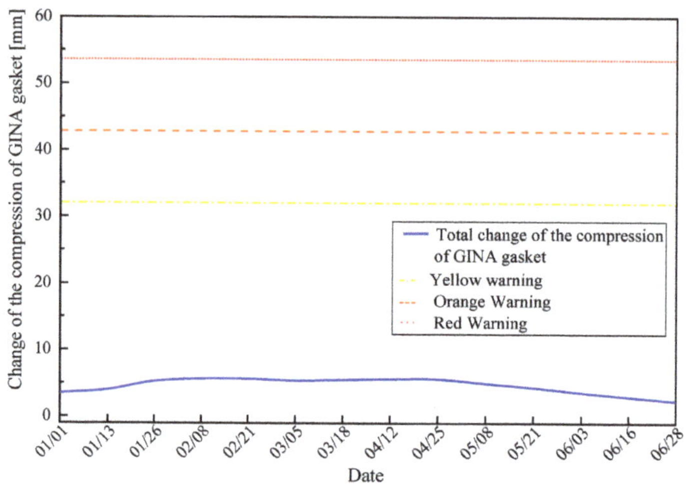

Figure 16. Total change of the compression of GINA gasket between E28 and E29 elements varying with time.

As shown in Figure 16, the maximum total change of the GINA gasket between E28 and E29 elements does not exceed 10 mm, which means that the remaining compression of the GINA gasket is greater than 130 mm. According to Table 6, the GINA gasket between E28 and E29 elements is in a safe state, and the risk of water leakage can be assessed to be very low. The results are also consistent with the actual situation on site.

4.3.2. Results Verified by Finite Element Analysis

To further verify whether the graded warning thresholds are reasonable, a finite element analysis of the GINA gasket between E28 and E29 elements is conducted in this paper. The geometry and finite element mesh of the GINA gasket are shown in Figure 17.

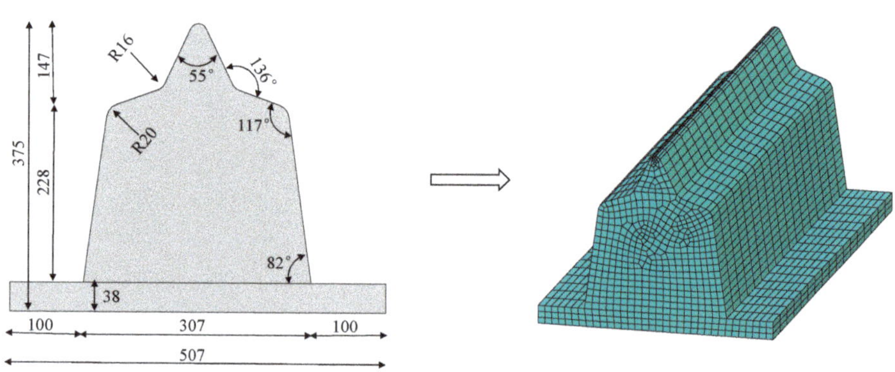

Figure 17. Geometry and finite element mesh of GINA gasket.

The GINA gasket adopted in the immersed tunnel of HZMB is a rubber material including two parts, the nose and main body, which have different hardness. The simulation was carried out by ABAQUS, using the rubber super-elastic Mooney–Rivlin constitutive model with a C3D8H mesh and a friction factor of 0.6 between the GINA gasket and the concrete part of the immersed tunnel joint. The parameters in the Mooney–Rivlin constitutive model are shown in Table 7.

Table 7. Parameters of the GINA gasket constitutive model.

Part	Hardness (Shore A)	C_{10} (MPa)	C_{01} (MPa)
Nose	50	0.012	0.309
Main body	65	0.7405	0.1851

The design compression of the GINA gasket is 140 mm. Based on the average water depths of E28 and E29 and the height of the pipe section, the water pressure p_w = 0.385 MPa. The design compression of 140 mm of GINA gasket is simulated in ABAQUS, and the results are shown in Figure 18. The stresses (pressure) at the top and bottom of the GINA gasket both exceed 1.5 MPa, which is much higher than the water pressure $3 \times p_w$ = 1.155 MPa. Therefore, the waterproofing capacity of the GINA gasket fully meets the requirements under the situation of design compression.

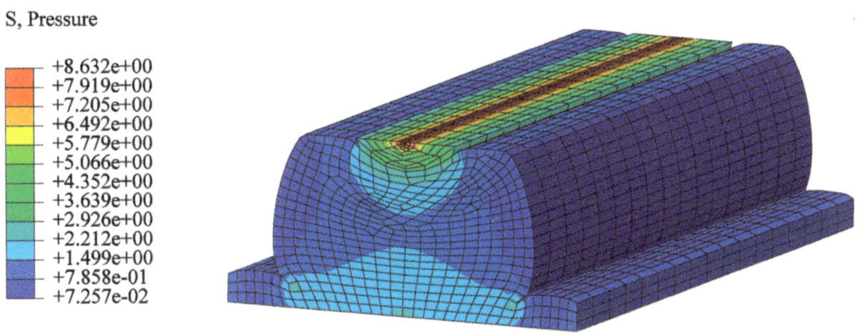

Figure 18. Stresses of GINA gasket under design compression (MPa).

Previous GINA gasket waterproof tests showed that the leakage parts are in the bottom of the main body, and the bottom pressure is also much smaller than the tip of the nose from simulation results; thus, the analysis of the bottom pressure of the GINA gasket is more significant in practical engineering. In this study, authors set different levels of warning thresholds (remaining compression = 108 mm, 97.2 mm, 86.4 mm, respectively) as the actual compression to simulate the bottom pressure distributions of the GINA gasket and compare the ratios between the bottom pressures and the water pressure. The numerical simulation results are shown in Figure 19.

As shown in Figure 19b–d, different characteristic values of the bottom pressure of the GINA gasket are extracted, and the results of their ratios to the water pressure are shown in Table 8.

From Table 8, it is concluded that the average bottom pressures of the GINA gasket are all greater than 1.5 times the water pressure at all warning thresholds of the remaining compression, which is consistent with the assumptions in Section 4.2. In addition, the remaining compression of 86.4 mm is the most dangerous situation, at which the minimum bottom pressure of the GINA gasket is 0.558 MPa, which is close to the value of water pressure, so it is reasonable to set this value as the threshold of the red warning alert, i.e., there is a possibility of water infiltration if the remaining compression is less than this value.

Through the analysis of numerical simulation results, it can be obtained that the graded warning thresholds proposed in this study have strong feasibility in practical engineering, and the proposed method can timely determine whether there is a risk of water leakage to provide safe operation of immersed tunnels.

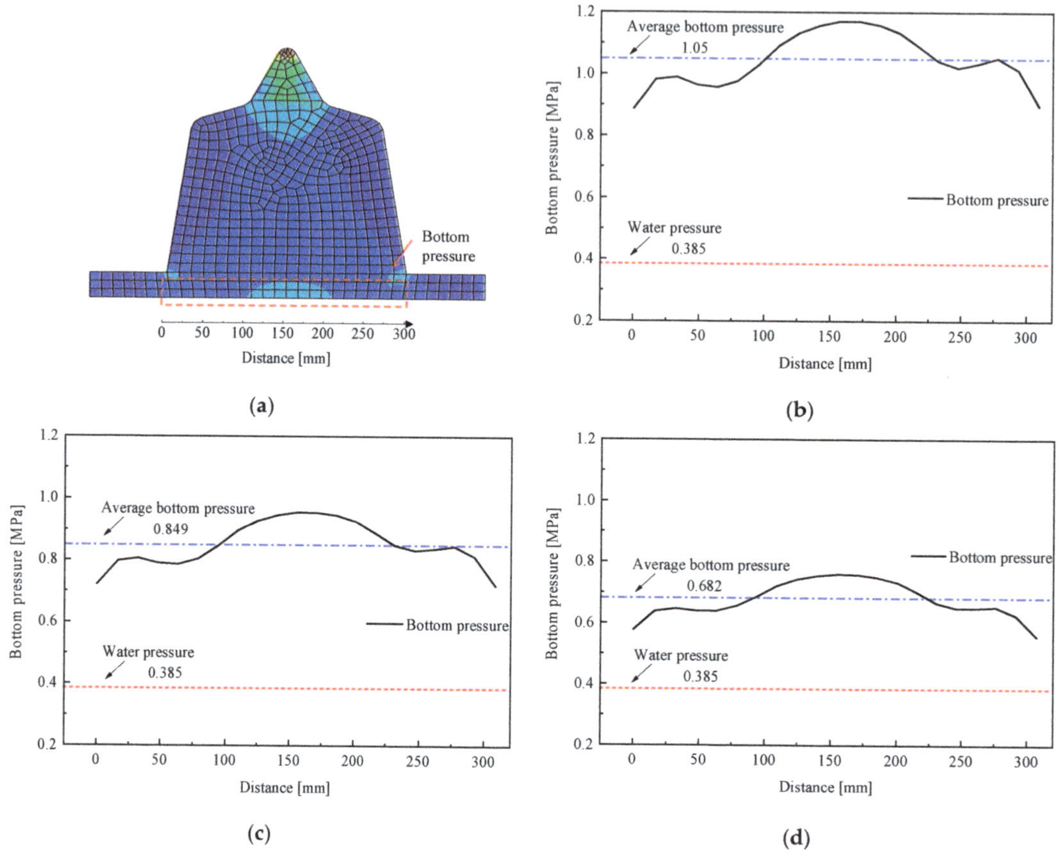

Figure 19. Bottom pressure of GINA gasket under different remaining compressions: (**a**) range of bottom pressure; (**b**) remaining compression = 108 mm; (**c**) remaining compression = 97.2 mm; (**d**) remaining compression = 86.4 mm.

Table 8. Ratios of bottom pressures of GINA gasket to water pressure.

Remaining Compression (mm)	Average Bottom Pressure/Water Pressure	Maximum Bottom Pressure/Water Pressure	Minimum Bottom Pressure/Water Pressure
108	2.73	3.04	2.30
97.2	2.20	2.48	1.87
86.4	1.77	1.97	1.45

5. Conclusions

This study analyzed the factors affecting the compression of the GINA gasket and summarized the computation model for the deformation of the GINA gasket due to uneven settlement. The calculation formulas for determining the graded warning thresholds were given, and their feasibility was verified by a real project. The following conclusions are drawn:

(1) The waterproof performance of the GINA gasket is directly related to the hardness of the rubber material and the cross-sectional shape. Properly increasing the rubber hardness can significantly improve the compression stiffness of the GINA gasket. The type of main part hole can significantly reduce the stress concentration of the top rib, which is more effective for long-term waterproofing.

(2) Uneven settlement is the main reason for the increase (decrease) in the compression of the GINA gasket during operation. The bending, shear, and expansion deformation will affect the compression of the GINA gasket. Therefore, to evaluate the waterproof status of the immersed tunnel during operation, monitoring the settlements of elements and the joint opening is indispensable.
(3) A material-to-mechanical analysis method is proposed to obtain the warning thresholds of the GINA gasket of immersed tunnels according to the material properties and mechanical computation model. This method is validated by the monitoring data at the joint of E28 and E29 of the HZMB Immersed Tunnel. The results show that there is no risk of leakage at this joint, which is consistent with the actual situation on site. The finite element analysis verified that the graded warning thresholds are feasible for different levels of leakage risks. Therefore, the proposed graded warning method for the GINA gasket is proven to be applicable to practical engineering.

Author Contributions: Conceptualization, H.D. and Q.A.; methodology, J.H. and Q.A.; software, J.H.; validation, J.H., X.J. and Y.Y.; investigation, J.C.; resources, Y.Y.; writing—original draft preparation, J.H.; writing—review and editing, Q.A. and S.D.; supervision, H.D. and S.D.; project administration, Y.Y.; funding acquisition, X.J. and H.D. All authors have read and agreed to the published version of the manuscript.

Funding: This study was funded by the National Key R&D Program of China (No.2019YFB1600702), the Chongqing Natural Science Foundation (Distinguished Youth Fund) Project (cstc2021jcyj-jqX0012), the National Natural Science Foundation of China (No.51978600), and the Natural Science Foundation of Chongqing Municipality (cstc2021jcyj-bshX0131).

Institutional Review Board Statement: Not applicable.

Informed Consent Statement: Not applicable.

Data Availability Statement: Data available on request to the authors.

Acknowledgments: We acknowledge the full support given by the Hong Kong-Zhuhai-Macao Bridge Authority.

Conflicts of Interest: The authors declare no conflict of interest.

References

1. Olsen, T.; Kasper, T.; de Wit, J. Immersed tunnels in soft soil conditions experience from the last 20 years. *Tunn. Undergr. Space Technol.* **2022**, *121*, 104315. [CrossRef]
2. Niu, Y.; Xie, Y.; Zhang, H.; Yue, X.; Han, Y.; Hu, Z. Study on Deformation Characteristics of Segment Joints of the Immersed Tunnel in Hong Kong-Zhuhai-Macau Bridge. *Adv. Mater. Sci. Eng.* **2022**, *2022*, 7152132. [CrossRef]
3. Wang, W.; Luo, Y.; Kong, L.; Zhang, Y.; Chen, Y. Numerical Simulation and Experimental Study on Mechanical Properties of GINA Waterstop. *Mod. Tunn. Technol.* **2021**, *58*, 237–243. (In Chinese)
4. Grantz, W.C. Immersed tunnel settlements. Part 1: Nature of settlements. *Tunn. Undergr. Space Technol.* **2001**, *16*, 195–201. [CrossRef]
5. Grantz, W.C. Immersed tunnel settlements: Part 2: Case histories. *Tunn. Undergr. Space Technol.* **2001**, *16*, 203–210. [CrossRef]
6. Ding, W.; Liu, P. Research on the Three-Dimensional Nonlinear Stiffness Mechanical Model of Immersed Tube Tunnel Joints. In Proceedings of the 2014 Geoshanghai International Congress, Shanghai, China, 26–28 May 2014.
7. Liu, P.; Chen, J.; Chen, Y.; Yang, J.; Tang, Q. Mechanical model for joints of immersed tunnel considering the influence of joint differential settlement. *Int. J. Geosynth. Ground Eng.* **2020**, *6*, 1–10. [CrossRef]
8. Wang, Y.N.; Zhou, H.Z.; Wang, L.C. Settlement mode analysis for an immersed tube tunnel considering a nonuniform foundation under tidal load. *China Ocean Eng.* **2022**, *36*, 427–438. [CrossRef]
9. Xiao, W.; Yu, H.; Yuan, Y.; Taerwe, L.; Chai, R. Compression–bending behavior of a scaled immersion joint. *Tunn. Undergr. Space Technol.* **2015**, *49*, 426–437. [CrossRef]
10. Xiao, W.; Yu, H.; Yuan, Y.; Taerwe, L.; Xu, G. Compression-shear behavior of a scaled immersion joint with steel shear keys. *Tunn. Undergr. Space Technol.* **2017**, *70*, 76–88. [CrossRef]
11. Yu, H.; Xiao, W.; Yuan, Y.; Taerwe, L. Seismic mitigation for immersion joints: Design and validation. *Tunn. Undergr. Space Technol.* **2017**, *67*, 39–51. [CrossRef]

12. Yu, H.; Yuan, Y.; Xu, G.; Su, Q.; Yan, X.; Li, C. Multi-point shaking table test for long tunnels subjected to non-uniform seismic loadings-part II: Application to the HZM immersed tunnel. *Soil Dyn. Earthq. Eng.* **2018**, *108*, 187–195. [CrossRef]
13. Liu, Z.G.; Huang, H.W.; Zhang, D.M. 3D nonlinear numerical simulation on immersed tunnel joint. *Undergr. Space Eng.* **2011**, *7*, 691–694. (In Chinese)
14. Huang, J.; Chen, X.K.; Li, H.; Zhang, Z.Y. Application of intelligent health monitoring system in underwater tunnel. *Undergr. Space Eng.* **2017**, *13* (Suppl. 1), 306–313. (In Chinese)
15. Song, E.; Li, P.; Lin, M.; Liu, X. The rationality of semi-rigid immersed tunnel element structure scheme and its first application in Hong Kong Zhuhai Macao bridge project. *Tunn. Undergr. Space Technol.* **2018**, *82*, 156–169. [CrossRef]
16. *GB/T 51318-2019*; Standard for design of immersed tunnel. China Building Industry Press: Beijing, China, 2019.
17. Wei, G.; Lu, S.J. Present Status and Prospects of Research on Flexible Joint Models of Immersed Tube Tunnels. *Mod. Tunn. Technol.* **2019**, *56*, 6–13. (In Chinese)
18. Xue, Y. Research on the joint of tube tunnel. *Spec. Struct.* **2003**, *20*, 4–8. (In Chinese)
19. Peng, L.Q.; Luo, Y.H.; Wu, X.L.; Li, B.; Lin, D.W.; Wang, J. Mechanical Property Test of Gina Seal Blet in Immersed Tunnel. *Special Purpose Rubber Products* **2020**, *41*, 56–60. (In Chinese)
20. What is a Shore A Hardness and Why Is It Important? Available online: https://www.barnwell.co.uk/shore-a-hardness/ (accessed on 6 February 2023).
21. Zhang, L.; Li, Z.; Ma, X. Study on Parameter Characteristics of Rubber Mooney-rivlin model. *Noise Vib. Control.* **2018**, *38* (Suppl. S2), 427–430. (In Chinese)
22. Jiang, Z.W.; Bai, Y.; Su, Q.K. Element Joint Stiffness Properties of Large Immersed Tube Tunnels. *Mod. Tunn. Technol.* **2017**, *54*, 168–174. (In Chinese)
23. Hu, Z.N.; Yang, P.; Shan, C.; Ren, Y.Z.; Dang, D. Comparative Study on Structural Types of GINA Gaskets Used in Immersed Tunnels. *Tunn. Constr.* **2014**, *34*, 937–943. (In Chinese)
24. Tang, Y.; Guan, M.; Wan, X. The analysis and study of rail joints in immersed tunnel. *China Railw. Sci.* **2002**, *23*, 67–72. (In Chinese)
25. Liu, Z.G.; Huang, H.W.; Zhao, Y.H.; Xie, X.Y. Immersed Tube Tunnel Real-time Health Monitoring System. *Undergr. Space Eng.* **2008**, *4*, 1110–1115. (In Chinese)
26. Xie, X.Y.; Yi, C.M.; Li, W.P.; Fang, Y.G. Safety analysis of settlement monitoring data of joints of Yongjiang immersed tube tunnel during operation period. *Chin. J. Geotech. Eng.* **2019**, *41*, 2338–2344. (In Chinese)
27. HPCLab. *A Review Report on the Performances of Immersed Tunnel Joint*; HPCLab, Tongji University: Shanghai, China, 2010. (In Chinese)
28. Lu, M.; Zhu, Z.X.; Zhang, Y. Experimental study on watertightness of connections of pipe sections used in a large sunk pipe tunnel. *China Build. Waterproofing* **2003**, *10*, 9–12. (In Chinese)
29. Huang, F. Numerical Simulation Analysis of GINA Rubber Water Stop. *Struct. Eng.* **2010**, *26*, 96–102. (In Chinese)
30. Hu, J.Z.; Wang, Y.; Xu, G.P.; Xu, Y.; Yu, G.Z.; Gong, Y. Experimental Study and Selection Design of Domestic GINA Gasket for the Immersed Tunnel. *Mod. Tunn. Technol.* **2020**, *57*, 171–177. (In Chinese)
31. Xu, X.; Tong, L.; Liu, S.; Li, H. Evaluation model for immersed tunnel health state: A case study of Honggu Tunnel, Jiangxi Province, China. *Tunn. Undergr. Space Technol.* **2019**, *90*, 239–248. [CrossRef]
32. Xu, X.; Liu, S.; Tong, L. Establishment of Nanchang Honggu Tunnel health monitoring and assessment system. *J. Southeast Univ.* **2019**, *35*, 206–212.
33. *JTG/T 3371-01—2022*; Specifications for Design of Highway Underwater Immersed Tunnel. Ministry of Transport of People's Republic of China: Bejing, China, 2022.
34. *DB32/T 4243-2022*; Technical Specification of Structure Health Monitoring for Underwater Tunnel. Jiangsu Provincial Administration of Market Supervision and Jiangsu Provincial Department of Housing and Urban-Rural Development: Nanjing, China, 2022.
35. Hu, Z.N.; Xie, Y.L.; Wang, J. Challenges and strategies involved in designing and constructing a 6 km immersed tunnel: A case study of the Hong Kong–Zhuhai–Macao Bridge. *Tunn. Undergr. Space Technol.* **2015**, *50*, 171–177. [CrossRef]
36. Hu, Z.; Xie, Y.; Xu, G.; Bin, S.; Liu, H.; Lai, J. Advantages and potential challenges of applying semi-rigid elements in an immersed tunnel: A case study of the Hong Kong-Zhuhai-Macao Bridge. *Tunn. Undergr. Space Technol.* **2018**, *79*, 143–149. [CrossRef]
37. Hu, Z.N.; Xie, Y.L.; Xu, G.P.; Bin, S.L.; Zhang, H.G.; Lai, H.P.; Liu, H.Z.; Yan, C.G. Segmental joint model tests of immersed tunnel on a settlement platform: A case study of the Hongkong-Zhuhai-Macao Bridge. *Tunn. Undergr. Space Technol.* **2018**, *78*, 188–200. [CrossRef]
38. Li, B.; Hou, J.; Min, K.; Zhang, J. Analyzing immediate settlement of Hong Kong-Zhuhai-Macao Bridge immersed tunnel based on monitoring data. *Ships Offshore Struct.* **2021**, *16* (Suppl. 2), 100–109. [CrossRef]
39. Jiang, X.; Lang, Q.; Jing, Q.; Wang, H.; Chen, J.; Ai, Q. An improved wavelet threshold denoising method for health monitoring data: A case study of the Hong Kong-Zhuhai-Macao Bridge immersed tunnel. *Appl. Sci.* **2022**, *12*, 6743. [CrossRef]
40. Chen, J.; Jiang, X.; Yan, Y.; Lang, Q.; Wang, H.; Ai, Q. Dynamic Warning Method for Structural Health Monitoring Data Based on ARIMA: Case Study of Hong Kong–Zhuhai–Macao Bridge Immersed Tunnel. *Sensors* **2022**, *22*, 6185. [CrossRef] [PubMed]

41. Lin, M.; Lin, W.; Wang, Q.; Wang, X. The deployable element, a new closure joint construction method for immersed tunnel. *Tunn. Undergr. Space Technol.* **2018**, *80*, 290–300. [CrossRef]
42. Lin, W.; Liu, X. Analysis of GINA uneven compression during hydraulic connection of immersed tunnel element at curved plane design line. *China Harbour Engineering* **2016**, *36*, 51–53, 76. (In Chinese)

mathematics

MDPI

Article

A Robust Learning Methodology for Uncertainty-Aware Scientific Machine Learning Models

Erbet Almeida Costa [1,†], Carine de Menezes Rebello [2,†], Márcio Fontana [1,†], Leizer Schnitman [1,†] and Idelfonso Bessa dos Reis Nogueira [3,*,†]

1 Programa de Pós-Graduação em Mecatrônica, Universidade Federal da Bahia, Rua Prof. Aristides Novis, 2, Federação, Salvador 40210-630, Brazil
2 Programa de Pós-Graduação em Engenharia Industrial, Universidade Federal da Bahia, Rua Prof. Aristides Novis, 2, Federação, Salvador 40210-630, Brazil
3 Department of Chemical Engineering, Norwegian University of Science and Technology (NTNU), 7491 Trondheim, Norway
* Correspondence: idelfonso.b.d.r.nogueira@ntnu.no
† These authors contributed equally to this work.

Abstract: Robust learning is an important issue in Scientific Machine Learning (SciML). There are several works in the literature addressing this topic. However, there is an increasing demand for methods that can simultaneously consider all the different uncertainty components involved in SciML model identification. Hence, this work proposes a comprehensive methodology for uncertainty evaluation of the SciML that also considers several possible sources of uncertainties involved in the identification process. The uncertainties considered in the proposed method are the absence of a theory, causal models, sensitivity to data corruption or imperfection, and computational effort. Therefore, it is possible to provide an overall strategy for uncertainty-aware models in the SciML field. The methodology is validated through a case study developing a soft sensor for a polymerization reactor. The first step is to build the nonlinear model parameter probability distribution (PDF) by Bayesian inference. The second step is to obtain the machine learning model uncertainty by Monte Carlo simulations. In the first step, a PDF with 30,000 samples is built. In the second step, the uncertainty of the machine learning model is evaluated by sampling 10,000 values through Monte Carlo simulation. The results demonstrate that the identified soft sensors are robust to uncertainties, corroborating the consistency of the proposed approach.

Keywords: scientific machine learning; robust learning; uncertainty; Markov Chain Monte Carlo

MSC: 68T01; 68T07; 65C05; 90B30

1. Introduction

Machine learning (ML) has been widespread in several application domains. Hence, this has given birth to a new field of study: Scientific Machine Learning (SciML). This field is concerned with the proper application of an ML model by taking into consideration all peculiarities of a given domain. As ML becomes more popular, several concerns have arisen [1–5]. It is possible to find recent work in the literature concerned with developing uncertainty-aware ML models [6,7]. These works seek to provide viable methods to evaluate the prediction uncertainty of the models. However, the literature still lacks a methodology for evaluating all the sources of uncertainty surrounding ML model identification and prediction. Uncertainty is an important topic, as developing robust models is essential for applying an ML in a real-case scenario. Most application domains have associated uncertainties caused by corrupted data, measurement noise, redundancies, and instrument uncertainties. Hariri et al. [8] discuss how uncertainty can impact big data in terms of analysis and the dataset. They show that if the learning algorithm uses corrupted training data, it will likely produce inaccurate results. When these issues are not considered, the ML tools may perform poorly and become inadequate. This might create general scepticism in the general scientific community towards ML tools. Hence, robust learning plays an essential role in the SciML literature.

Despite its increasing interest, there are still a lack of algorithms that efficiently cope with the epistemic and aleatory uncertainties in real case scenarios [6,9]. For instance, Gal and Ghahramani [10] present a seminal work regarding this topic. The authors proposed evaluating reinforcement learning models using a Bayesian approximation technique. The referred article points toward issues that still needs to be addressed in this field. Some of these issues are addressed in the present work.

Fully understanding the uncertainty of ML models is still a complex issue, as it means evaluating the uncertainty of predictions. Similar approaches in different fields have been proposed to address uncertainty analysis of model prediction [11,12]. For instance, Gneiting, Tilmann; Balabdaoui, Fadoua; Raftery [13] propose an efficient method to calibrate the distribution of a known random variable. This work addresses the issues related to non-deterministic variables and their effect on model prediction. Abdar et al. [14] and Siddique et al. [15] present comprehensive reviews of this topic and reinforce the increasing necessity for further development. Costa et al. [16] propose a novel strategy for developing uncertainty-aware soft sensors based on a deep learning architecture. The authors mention the need for developing methods that simultaneously evaluate the different uncertainty components involved in an ML model identification. Table 1 compares different methods for evaluating uncertainty in neural networks based on the work of Abdar et al. [14].

Table 1. Comparison of methods for quantifying uncertainty.

Method	Advantage	Disadvantage
Bayesian Approaches	Handle small and large datasets;	Needs multiple samplings;
	Easy to implement;	Fails to find poor convergence;
	Low training complexity; Posterior over the weights.	Depends on the starting point
Ensemble Approaches	Robust prediction; Robust uncertainty estimates; Emulating the analytic posterior predictive.	More resource-consuming; Time-consuming; Weak performance on smaller problems.

While identifying an ML model, several perspectives must be considered. For instance, Abdar et al. [14] proposed three primary uncertainties related to an ML application, the absence of theory and causal models, the sensitivity to data corruption or imperfection, and the computational effort. Levi et al. [17] proposed a simple recalibration method that significantly improves real-world applications. However, they indicate that further work is needed to test the method's generalizability. Levi et al. [17] also assume that the prediction is a known distribution. As mentioned, several methodologies in the literature address one of these listed points. However, the literature lacks methods to address them in the same framework. Additionally, Abdar et al. [14] present some methods for quantifying uncertainty, i.e., bootstrapping and ensemble. On the other hand, in identifying soft sensors for real-time applications, the computational cost associated with the calculations can make their use infeasible.

Hence, this work proposes a comprehensive methodology for uncertainty evaluation of an ML model for SciML. The proposed method considers the epistemic and aleatory uncertainties related to both data used to train the models and the models themselves. Therefore, it is possible to provide an overall strategy for uncertainty-aware models in the SciML field. This work contributes to the robust learning literature as it allows for an approach that considers the several sources of uncertainty involved in SciML model identification. The proposed methodology uses Bayesian inference to evaluate non-linear models' uncertainty propagation for ML models through Monte Carlo methods.

The following sections of this work present the proposed methodology and a case study with soft sensors for a polymerization reactor. Thus, Section 2 presents the methodology, Section 3 is the results and discussions, Section 4 presents the conclusions, and supplementary information on the results is shown in Appendix A.

2. Methodology for Monte Carlo Uncertainty Training

This paper proposes a general methodology to build surrogate models based on artificial intelligence (AI) with uncertainty assessment. The proposed methodology is divided into five steps to obtain the validated machine learning models with uncertainty assessment. Figure 1 presents the general scheme of the proposed method as follows.

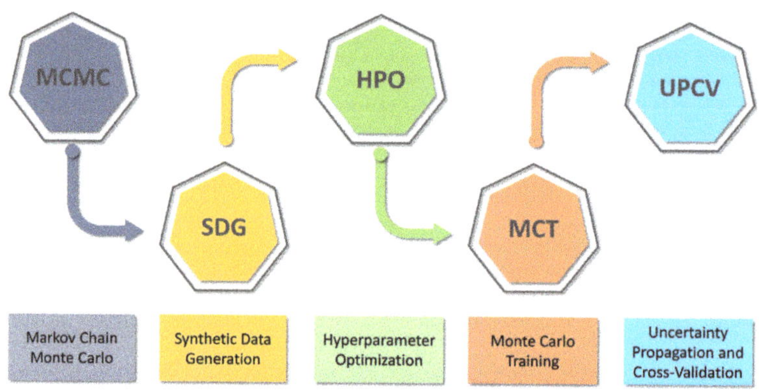

Figure 1. General methodology scheme.

The first step is to use the Markov Chain Monte Carlo method to obtain the uncertainty of the non-linear model parameters that represent the system. Following the methodology, the validated model is used to generate synthetic data. These synthetic data are used to build the neural networks in two steps. The first step is to define the type and the general architecture of the neural network before optimising the hyperparameters. After finding the best network architecture, the second step is to perform Monte Carlo simulation training to propagate the uncertainty from the non-linear model (i.e., synthetic data) to the AI model. The last step of the proposed methodology is to perform validation and uncertainty assessment of the trained model. In that step, the AI model prediction and simulation are collated with the non-linear model and experimental data when available. Further, uncertainty assessment is performed with the appropriate hypothesis in that step. The following subsections provide specific details about each stage of the proposed methodology.

2.1. *Markov Chain Monte Carlo*

Phenomenological and empirical models have common parameters that interfere with their respective output behaviour. In these models, parameter estimation is a challenge because their choice contributes to the prediction uncertainty of the model. Consider a non-linear dynamic model written as:

$$\dot{\mathbf{y}} = \mathbf{f}(t, \mathbf{x}, \mathbf{u}, \boldsymbol{\theta}), \tag{1}$$

where $\mathbf{f}$ is the relationship function between the time t, states $\mathbf{x}$, the input vector $\mathbf{u}$, parameters $\boldsymbol{\theta}$, and the output vector $\mathbf{y}$. In this scenario, if $\boldsymbol{\theta} = [\theta_1, \theta_2, \ldots, \theta_{np}]$ is a set of np parameters. If they have a low predictive probability, the model will not provide a good forecast or adjustment to experimental data [18]. Thence, it is essential to know the model's parameter probability density function (PDF) and, consequently, the model uncertainty to ensure that the model and the parameters are good enough.

Several methods are available in the literature to solve the inference problem and to estimate parameters and the associated uncertainty. Bard [19] presents several tools to obtain the variance of models from the frequentist approach, including the Least Squares and Maximum Likelihood methods. The main drawback of the Bard [19] methods is the hypothesis imposed to obtain the variance of the parameters, including Gaussian distribution. However, the Bayesian approach estimates the joint probability distribution using all available information about the system without assumptions about the target distribution [20].

The Bayesian approach to inference allows obtaining the posterior PDF of any set of parameters $(g_\theta(\eta \mid D, I))$ using as information the inferred data (D) and any previous information about the system (I). Therefore, using the Bayes Theorem, it is possible to write the following relationship between the earlier variables [20]:

$$g_{\boldsymbol{\theta}}(\eta \mid D, I) \propto L(\eta \mid D) g_{\boldsymbol{\theta}}(\eta \mid I), \quad (2)$$

where η represents sampled values of $\boldsymbol{\theta}$, L is the likelihood function, and $g_{\boldsymbol{\theta}}(\eta \mid I)$ is the prior distribution of $\boldsymbol{\theta}$ that is a new observation of $\boldsymbol{\theta}$. Equation (2) allows updating the actual knowledge of the system represented by the posterior $g_{\boldsymbol{\theta}}(\eta \mid D, I)$.

The likelihood $L(\eta \mid D)$ is defined by Migon et al. [18] as a function that associates the value of the probability $g_\theta(\eta \mid I)$ with each η value. By defining the estimation process as a least square problem, the objective is to minimize a loss function that can be represented by a weighted least square estimator (WLSE). Thus, the likelihood function can be defined as:

$$L(\eta \mid D) \propto -\frac{1}{2}\sum_{i=1}^{n}\left(y_i^{exp} - y_i^m\right)^\top \boldsymbol{\Phi}^{-1}\left(y_i^{exp} - y_i^m\right), \quad (3)$$

where $(y_i^{exp} - y_i^m)$ is the residual between the experimental data (y_i^{exp}) and that obtained with the prediction model (y_i^m). Further, the use of the WLSE estimator implies the use of the variance of the residual between the y^{exp} and y^m for the ny outputs of the system, represented in Equation (3) as $\boldsymbol{\Phi} = diag[\Phi_1, \Phi_2, \ldots, \Phi_{ny}]$.

The posterior PDF of each θ_i parameter of the vector $\boldsymbol{\theta}$, $g_{\boldsymbol{\theta}}(\eta \mid D, I)$ is obtained from the marginal posterior density function $g(\theta_1, \theta_2, \ldots, \theta_{np})$ and is defined by Gamerman and Lopes [20] as:

$$g_{\boldsymbol{\theta}}(\eta \mid D, I) \propto \int_\theta (L(\eta \mid D) g_{\boldsymbol{\theta}})(\eta \mid I) d\theta_{n-j} \quad (4)$$

Chapter 5 by Gamerman and Lopes [20] presents several methods for solving the inference problem of Equation (4). The Markov Chain Monte Carlo methods have some interesting features among the numerical integration methods. Among these characteristics is convergence, because when chains are adequately constructed, after a sufficiently high number of iterations, the chains converge to an equilibrium distribution. Thus, Figure 2 shows a schematic diagram of the solution to the inference problem using the MCMC method. The general idea is that the MCMC uses existing information, such as experimental data and a likelihood function, to provide a mathematical model and the associated PDF of the estimated parameters.

On the other hand, this paper proposes using the DRAM (Delayed Rejection Adaptive Metropolis) MCMC algorithm Haario et al. [21] presented to solve the inference problem. The DRAM algorithm combines the Adaptive Metropolis, which provides global adaptation, and the Delayed Rejection, which offers local adaptation. Further, the main idea of the DRAM algorithm is to collect information during the chain run and tune the target PDF by using the learned information.

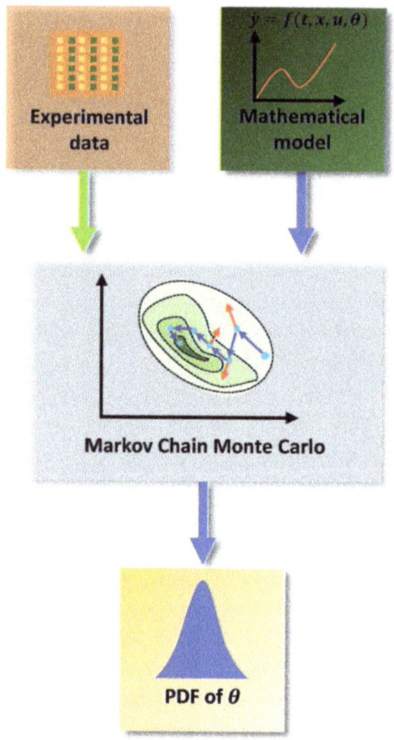

Figure 2. MCMC method.

2.2. Synthetic Data Generation

In building AI models, data quality is crucial to obtain great adjusted models. This paper proposes a methodology to build AI models using synthetic data from a non-linear model. Further, the methodology is based on the uncertainty propagation law established in BIPM et al. [22], Bipm et al. [23], BIPM et al. [24]. In this sense, the quantity and quality of data used in training must be adequate, which means the inputs must be uncorrelated and the amount of data needs to be enough to provide information to the training process. Then, Sections 3.1 and 3.4.2 present results that illustrate this issue by providing numerical information regarding the adequate amount of data and distribution and input features. It is important to highlight that the inadequate use of data can lead to underestimation of uncertainty. Such a situation can undermine the uncertainty assessment.

This paper proposes to build a training database by drawing a sample of the parameters of PDF and propagating it to the outputs of the non-linear model. In this way, the data used for training the models need to be representative of the operating conditions of the system and characterize the uncertainties of the non-linear model. Figure 3 presents a generic Monte Carlo Method (MCM) simulation scheme for synthetic data generation. The scheme in Figure 3 is inspired by the algorithm for implementing the Monte Carlo Method presented in Supplements 1 and 2 and to the "Guide to the expression of uncertainty in measurement" [22,24].

The first step of the algorithm is to determine the number m of trials to be performed. In general, the MCM produces better responses with a greater number of shots, and the recommendation is to use a value $m = 10^6$ [18]. However, smaller values can be used when evaluating complex models requiring high computational costs for numerical solutions. This reduction in the number of tests may not allow the correct characterization of the PDF of the output values and may produce less reliable results [22].

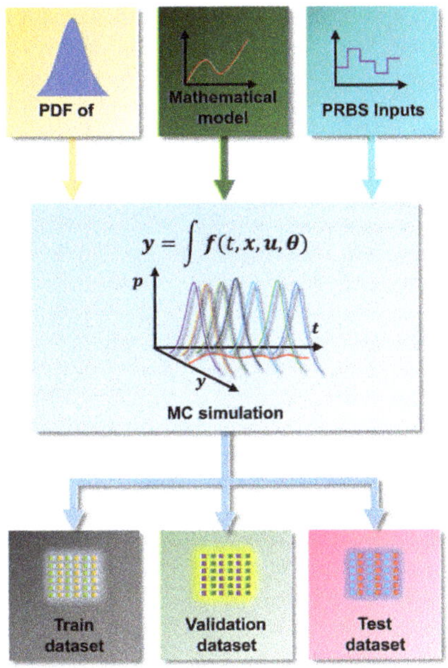

Figure 3. Monte Carlo simulation method for data generation.

After defining the number of tests to be performed, a matrix Θ containing m vectors of PDF samples of $g_\theta(\eta \mid D, I)$ is built:

$$\boldsymbol{\Theta} = \begin{pmatrix} \boldsymbol{\theta}_{1,1} & \cdots & \boldsymbol{\theta}_{1,np} \\ \vdots & \ddots & \vdots \\ \boldsymbol{\theta}_{m,1} & \cdots & \boldsymbol{\theta}_{m,np} \end{pmatrix}. \tag{5}$$

Thus, m distinct sets of model parameters are obtained such that it is possible to write

$$\dot{\mathbf{y}}_{1,\dots,m} = \mathbf{f}(t, \mathbf{f}, \mathbf{u}, \boldsymbol{\Theta}), \tag{6}$$

in this way, it is possible to integrate the model so that the m dynamic responses are obtained for the output variables y.

As it is a dynamic model, it is necessary to obtain representative data from the entire operating region. An independent Pseudo-Random Binary Sequence (PRBS) signal for each of the inputs is generated through a Latin Hypercube Sampler (LHS). The PRBS signals are then combined with the non-linear mathematical model of the system. A dynamic response is received for each parameter combination obtained from the PDF of the parameters. Additionally, the system's dynamic response is represented by a set of curves obtained from this MC simulation. In this scenario of propagation of uncertainties by MCM in dynamical systems, the true value must be calculated for each sampling instant in which the equations are solved. In this way, it is considered that for each sampling instant, a PDF sample is obtained for each system output response $\mathbf{y}(t)$.

From Figure 3, it is also possible to observe that the data generated through the MC simulation will be divided into three sets: training, testing, and validation. This division follows the common literature guidelines for training AI models [25]. The first two sets are used during supervised training of the models, since the algorithms need two data sets for training and validation. The third set, the test dataset, is used for final cross-validation as these data are "unknown" to the AI model. Thus, the ability to predict and extrapolate to new data is evaluated. Additionally, dividing the data into three sets must consider that the training process has consistent information. In this sense, sets are typically divided into: Train—70%, Validate—15%, and Test—15%.

2.3. Data Curation

A database to train a dynamic data-driven model should be systematically organized to represent the system dynamics. Hence, the identified model can approximate the observed dynamic phenomena. There are several ways to manage a data set to incorporate the system's time dependence. The most common is non-linear autoregressive with exogenous inputs (NARX) predictors. The general NARX structure is composed of a prediction of the actual output as:

$$y_k = f(x_k, x_{(k-1)}, x_{(k-2)}, \ldots, x_{(k-n)}, y_{(k-1)}, y_{(k-2)}, \ldots, y_{(k-p)}, \gamma) + \epsilon \quad (7)$$

where $x_{(k-1)}, x_{(k-2)}, \ldots, x_{(k-n)}$ is the input delay, and $y_{(k-1)}, y_{(k-2)}, \ldots, y_{(k-p)}$ are the p of past values for the output and input, respectively. The noise, ϵ, is additive: for the NARX, the error information is assumed to be filtered through the system's dynamic. In its turn, γ is a parameter that represents the model parameters' uncertainty. As observed from Equation (7), the NARX predictor has two hyperparameters: n and p. These parameters should be defined correctly to improve the dynamic representativeness of the data. For this purpose, He and Asada [26] proposed the Lipschitz coefficient analysis. A Lipschitz coefficient is then calculated for each pair of measurements. For further information about the Lipschitz coefficient calculations, see He and Asada [26].

2.4. Building the AI Model

Figure 4 shows a methodology step responsible for finding the hyperparameters of the network. That step defines the appropriate architecture and network format that one wants to get before starting the training. The type of network is the first aspect to be evaluated when building an AI model. In this way, expert knowledge must be considered to define whether a network is to be used, e.g., recurrent, convolutional, or dense. Choosing the network format depends on the characteristic of the system being modelled and the main application of the model.

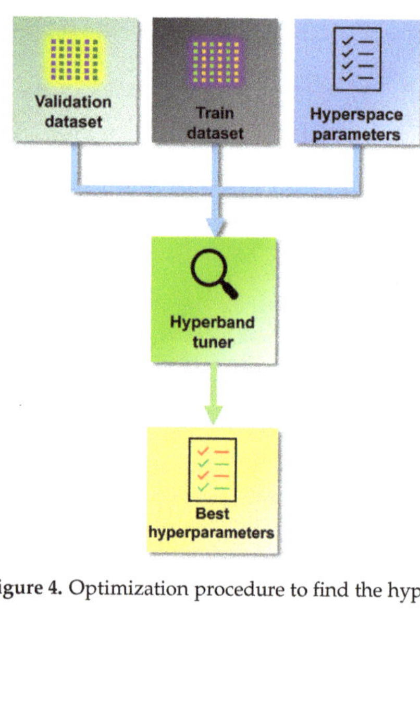

Figure 4. Optimization procedure to find the hyperparameters of the neural network.

Once the general format of the type of network is defined, the next step is to define its architecture. There are some powerful algorithms available in the literature for this means. The optimal number of layers determines the architecture of a neural network, the number of neurons per layer, and activation functions, among other parameters [27]. Determining these parameters is one source of uncertainty during the modelling process that needs to be considered.

2.5. Monte Carlo Training

The fourth step of the methodology proposed in this work is the uncertainty training of networks through Monte Carlo simulations. The stages of generating data, obtaining the architecture of the neural network, and the hyperparameters provide the necessary information for the uncertainty training of the networks. In this way, it is sought to characterize the prediction region of the identified non-linear system, obtained in Section 2.1, through a set of networks capable of representing each of the probable outputs of the model.

Figure 5 presents a simplified schematic diagram of this step in the methodology. It is possible to observe that the MC training stage boils down to massive training on top of the generated data. The result is a set of equally probable trained AI models that comprehensively account for the uncertainty sources.

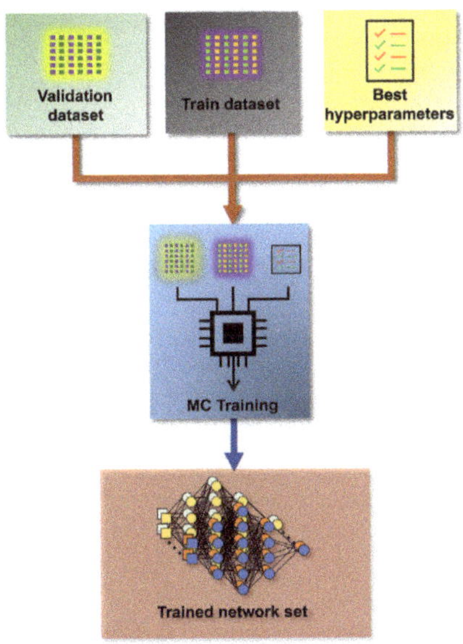

Figure 5. Monte Carlo training method.

This training step follows the concepts of Monte Carlo simulations. It is the step that has the most significant computational effort. The simulation is built to train an AI model with pre-defined optimal architecture for each element in the training, validation, and test datasets. In addition to the computational effort required to perform this step, the volume of data generated is also significant. However, the amount of data generated has a less relevant impact.

On the other hand, nowadays, SciML model training has become increasingly efficient. The literature has presented algorithms that extract maximum performance from the available hardware. Additionally, manufacturers have built hardware with specific characteristics for application training and execution of artificial intelligence. In this scenario, the available technology makes it feasible to run a Monte Carlo simulation for training neural networks. The proposed method obtains the network uncertainty by a set of identically retrained networks. Therefore, the predicted most likely value is obtained through the expectation of all networks set at each instant. Then, the Monte Carlo training step allows for obtaining the necessary network parameters to perform the prediction.

2.6. Propagation and Cross-Validation

The methodology proposed in this article includes a supplementary validation stage of the built AI model. In this step, the data used for cross-validation are labelled "Test data" in Figure 3 (Note that the set called "validation" is used during training). In a complementary way, validation in the context of dynamic models with uncertainty needs to be evaluated to compare the coverage regions. In this context, a model is considered validated when the coverage of regions of models is overlapping, implying that the values are statistically equal.

The main issue involved is the method used to assess the uncertainty of the model. For both the non-linear phenomenological model and the AI model, this article proposes to use the Monte Carlo method. Thus, the uncertainty of the evaluated model can be obtained assuming the same hypotheses proposed by Haario et al. [21,28]; that is: the variance is approximated by an inverse Gamma distribution. Then:

$$V[y] \approx \Gamma^{-1}(x, \alpha, \beta) \tag{8}$$

where the distribution is supported in $x > 0$ and represented by Γ^{-1}, and the α and β parameters are the shape and scale of the distribution, respectively.

In turn, to obtain the parameters α and β, Gelman et al. [29] suggest using:

$$\alpha(j) = \frac{N_{prior}(j) + N_{data}(j)}{2}, \tag{9}$$

$$\beta(j) = \frac{2}{N_{prior}(j) \cdot V_0^2 + SSE(j)}, \tag{10}$$

where $j = 1, 2, \ldots, ny$ is the number of outputs of the model. On the other hand, V_0^2 is the variance of the prior, and $SSE(j)$ is the sum of the squared errors between the prediction and the experimental data.

Using the hypothesis of a non-informative prior, the variance of the prior and the number of points are unknown. In this way, the previous equations can be approximated by:

$$\alpha(j) = \frac{N_{data}(j)}{2}, \tag{11}$$

$$\beta(j) = \frac{2}{SSE(j)}. \tag{12}$$

The methodology of this article implies obtaining two sets of model parameters that each have their associated uncertainty. Thus, the proposal is that the variance calculation is performed using the SSE obtained through the estimation data when the MCMC is performed. The SSE is obtained with the training data for the training of networks. Then, the uncertainty of a prediction will be based on the variance of the model that will follow the inverse gamma distribution. This methodology allows for characterizing the epistemic uncertainty of the model.

3. Results and Discussion

This section presents the results of applying the proposed methodology in a case study. A polymerization reactor with synthetic data is used as a case study. The detailed polymerization model is presented in Section 3.1. Following the proposed methodology, Section 3.2 explains network construction using the Monte Carlo method, uncertainty propagation, and final cross-validation.

3.1. Case Study: Polymerization Reactor

The reactor model is presented in detail by Hidalgo and Brosilow [30], Alvarez and Odloak [31]. It is composed of a system of algebraic differential equations (DAE) with thirteen equations as follows:

$$\frac{d[I]}{dt} = \frac{Q_i[i_f] - Q_t[I]}{V} - k_d[I], \tag{13}$$

$$\frac{d[M]}{dt} = \frac{Q_m[M_f] - Q_t[M]}{V} - k_p[M][P], \tag{14}$$

$$\frac{dT}{dt} = \frac{Q_i[T_f - T]}{V} + \frac{-\Delta H_r}{\rho C_p} k_p[M][P] - \frac{hA}{\rho C_p V}(T - T_c), \tag{15}$$

$$\frac{dT_c}{dt} = \frac{Q_c(T_{cf} - T_c)}{V_c} + \frac{hA}{\rho C_p V}(T - T_c), \tag{16}$$

$$\frac{dD_0}{dt} = 0.5k_t[P]^2 - \frac{Q_t D_0}{V}, \tag{17}$$

$$\frac{dD_1}{dt} = M_m k_p[M][P] - \frac{Q_t D_1}{V}, \tag{18}$$

$$\frac{dD_2}{dt} = 5M_m k_p[M][P] + M_m \frac{k_p^2}{k_t}[M]^2 - \frac{Q_t D_2}{V}, \tag{19}$$

$$[P] = \left[\frac{2f_i k_d[I]}{k_t}\right]^{0.5}, \tag{20}$$

$$Q_t = Q_i + Q_s + Q_m, \tag{21}$$

$$\bar{M}_w = M_m \frac{D_2}{D_1}, \tag{22}$$

$$PD = M_m \frac{D_2 D_0}{D_1^2}, \tag{23}$$

$$\eta = 0.0012(\bar{M}_w)^{0.71}. \tag{24}$$

In the above DAE system, Equations (13)–(16) represent the mass and energy balance of the monomer and the initiator. Equations (17)–(19) are the moment equations of the dead polymer, in which D_0, D_1, and D_2 represent the moments of the dead polymer. Algebraic equations are used to describe the relationship between supplementary variables. Equation (22) represents the weight-average molecular weight, and Equation (24) represents the viscosity. Tables 2–4 show the model parameters general definitions, the initial condition values of inputs, and the steady-state output system variables.

Alvarez and Odloak [31] developed this model based on seven hypotheses: the lifetime of the radical polymer is shorter than that of other species; Long Chain Assumption (LCA) is related to monomer consumption; the chain transfer reaction to monomer and solvent can be neglected; operation below 373 K because greater temperatures cause monomer thermal initiation; termination by disproportionation is not considered; the rate of termination is dominant; and only the heat of polymerization is considered.

Alvarez and Odloak [31] discuss the polymerization reactor from the control and optimization point of view. However, other relevant aspects are pointed out. One of these, Alvarez and Odloak [31], uses Equation (23) as a virtual analyser for the viscosity because this is a difficult variable to measure in the studied reactor. The authors use the temperature and the viscosity as controlled variables, manipulating the initiator flow rate and the rate of the cooling jacket. Therefore, this case study is used to validate the proposed methodology for the uncertainty assessment of neural networks. Further, using an AI model reduces the computational efforts of the control and optimization loops.

Table 2. Parameters and initial conditions.

Nominal Process Parameters	Value
Frequency factor for initiator decomposition, A_d (h^{-1})	2.142×10^{17}
Activation energy for initiator decomposition, E_d (K)	14,897
Frequency factor for propagation reaction, A_p ($L \cdot mol^{-1} \cdot h^{-1}$)	3.81×10^{10}
Activation temperature for propagation reaction, E_p (K)	3557
Frequency factor for termination reaction, A_t ($Lmol^{-1}h^{-1}$)	4.50×10^{12}
Activation temperature for termination reaction, E_t (K)	843
Initiator efficiency, f_i	0.6
Heat of polymerization, $-\Delta H_r$ ($J \cdot mol^{-1}$)	6.99×10^4
Overall heat transfer coefficient, hA ($J \cdot K^{-1} \cdot L^{-1}$)	1.05×10^6
Mean heat capacity of reactor fluid, ρC_p ($JK^{-1}L^{-1}$)	1506
Heat capacity of cooling jacket fluid, $\rho_c C_p c$ ($JK^{-1}L^{-1}$)	4043
Molecular weight of the monomer, M_m ($g \cdot mol^{-1}$)	104.14
Initial conditions	Value
Reactor volume, V (L)	3000
Volume of cooling jacket fluid, Vc (L)	3312.4
Concentration of initiator in feed, I_f ($mol \cdot L^{-1}$)	0.5888
Concentration of monomer in feed, M_f ($mol \cdot L^{-1}$)	8.6981
Temperature of reactor feed, T_f (K)	330
Inlet temperature of cooling jacket fluid, Tcf (K)	295

As no experimental data are available regarding this system, this paper proposes using random white noise to simulate the interferences that usually occur in an experimental setup. The system is simulated with the initial and steady-state conditions in Tables 2 and 3, respectively.

Table 3. Steady-state input conditions and LHS region.

Variable	Steady-State	Minimum	Maximum
Flow rate of initiator, Q_i ($L \cdot h^{-1}$)	108	91.8	124.2
Flow rate of solvent, Q_s ($L \cdot h^{-1}$)	3312.4	2815.5	3809.26
Flow rate of monomer, Q_m ($L \cdot h^{-1}$)	0.5888	0.5005	0.6771
Flow rate of cooling jacket fluid, Q_c ($L \cdot h^{-1}$)	8.6981	7.3934	10.0028

Table 4. Output variables at steady-state.

Variable	Value
Concentration of initiator in the reactor, I ($mol \cdot L^{-1}$)	330
Concentration of monomer in the reactor, I ($mol \cdot L^{-1}$)	295
Temperature of the reactor, T (K)	323.56
Temperature of cooling jacket fluid, T (K)	305.17
Molar concentration of dead polymer chains, D_0 ($mol \cdot L^{-1}$)	2.7547×10^{-4}
Mass concentration of dead polymer chains, D_1 ($g \cdot L^{-1}$)	16.110

Figure 6 shows the LHS generated with $\pm 15\%$ of the steady-state input value and used as input in the simulation. A total of 30 steps, with 150 h of simulation each, were developed to compose the synthetic data.

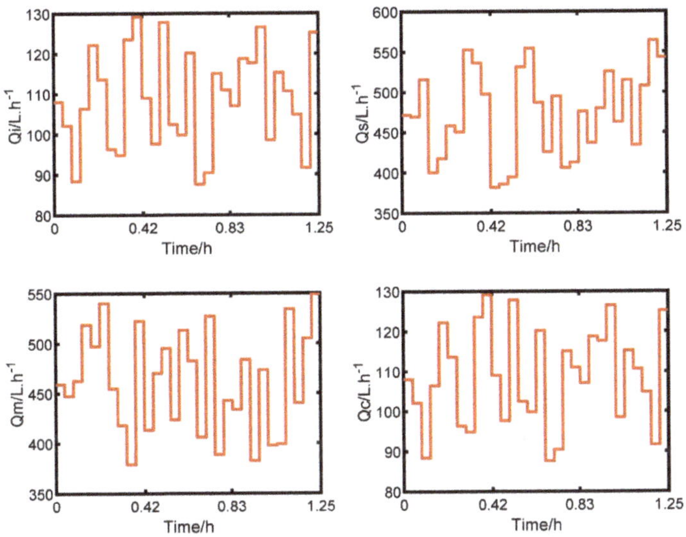

Figure 6. LHS inputs.

Figure 7 presents the correlation heat map for the variables set by the LHS. The main diagonal presents high correlations as it pairs the variables with themselves. In contrast, the pairing between the other entries produces a value that allows verifying if the generated values are uncorrelated. The lower these values, the less correlated they are. As shown in Figure 7, the correlations are close to null, demonstrating that the LHS can efficiently generate uncorrelated samples.

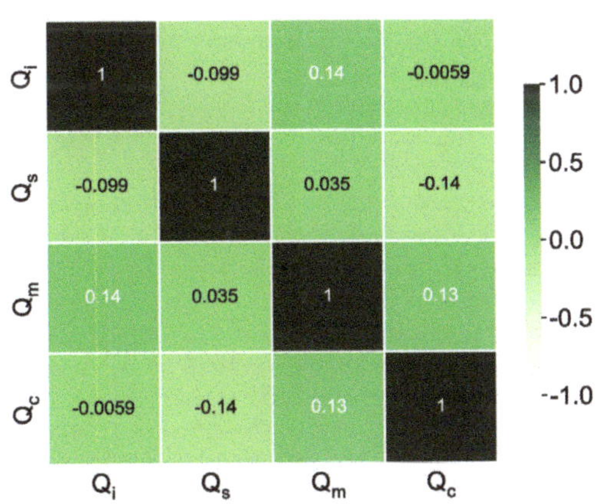

Figure 7. Input correlation map.

The synthetic output dataset is shown in Figure 8. As mentioned, random noise with −20 dB and 10% of the output range is included in the signal to emulate the field conditions. All these variables are used in the likelihood function presented in Equation (3). A total of 70% of these data are used for the SciML model identification, and the rest are used for the methodology cross-validation step, as discussed in the subsequent sections.

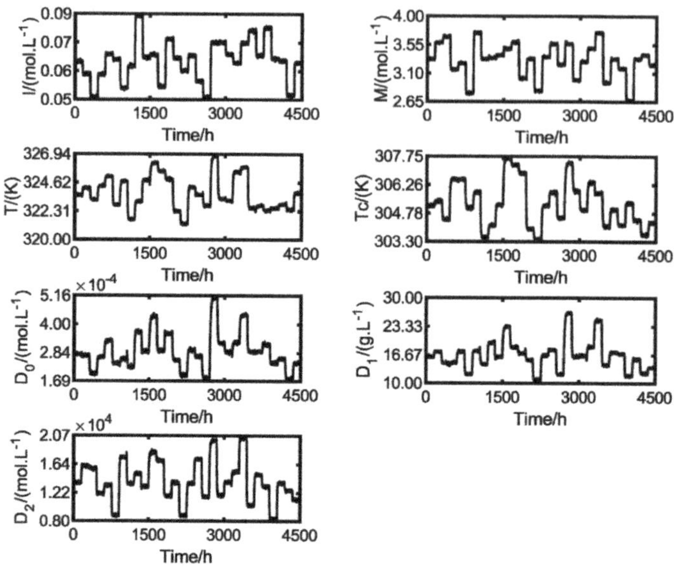

Figure 8. Synthetic output data with white noise.

3.2. MCMC

The generated synthetic data allows the uncertainty assessment of the Alvarez and Odloak [31] model, done through the MCMC methodology. Therefore, 12 model parameters and 6 initial conditions were used as decision variables for the MCMC algorithm. The DRAM algorithm proposed by Haario et al. [21] allows limiting the parameter search region. Therefore, in this paper, the search region was limited to $\pm5\%$ of the nominal value of the parameter. Further, all parameters were normalized to the nominal value to facilitate the algorithm's convergence.

Other algorithm aspects must be set. The first is the number of samples sorted to build the joint PDF. At this point, the algorithm was configured to build a set with 30,000 samples of the targeted joint PDF. The algorithm was also configured to use a non-informative prior. Therefore, to estimate the variance of the parameter, the algorithm chooses 5000 samples to update the prior and discards the chain. After the burn step, the MCMC algorithm restarts building the chains and evaluates the parameters in the search region.

Table 5 shows the resulting normalized parameters obtained from the Markov Chains. The MCMC algorithm does not make any assumptions about the target distribution. The mean and median in normal distributions converge to the same number. However, it is more conservative to assume that the distribution is not Gaussian and to use the median as a value for the most probable value. In Table 5, it is possible to see the difference between the parameter's mean and median. Table 5 also shows the standard deviation (std) and the Geweke diagnostic parameter [32]. For some parameters, the std value is relatively high. However, the Geweke parameter indicates that the chain converges [32]. Figures A1–A11 in the Supplementary Material (Appendix A) show the confidence region and the full Markov Chain. Those figures compare Gaussian and unshaped regions proposed by Possolo [33].

The MCMC algorithm has the particularity of being unable to be parallelised. This comes from the need to carry out the random walk sequentially. In this way, this procedure implies the use of few computational resources but for a long time. Then, the algorithm sampled 72,672 sets to obtain the 30,000 samples for the posterior PDF. It used a computational time of about 76.10 h of processing on a computer with two AMD EPYC 7252 processors and 32 Gb of memory.

Table 5. Normalized parameters obtained by DRAM algorithm.

Parameter	Mean	Median	STD	Geweke
A_d	1.00×10^{0}	1.01×10^{0}	1.96×10^{-2}	9.95×10^{-1}
E_d	1.00×10^{0}	1.00×10^{0}	6.97×10^{-4}	9.99×10^{-1}
A_p	9.99×10^{-1}	9.98×10^{-1}	1.99×10^{-2}	9.96×10^{-1}
E_p	9.98×10^{-1}	9.98×10^{-1}	3.17×10^{-3}	9.99×10^{-1}
A_t	1.00×10^{0}	1.00×10^{0}	2.06×10^{-2}	9.83×10^{-1}
E_t	9.91×10^{-1}	9.88×10^{-1}	2.42×10^{-2}	9.91×10^{-1}
f_i	1.00×10^{0}	1.01×10^{0}	2.33×10^{-2}	9.94×10^{-1}
$-\Delta H_r$	9.99×10^{-1}	1.00×10^{0}	7.93×10^{-3}	9.96×10^{-1}
hA	1.00×10^{0}	1.00×10^{0}	8.11×10^{-3}	9.96×10^{-1}
ρC_p	9.97×10^{-1}	9.98×10^{-1}	9.80×10^{-3}	9.96×10^{-1}
$\rho_c C_{pc}$	1.01×10^{0}	1.01×10^{0}	9.63×10^{-3}	9.97×10^{-1}
M_m	9.99×10^{-1}	9.99×10^{-1}	6.41×10^{-4}	9.99×10^{-1}
V	9.98×10^{-1}	9.99×10^{-1}	3.71×10^{-3}	9.99×10^{-1}
Vc	1.00×10^{0}	1.00×10^{0}	1.34×10^{-2}	9.99×10^{-1}
If	1.00×10^{0}	1.00×10^{0}	3.15×10^{-4}	9.99×10^{-1}
Mf	9.99×10^{-1}	9.99×10^{-1}	2.79×10^{-4}	9.99×10^{-1}
Tf	9.99×10^{-1}	9.99×10^{-1}	1.83×10^{-4}	9.99×10^{-1}
Tcf	1.00×10^{0}	1.00×10^{0}	4.32×10^{-4}	9.99×10^{-1}

3.3. Synthetic Data Generation for Training

The results of the MCMC allow the construction of the parameter PDF of the phenomenological model capable of representing the uncertainty of the non-linear system. Thus, it is possible to build a set of non-linear responses by randomly selecting a set of parameters. This work randomly selected a sample of 10,000 distinct non-linear parameters. Subsequently, all resulting models were excited with the same LHS signal as in Figure 6, and the result was 10,000 different dynamic responses.

With these dynamic trajectories, it was possible to establish the number of embedded dimensions of the NARX model. The Lipschitz method is presented in Section 2.3 and was used to define the NARX parameters. Figure 9a,b show these results. In Figure 9a,b, the decisive factor is the slope of the surface, because when there is high variation between two delays, the increase is considered important. However, if the slope variation is low, it can be considered that this inclusion is not necessary. Then, it is possible to observe that a delay of four sampling instants for the inputs and one for the variables is reasonable for good representation, as after these values, the slope starts to be constant.

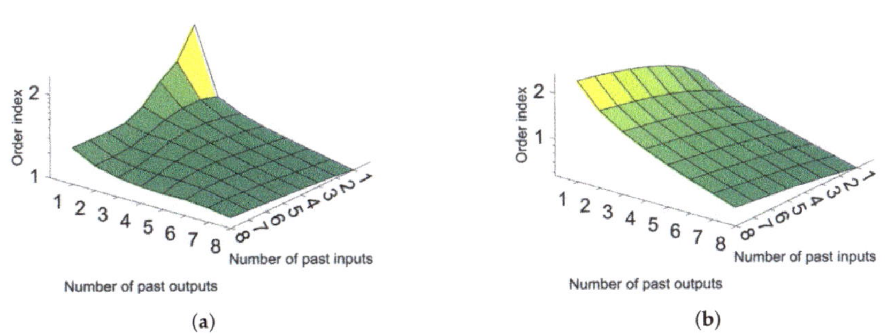

Figure 9. (**a**) Lipschitz surface for reactor temperature; (**b**) Lipschitz surface for polymer viscosity.

3.4. Monte Carlo Training

The proposed methodology includes a step called 'Monte Carlo training', which is composed of smaller steps. It starts with the identification of the hyperparameters. It is followed by defining the data needed for training. Then, finally, the final Monte Carlo training is done.

3.4.1. Monte Carlo Training

The network's optimal structure is found by a search in a hyperspace formed by the structural parameters that constitute the networks. Table 6 shows the initial configuration included in the hyperband algorithm [27].

Table 6. Hyperband hyperspace search.

Parameter	Search Space
Type of layer	Dense
Number of layers	2–6
Output layer	1
Activation function	*Relu* or *Tanh*
Number of neurons per layer	[30, 50, 70, 90, 100, 120, 130, 160]
Learning rate	0.0001, 0.001, and 0.1
Metrics	MAE—Mean Absolute Error
Loss	MSE—Mean Square Error

The results obtained from the hyperparameter search are presented in Table 7. It is possible to observe that a relatively simpler network was necessary to represent the temperature than the viscosity. This simpler architecture implies a big difference in the computational cost. The viscosity network required 6.4 times longer to be trained than the network for the temperature. On the other hand, the networks have the same activation functions in the layers and the same learning rate. Table 7 also shows the MAE and MSE values resulting from the hyperband search. The hyperband algorithm uses the training and validation datasets during training. Then, the test dataset is used after the training to test the final model parameters. It is noteworthy, however, that this methodology assumes that the network's architecture does not change to a variable. In this way, it is considered that it is only necessary to execute the hyperparameter search process once. With the network structure identified, it is trained for all trajectories obtained from each non-linear model. Hence, a set of networks is identified, as described in Section 2.5.

Table 7. Resulting network hyperparameters.

Hyperparameters	T	η
Number of layers	3	7
Number of neurons in the dense layers	$[100, 90, 1]$	$[150, 90, 150, 90, 150, 90, 1]$
Activation function	$[tanh, tanh]$	$[tanh, tanh, tanh, tanh, tanh, tanh]$
Initial learning rate	1×10^{-3}	1×10^{-3}
Total number of trainable parameters	11,081	71,011
MSE Test	2.37×10^{-5}	5.84×10^{-4}
MAE Test	4.30×10^{-3}	2.03×10^{-2}

3.4.2. Data Size

An important aspect to be analysed in neural network training is the guarantee of adequate training. In this sense, assessing whether the amount of information added in training the model is sufficient for the training algorithm to obtain a suitable model is necessary. Figure 10 shows this analysis for the polymer viscosity and reactor temperature. This evaluation was based on a set of independent training sets in which each one was repeated 25 times. The first 25 training sets were carried out with 100 experiments. The average values for MAE and the final MSE were calculated. For the next 25, 100 experiments were added, and so on. In Figure 10, it is possible to observe that for viscosity, after about 1750 experiments, there is no significant change in the MSE; however, for MAE, this value is about 1500. On the other hand, when the reactor temperature is evaluated, this value is higher, and more than 2500 experiments were needed for convergence. Thus, to ensure convergence, 3100 were used for both networks.

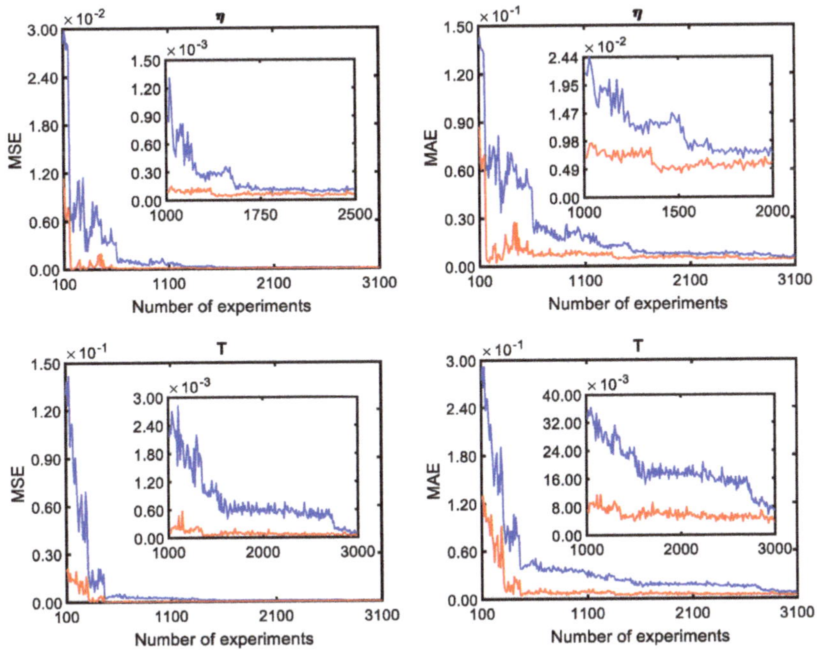

Figure 10. Training performance as a function of experiments.

3.4.3. Training

The adaptive moment estimation algorithm (ADAM) proposed by [34] was used to train the chosen structure. ADAM is an optimization method based on the descending gradient technique, making the ADAM algorithm efficient for problems involving extensive data and parameters. It also requires less memory than other training algorithms because the data are sliced into several packages and treated.

Building the networks involves an exhaustive training process called 'Monte Carlo training'. The proposed methodology is based on the Monte Carlo method for PDF propagation. Thus, the assumed hypothesis is that the different trajectories generated through the non-linear model can represent the model's uncertainty. Therefore, training networks capable of representing these distinct trajectories imply obtaining a PDF of trained parameters of an AI model that also represents the uncertainty of the model.

Convergence analysis of training networks via MC training can be performed by analysing MAE and MSE values similar to conventional training. However, given the number of trained networks, it is more convenient to evaluate in histogram format, as in Figure 11. In the first analysis, Figure 11 shows the histograms of the MAE and MSE indicators, both for the test and validation data. It is possible to observe that the histograms do not follow a Gaussian distribution. Thus, the mean may not be a good reference in statistical terms. Thus, Table 8 shows the minimum, maximum, median, and standard deviation of the MAE and MSE. Generally, it is possible to affirm that the networks converged sufficiently.

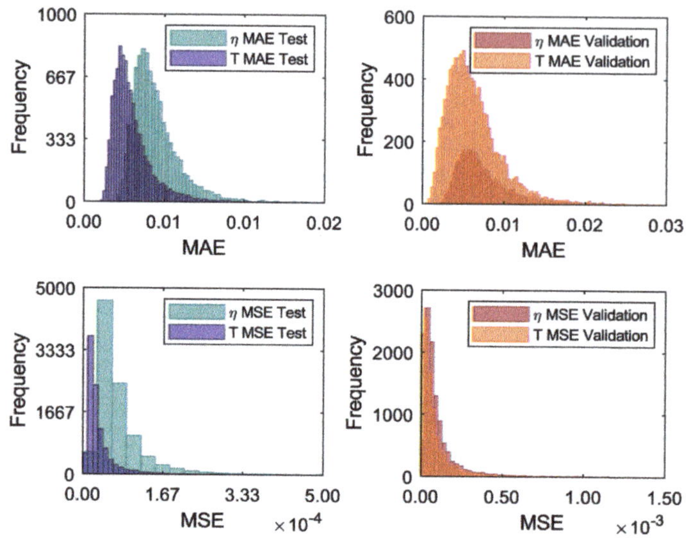

Figure 11. Monte Carlo Training convergence evaluation.

Table 8. Training network performance.

	MAE Test	MAE Valid	MSE Test	MSE Valid
		T		
Min	1.49×10^{-3}	7.91×10^{-4}	5.64×10^{-6}	2.73×10^{-6}
Max	2.26×10^{-3}	6.30×10^{-2}	1.05×10^{-3}	4.82×10^{-3}
Median	3.57×10^{-3}	5.77×10^{-3}	2.37×10^{-5}	4.98×10^{-5}
STD	1.82×10^{-3}	3.72×10^{-3}	4.37×10^{-5}	1.24×10^{-4}
		η		
Min	2.35×10^{-3}	2.06×10^{-3}	1.20×10^{-5}	1.06×10^{-5}
Max	7.35×10^{-2}	2.01×10^{-1}	1.82×10^{-2}	5.27×10^{-2}
Median	5.55×10^{-3}	6.79×10^{-3}	5.87×10^{-5}	7.22×10^{-5}
STD	3.38×10^{-3}	6.23×10^{-3}	4.55×10^{-4}	9.25×10^{-4}

In the Monte Carlo Training process, an early stopping option in MC training was used to reduce the computational cost. Thus, training was aborted if there ewas no decrease in the LOSS value for 100 epochs. Figure 12 shows the histograms of the number of epochs trained during MC training for the two modelled variables. In the graph of Figure 12, the minimum number of epochs was 50, and the maximum number was 300. Lognormal distributions with lower or upper bounds should be the best representation for this data type. Figure 12 also shows that the data do not fit a lognormal distribution. Hence, no assumptions were made about the type of distribution of variables. Additionally, Figure 12 shows the distribution of each network's time consumption during the Monte Carlo training process. With the early stopping option, the number of epochs trained is variable, and the time consumption during the training differs for each Monte Carlo trail. The training calculation through CM was performed using a computer with a dedicated Tesla T4 16 Gb GPU, two AMD EPYC 7252 processors, and 32 Gb of memory. The MC method can be parallelised when GPU processing is not used. Then, the training was carried out sequentially and totalled 155 h of training, which is the sum of all values presented in Figure 12.

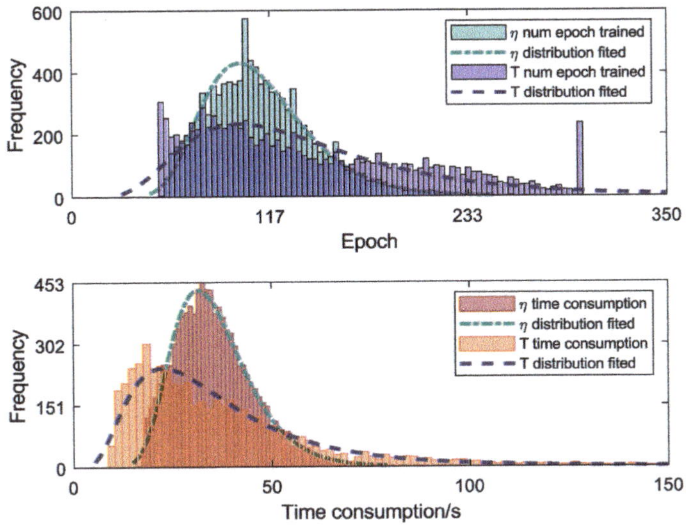

Figure 12. Trained epochs and training time of Monte Carlo training.

3.5. Uncertainty Propagation and Validation

The last step of the proposed methodology is the propagation of uncertainty and methodology cross-validation. The proposal is based on constructing the uncertainty regions of the neural network's prediction and comparison with the uncertainty regions of the non-linear phenomenological model. With the prediction values, it is possible to calculate the variance of the networks using the same assumptions used to calculate the uncertainty of the phenomenological model Equations (13)–(24). Figures 13 and 14 show the comparisons between the predictions for the two modelled variables: T and η.

Figures 13 and 14 present the entire output dataset used for training, testing, and validation. A zoom is given to verify the variables' behaviour in each region. It is pointed out, however, that the training and validation data sets are used during the training of the networks. In this way, the networks' only unknown is the test data set, which is used to certify their performance.

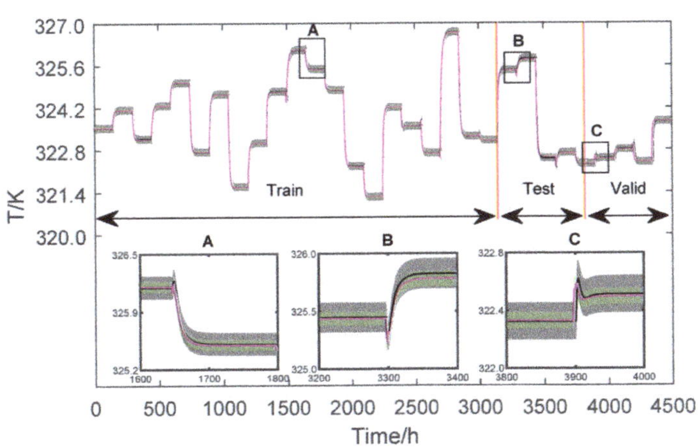

Figure 13. Training and validation data of T.

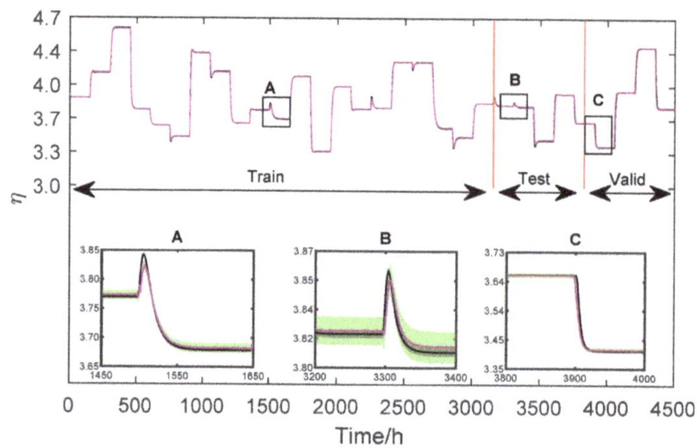

Figure 14. Training and validation data of η.

From a statistical point of view, when two measurements have overlapping coverage regions, they are impossible to differentiate, and they are considered equal. Therefore, validation of the AI model against the non-linear phenomenological model is achieved when the dynamic range regions are superimposed. In this sense, the graphs of Figures 13 and 14 allow us to conclude that both models statistically produce the same dynamic response.

4. Conclusions

This work presented a novel methodology for evaluating the uncertainty of Scientific Machine Learning Models. A comprehensive approach was proposed that considered several uncertainties associated with the SciML model structure, the data used, and the original data source. The proposed strategy was composed of five steps: Markov Chain Monte Carlo method to obtain the uncertainty of the non-linear model parameters; generation of synthetic data; neural network structure identification; Monte Carlo simulation training; and methodology validation and uncertainty assessment of the trained mode.

The proposed method considers epistemic and aleatory uncertainties. These uncertainties are considered in the context of the data used to train the models and the model itself. Therefore, it is possible to provide an overall strategy for the uncertainty-aware models in the SciML field. The proposed approach can be applied to different ML models for numerical data prediction. On the other hand, it is not applied to categorical or image classification ML. This limitation exists, as it requires methods that allow quantifying the uncertainty of categorical variables and classification. Another limitation of this method is the computing effort required by it. This issue limits its application in online learning, as the computational effort can make the application unfeasible. This last limitation should be a topic of further development of the proposed methodology.

A case study demonstrated the method's consistency. Hence, two soft sensors were identified to provide information about the temperature and viscosity of a polymerization reactor. The results indicated that the soft sensor predictions are statistically equal to the validation data in both dynamic and stationary regimes. Therefore, a practical implication of the proposed method is that, for the prediction and evaluation of uncertainty in real-time applications, the computational cost is not high since the process of prediction and evaluation of uncertainty is performed only by consulting and calculating the most probable value of the prediction. This allows the use of soft sensors in real-time predictions with uncertainty evaluation.

The proposed methodology was validated using a publicly available data set: the polymerization process dataset. The proposed methodology can be experimentally validated as long as experimental data and their associated uncertainties exist. However, identifying the experimental uncertainties needs to be carried out in detail, which is out of the scope of the present work. As the results of this work demonstrate the efficiency of the proposed approach, a further natural development of this work is the application of the proposed methodology in an experimental case.

Author Contributions: Conceptualization, E.A.C.; Methodology, E.A.C., C.d.M.R., L.S. and I.B.d.R.N.; Software, E.A.C.; Formal analysis, M.F., L.S. and I.B.d.R.N.; Resources, M.F.; Data curation, C.d.M.R.; Writing—original draft, C.d.M.R.; Writing—review & editing, M.F., L.S. and I.B.d.R.N.; Supervision, L.S.; Project administration, L.S.; Funding acquisition, L.S. All authors have read and agreed to the published version of the manuscript.

Funding: This research received no external funding

Data Availability Statement: Not applicable.

Conflicts of Interest: The authors declare no conflict of interest.

Appendix A

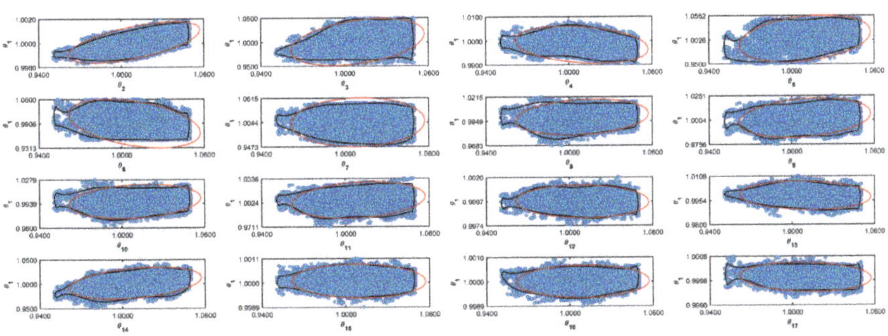

Figure A1. Coverage regions of parameters 01: (—) Gaussian region; (—) Possolo [33] region.

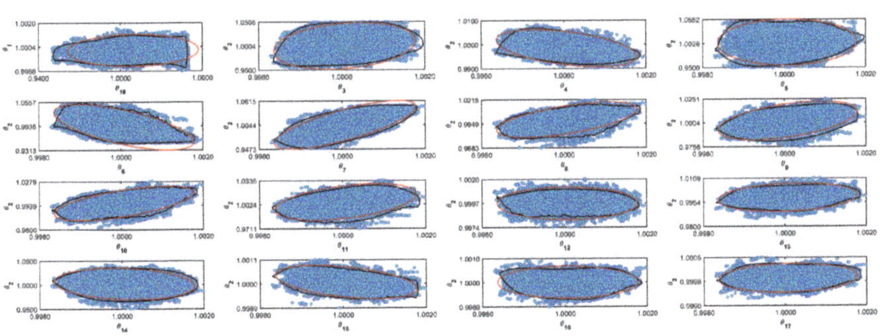

Figure A2. Coverage regions of parameters 02: (—) Gaussian region; (—) Possolo [33] region.

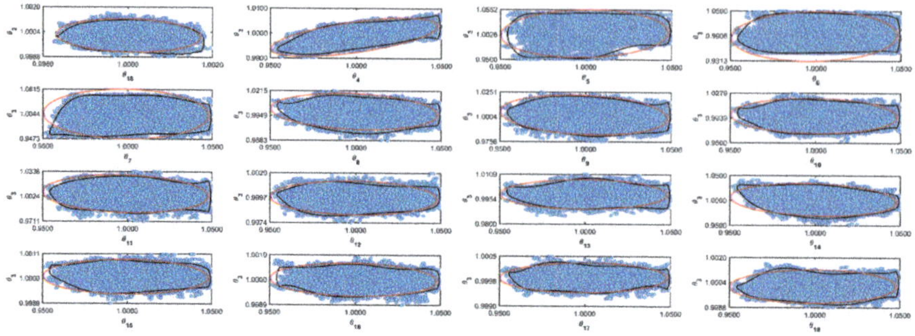

Figure A3. Coverage regions of parameters 03: (—) Gaussian region; (—) Possolo [33] region.

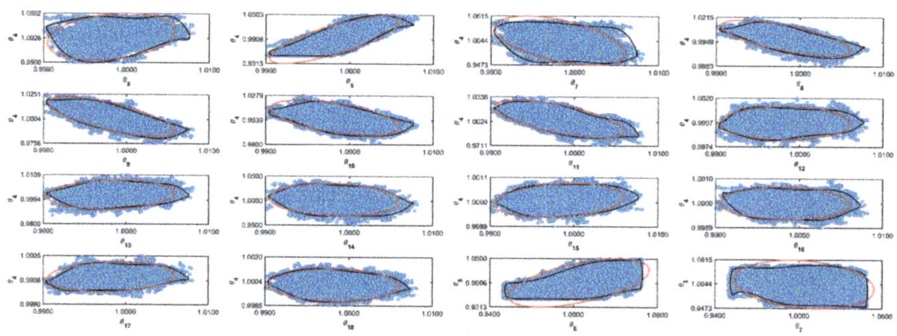

Figure A4. Coverage regions of parameters 04: (—) Gaussian region; (—) Possolo [33] region.

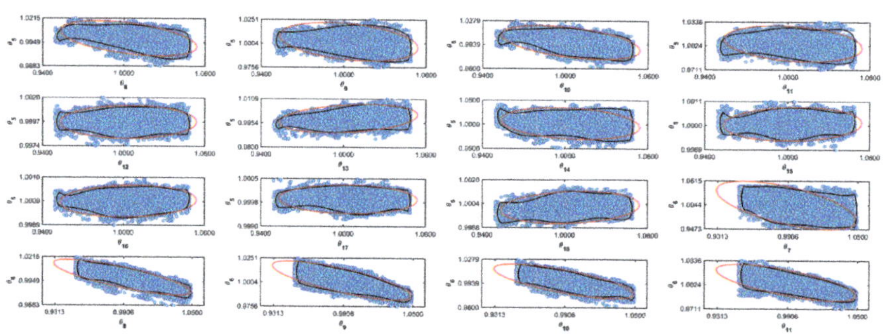

Figure A5. Coverage regions of parameters 05: (—) Gaussian region; (—) Possolo [33] region.

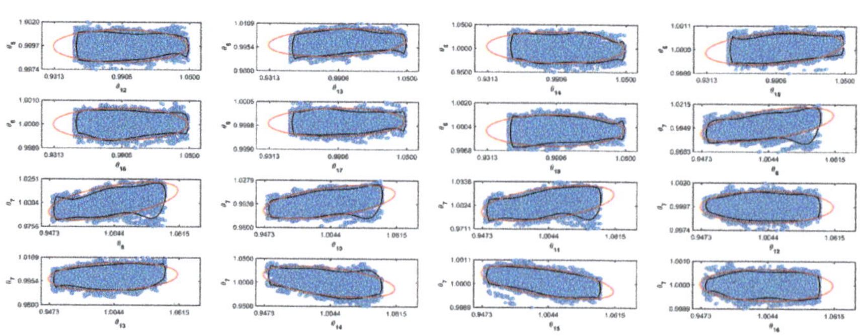

Figure A6. Coverage regions of parameters 06: (—) Gaussian region; (—) Possolo [33] region.

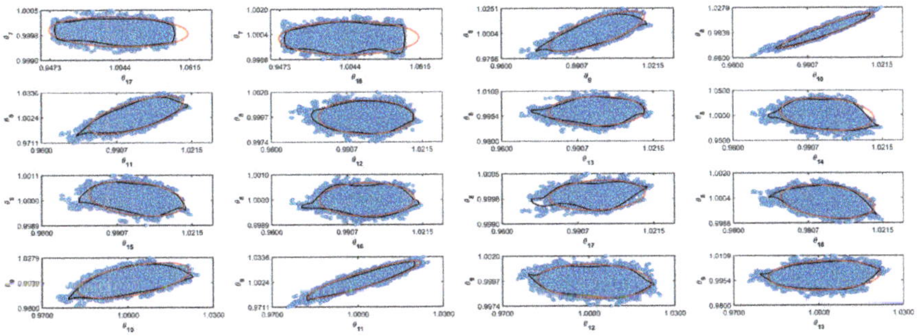

Figure A7. Coverage regions of parameters 07: (—) Gaussian region; (—) Possolo [33] region.

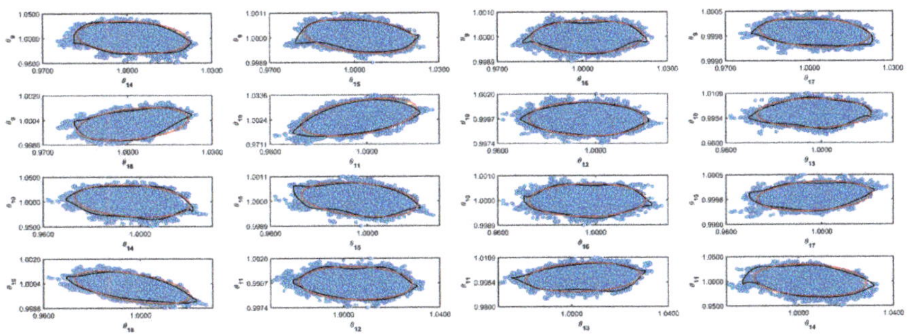

Figure A8. Coverage regions of parameters 08: (—) Gaussian region; (—) Possolo [33] region.

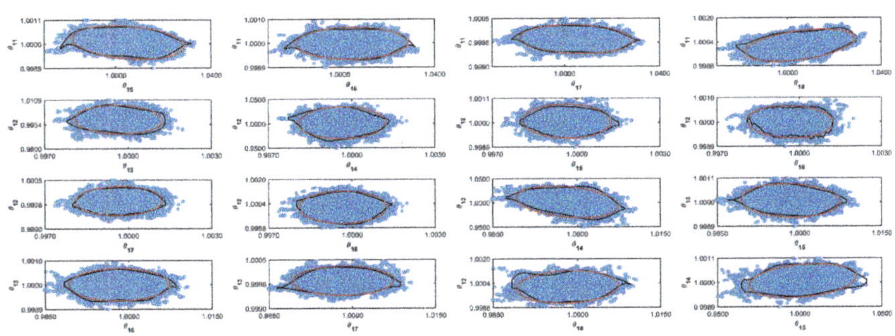

Figure A9. Coverage regions of parameters 09: (—) Gaussian region; (—) Possolo [33] region.

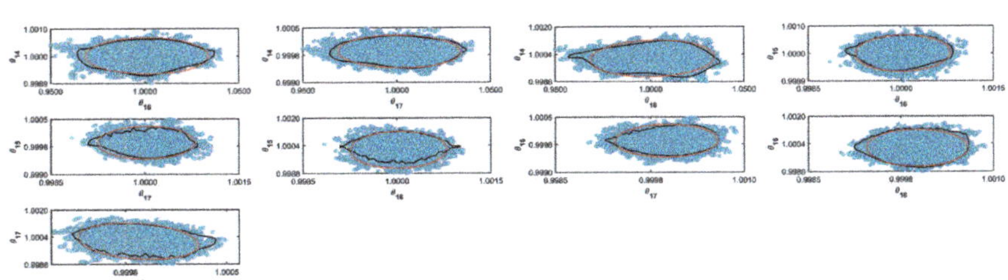

Figure A10. Coverage regions of parameters 10: (—) Gaussian region; (—) Possolo [33] region.

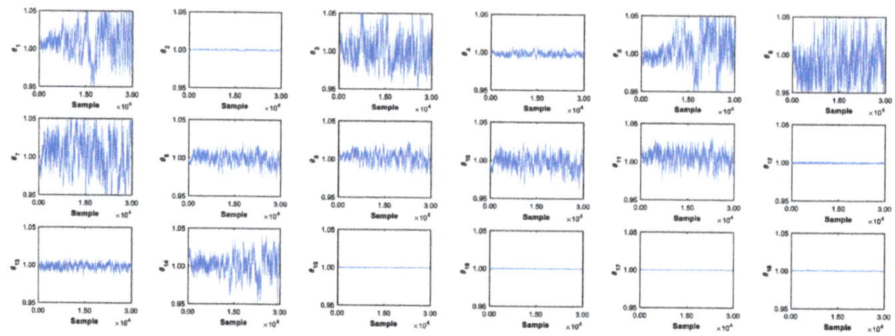

Figure A11. Parameters random walk.

References

1. Rackauckas, C.; Ma, Y.; Martensen, J.; Warner, C.; Zubov, K.; Supekar, R.; Skinner, D.; Ramadhan, A.; Edelman, A. Universal Differential Equations for Scientific Machine Learning. *arXiv* **2020**, arXiv:2001.04385. [CrossRef]
2. Chuang, K.V.; Keiser, M.J. Adversarial Controls for Scientific Machine Learning. *ACS Chem. Biol.* **2018**, *13*, 2819–2821. [CrossRef] [PubMed]
3. Gaikwad, A.; Giera, B.; Guss, G.M.; Forien, J.B.; Matthews, M.J.; Rao, P. Heterogeneous sensing and scientific machine learning for quality assurance in laser powder bed fusion—A single-track study. *Addit. Manuf.* **2020**, *36*, 101659. [CrossRef]
4. Nogueira, I.B.R.; Santana, V.V.; Ribeiro, A.M.; Rodrigues, A.E. Using scientific machine learning to develop universal differential equation for multicomponent adsorption separation systems. *Can. J. Chem. Eng.* **2022**, *100*, 2279–2290. [CrossRef]
5. Meng, X.; Yang, L.; Mao, Z.; del Águila Ferrandis, J.; Karniadakis, G.E. Learning functional priors and posteriors from data and physics. *J. Comput. Phys.* **2022**, *457*, 111073. [CrossRef]
6. Das, W.; Khanna, S. A Robust Machine Learning Based Framework for the Automated Detection of ADHD Using Pupillometric Biomarkers and Time Series Analysis. *Sci. Rep.* **2021**, *11*, 16370. [CrossRef]
7. Psaros, A.F.; Meng, X.; Zou, Z.; Guo, L.; Karniadakis, G.E. Uncertainty Quantification in Scientific Machine Learning: Methods, Metrics, and Comparisons. *arXiv* **2022**, arXiv:2201.07766. [CrossRef]
8. Hariri, R.H.; Fredericks, E.M.; Bowers, K.M. Uncertainty in big data analytics: Survey, opportunities, and challenges. *J. Big Data* **2019**, *6*, 44. [CrossRef]
9. Li, J.Z. Principled Approaches to Robust Machine Learning and Beyond. Ph.D. Thesis, Massachusetts Institute of Technology, Cambridge, MA, USA, 2018.
10. Gal, Y.; Ghahramani, Z. Dropout as a Bayesian Approximation: Representing Model Uncertainty in Deep Learning. In Proceedings of the 33rd International Conference on Machine Learning, New York, NY, USA, 19–24 June 2016.
11. Yu, D.; Wu, J.; Wang, W.; Gu, B. Optimal performance of hybrid energy system in the presence of electrical and heat storage systems under uncertainties using stochastic p-robust optimization technique. *Sustain. Cities Soc.* **2022**, *83*, 103935. [CrossRef]
12. Nogueira, I.B.; Faria, R.P.; Requião, R.; Koivisto, H.; Martins, M.A.; Rodrigues, A.E.; Loureiro, J.M.; Ribeiro, A.M. Chromatographic studies of n-Propyl Propionate: Adsorption equilibrium, modelling and uncertainties determination. *Comput. Chem. Eng.* **2018**, *119*, 371–382. [CrossRef]
13. Gneiting, T.; Balabdaoui, F.; Raftery, A. Probabilistic and sharpness forecasts , calibration. *Jrssb* **2013**, *69*, 243–268. [CrossRef]
14. Abdar, M.; Pourpanah, F.; Hussain, S.; Rezazadegan, D.; Liu, L.; Ghavamzadeh, M.; Fieguth, P.; Cao, X.; Khosravi, A.; Acharya, U.R.; et al. A review of uncertainty quantification in deep learning: Techniques, applications and challenges. *Inf. Fusion* **2021**, *76*, 243–297. [CrossRef]
15. Siddique, T.; Mahmud, M.; Keesee, A.; Ngwira, C.; Connor, H. A Survey of Uncertainty Quantification in Machine Learning for Space Weather Prediction. *Geosciences* **2022**, *12*, 27. [CrossRef]
16. Costa, E.; Rebello, C.; Santana, V.; Rodrigues, A.; Ribeiro, A.; Schnitman, L.; Nogueira, I. Mapping Uncertainties of Soft-Sensors Based on Deep Feedforward Neural Networks through a Novel Monte Carlo Uncertainties Training Process. *Processes* **2022**, *10*, 409. [CrossRef]
17. Levi, D.; Gispan, L.; Giladi, N.; Fetaya, E. Evaluating and Calibrating Uncertainty Prediction in Regression Tasks. *Sensors* **2022**, *22*, 5540. [CrossRef] [PubMed]
18. Migon, S.H.; Gamerman, D.; Louzada, F. *Statistical Inference: An Integrated Approach*, 2nd ed.; CRC Press: Boca Raton, FL, USA, 2014; p. 385.
19. Bard, Y. *Nonlinear Parameter Estimation*; Academic Press: Cambridge, MA, USA, 1974; p. 341.
20. Gamerman, D.; Lopes, H.F. *Markov Chain Monte Carlo: Stochastic Simulation for Bayesian Inference*, 2nd ed.; Chapman and Hall/CRC: London, UK, 2006; p. 343.
21. Haario, H.; Laine, M.; Mira, A.; Saksman, E. DRAM: Efficient adaptive MCMC. *Stat. Comput.* **2006**, *16*, 339–354. [CrossRef]

22. BIPM; IEC; IFCC; ILAC; ISO; IUPAC; IUPAP; OIML. *Evaluation of Measurement Data—Guide to the Expression of Uncertainty in Measurement*; BIPM: Sèvres, France, 2008.
23. BIPM; IEC; IFCC; ILAC; ISO; IUPAC; IUPAP; OIML. *Evaluation of Measurement Data—Supplement 1 to the "Guide to the Expression of Uncertainty in Measurement"—Propagation of Distributions Using a Monte Carlo Method*; BIPM: Sèvres, France, 2008.
24. BIPM; IEC; IFCC; ILAC; ISO; IUPAC; IUPAP; OIML. *Evaluation of Measurement Data—Supplement 2 to the "Guide to the Expression of Uncertainty in Measurement"—Models with Any Number of Output Quantities*; BIPM: Sèvres, France, 2011.
25. Haykin, S. *Neural Networks and Learning Machines*, 2nd ed.; Pearson Prentice Hall: Hoboken, NJ, USA, 1999; Volume 1–3. p. 938.
26. He, X.; Asada, H. New method for identifying orders of input-output models for nonlinear dynamic systems. In Proceedings of the 1993 American Control Conference, San Francisco, CA, USA, 2–4 June 1993. [CrossRef]
27. Li, L.; Jamieson, K.; DeSalvo, G.; Rostamizadeh, A.; Talwalkar, A. Hyperband: A Novel Bandit-Based Approach to Hyperparameter Optimization. *J. Mach. Learn. Res.* **2016**, *18*, 1–52.
28. Haario, H.; Saksman, E.; Tamminen, J. An Adaptive Metropolis Algorithm. *Bernoulli* **2001**, *7*, 223. [CrossRef]
29. Gelman, A.; Carlin, J.B.; Stern, H.S.; Dunson, D.B.; Vehtari, A.; Rubin, D.B. *Bayesian Data Analysis Third Edition (with Errors Fixed as of 13 February 2020)*; Routledge: London, UK, 2013.
30. Hidalgo, P.M.; Brosilow, C.B. Nonlinear model predictive control of styrene polymerization at unstable operating points. *Comput. Chem. Eng.* **1990**, *14*, 481–494. [CrossRef]
31. Alvarez, L.A.; Odloak, D. Optimization and control of a continuous polymerization reactor. *Braz. J. Chem. Eng.* **2012**, *29*, 807–820. [CrossRef]
32. Brooks, S.; Roberts, G. Assessing Convergence of Markov Chain Monte Carlo Algorithms. *Stat. Comput.* **1998**, *8*, 319–335. [CrossRef]
33. Possolo, A. Copulas for uncertainty analysis. *Metrologia* **2010**, *47*, 262–271. [CrossRef]
34. Kingma, D.P.; Ba, J. Adam: A Method for Stochastic Optimization. *arXiv* **2014**, arXiv:1412.6980. [CrossRef]

mathematics

MDPI

Article

Optimization of Analog Circuit Parameters Using Bidirectional Long Short-Term Memory Coupled with an Enhanced Whale Optimization Algorithm

Hengfei Yang [1], Shiyuan Yang [2,*], Debiao Meng [1,3,*], Chenghao Hu [1], Chaosheng Wu [1], Bo Yang [1], Peng Nie [1], Yuan Si [4] and Xiaoyan Su [5]

1 School of Mechanical and Electrical Engineering, University of Electronic Science and Technology of China, Chengdu 611731, China
2 Faculty of Engineering, University of Porto, 4200-465 Porto, Portugal
3 Institute of Electronic and Information Engineering of UESTC in Guangdong, Dongguan 523808, China
4 Glasgow College, University of Electronic Science and Technology of China, Chengdu 611731, China
5 School of Automation Engineering, Shanghai University of Electric Power, Shanghai 200090, China
* Correspondence: syyang214000@gmail.com (S.Y.); dbmeng@uestc.edu.cn (D.M.)

Abstract: The development of surrogate models based on limited data is crucial in enhancing the speed of structural analysis and design optimization. Surrogate models are highly effective in alleviating the challenges between design variables and performance evaluation. Bidirectional Long Short-Term Memory (BiLSTM) is an advanced recurrent neural network that exhibits significant advantages in processing sequential data. However, the training of BiLSTM involves the adjustment of multiple hyperparameters (such as the number of layers, the number of hidden units, and the learning rate), which complicates the training process of the model. To enhance the efficiency and accuracy of neural network model development, this study proposes an Improved Whale Optimization Algorithm-assisted BiLSTM establishment strategy (IWOA-BiLSTM). The new algorithm enhances the initial population design and population position update process of the original Whale Optimization Algorithm (WOA), thereby improving both the global search capability and local exploitation ability of the algorithm. The IWOA is employed during the training process of BiLSTM to search for optimal hyperparameters, which reduces model training time and enhances the robustness and accuracy of the model. Finally, the effectiveness of the model is tested through a parameter optimization problem of a specific analog circuit. Experimental results indicate that, compared to traditional neural network models, IWOA-BiLSTM demonstrates higher accuracy and effectiveness in the optimal parameter design of analog circuit engineering problems.

Keywords: analog circuit parameters; whale optimization algorithm; long short-term memory neural networks

MSC: 65K10; 68T07; 90C23

1. Introduction

With the rapid development of the electronics industry, the integration level of chips has been increasing. This has led to a rapid growth in the complexity of chips, making the design of integrated circuits increasingly reliant on efficient optimization design methods and design tools [1]. Therefore, the development of superior tools to assist in the design of complex engineering structures has become increasingly important.

With the continuous development of computer simulation technology, its powerful computational derivation capabilities, reliability, and accuracy have gradually gained favor among scholars and engineers. However, to ensure the accuracy and reliability of engineering optimization design and analysis results, increasingly higher precision requirements are being placed on simulation models [2–5]. This has led to a growing demand for computational resources and time in engineering design and analysis based on computer simulation technology [6]. Consequently, to reduce the high computational costs associated with high-fidelity simulation models, surrogate model techniques based on limited data have been widely developed and applied. In the field of optimization design for analog circuits, commonly used surrogate model techniques include Gaussian Processes [7,8], Artificial Neural Networks (ANN) [9–12], Support Vector Machines [13,14], and Response Surface Methodology [15]. Sanabria-Borbón et al. [16] proposed a low-cost multi-objective surrogate model for the automatic design of analog integrated circuits: the Gaussian Process Regression model. Zhang et al. [17] proposed a neural network-based Bayesian optimization method for the synthesis of analog circuits. Budak et al. [18] introduced a novel construction method for artificial neural network models to assist in the sizing of high-performance analog components. Wang et al. [19] proposed a semi-supervised support vector machine to aid in feature extraction and dimensionality reduction of frequency domain response data in the event of soft faults in analog circuits. Binu et al. [20] developed a Long Short-Term Memory (LSTM)-based fault prediction model for analog circuits, effectively addressing the challenge of tracking faults before they occur. A review of numerous previous studies indicates that surrogate model techniques play a significant role and hold considerable potential in the analysis and optimization design of analog circuits [21–24]. Among these, the performance of ANN is often more competitive under limited data conditions [25]. However, ANN models can face challenges during their establishment, such as an excessive number of parameters that need to be adjusted, a heavy reliance on the quality of training data, and the risk of overfitting when fitting small datasets. Therefore, the development of new neural network surrogate models remains highly relevant in the field of engineering applications.

Enhancing the efficiency and accuracy of surrogate model construction through the assistance of optimization algorithms is an effective strategy [26–29]. Numerous optimization algorithms have been developed in previous research, including Bayesian optimization, genetic algorithms, simulated annealing, and other heuristic algorithms [30–34]. Among these, many high-performing optimization algorithms have been applied in the analysis and optimization of analog circuits [35–38]. However, the challenge of balancing the global exploration capability and local exploitation ability of these algorithms persists. He et al. [39] proposed a Bayesian optimization based on the Gaussian process model to optimize expensive black-box functions. The experimental results show that the Bayesian optimization based on the Gaussian process can reduce the computational cost without sacrificing the modeling ability of the surrogate model. Liu et al. [40] applied a differential optimization algorithm to an antenna optimization algorithm based on an adaptive Bayesian neural network model. The results show that the optimization method proposed in this study has higher progress in convergence speed and computational cost saving. Li et al. [41] proposed an analog circuit optimization system based on a genetic algorithm. The study reduces the number of simulation calls through the ANN model, and the results show that the proposed global optimization algorithm has very high computational efficiency. Majeed et al. [42] proposed an optimization design of a Complementary Metal-Oxide-Semiconductor (CMOS) differential amplifier circuit and a two-stage CMOS operational amplifier circuit based on a Whale Optimization Algorithm (WOA). The research results reflect the effect of the WOA algorithm on improving the efficiency and accuracy of optimization design. The above research reflects the important role of excellent optimization algorithms in the parameter optimization of analog circuits. However, these optimization algorithms still face challenges when dealing with complex engineering problems. As the dimensionality of the problem increases, the volume of the search space grows exponentially. This results in the population of the optimization algorithm becoming sparse in space, hindering effective exploration. Second, when confronted with highly complex optimization objectives, traditional optimization algorithms are prone to premature convergence to local optima. Third, traditional algorithms are sensitive to parameter settings. In the context of high-dimensional problems, multiple trials and adjustments may be necessary to find suitable parameter combinations. Therefore, the development of more advanced optimization methods remains a significant challenge.

To this end, this study proposes a reliable method for constructing surrogate models. Considering that the establishment of a neural network model is prone to over-fitting or under-fitting and lack of memory ability, a new Bidirectional Long Short-Term Memory (BiLSTM) network is proposed. The proposed surrogate model improves the accuracy and robustness of the prediction results by capturing the aspects ignored by the early model. In addition, this study proposes an improved WOA optimization algorithm. Although the WOA optimization algorithm has the advantages of being able to balance exploration and development, is simple and efficient, and is suitable for a variety of optimization problems, it is sensitive to parameter settings has difficulty dealing with high-dimensional problems. Therefore, this study proposes an improved WOA algorithm for automatically adjusting the parameter values of BiLSTM. It is noteworthy that this study evaluates the effectiveness of the proposed Improved Whale Optimization Algorithm-assisted BiLSTM (IWOA-BiLSTM) solely through the parameter optimization problem of complex analog circuits. However, the proposed model construction method is equally applicable to other engineering problems, including simulations of different types of analog circuits or numerical simulation analyses (such as finite element analysis) and other engineering challenges.

The rest of this article is organized as follows. In Section 2, the original WOA algorithm and LSTM are introduced. In Section 3, the improved WOA algorithm is described, and the proposed optimization algorithm is compared with the latest optimization algorithms. Section 4 provides a detailed explanation of the proposed IWOA-BiLSTM model construction method. In Section 5, a common optimization problem related to analog circuit parameters is selected to evaluate the stability and accuracy of the IWOA-BiLSTM model. In Section 6, the work done in this study and the outlook for the future are described.

2. Relevant Theory Review

2.1. Whale Optimization Algorithm

S. Mirjalili and A. Lewis proposed a novel intelligence optimization technique inspired by the instinctive hunting techniques of humpback whales, which is called "The WOA" [43]. This algorithm simulates the whale pods' hunt for prey, which is composed of three parts: seeking prey, a spiral movement of positions, and encircling shrinkage.

The WOA is inspired by two hunting behaviors of humpback whales, exhibiting highly effective global exploration and local search capabilities. It has shown impressive performance in a variety of numerical optimization and engineering problems. Compared to Ant Colony Optimization [44] and Particle Swarm Optimization [45], the WOA demonstrates better convergence capability and optimization speed.

During the hunting process, whales identify an optimal location, known as the best spot discovered. They employ two possible strategies, either encircling and shrinking their position around the best whale or searching for prey in the immediate vicinity. The first strategy enables movement closer to the optimal location, while the second ensures exploration of nearby areas without overlooking potential opportunities. When a better location is found, the optimal position is updated, and this process continues until no further improvements are observed. Simulating this can achieve global optimization efficiently. The foraging mechanism can be expressed by Equations (1) and (2).

$$\vec{D} = \left| \vec{C} \cdot \overrightarrow{X_{\text{rand}}} - \vec{X} \right| \tag{1}$$

$$\vec{X}_{(t+1)} = \overrightarrow{X_{\text{rand}}} - \vec{A} \cdot \vec{D} \tag{2}$$

where t represents the current iteration count. $\vec{D}$ indicates the distance vector that measures the space between the current whale and the randomly selected whale. The vector $\overrightarrow{X_{\text{rand}}}$ represents the position of a randomly selected whale from the existing whale population. The vector $\vec{X}_{(t+1)}$ shows the position of the next generation of whales. $\vec{A}$ and $\vec{C}$ are coefficient vectors which are specified in Equations (3) and (4).

$$\vec{A} = 2\vec{a} \cdot \vec{r} - \vec{a} \tag{3}$$

$$\vec{C} = 2\vec{r} \tag{4}$$

where $\vec{r}$ is a random vector which is distributed between [0, 1], and the vector $\vec{a}$ is a control parameter which gradually drops from 2 to 0 in a linear fashion as the iterations move forward.

The definition of the contraction enclosure strategies in mathematical terms is presented below:

$$\vec{D} = \left| \vec{C} \cdot \overrightarrow{X^*}(t) - \vec{X}(t) \right| \tag{5}$$

$$\vec{X}(t+1) = \overrightarrow{X^*}(t) - \vec{A} - \vec{D} \tag{6}$$

where $\overrightarrow{X^*}(t)$ represents the position of the individual whale in the current population that has the best function value. $\vec{D}$ indicates the distance factor for surrounding the current whale. A smaller value of $\vec{A}$ leads to shorter steps in the whale's movement.

The mathematical model for the spiral update position stage can be represented as

$$\vec{X}(t+1) = \overrightarrow{D'} \cdot e^{bl} \cdot \cos(2\pi l) + \overrightarrow{X^*}(t) \tag{7}$$

$$\overrightarrow{D'} = \left| \vec{X}^*(t) - \vec{X}(t) \right| \tag{8}$$

where $\overrightarrow{D'}$ is a vector representing the distance between the optimal-position whale and the whale under consideration. The shape of the spiral is determined by the constant coefficient b as the process continues. When b equals 1, it generates a standard logarithmic spiral. l is a random value chosen within the range $[-1, 1]$.

The changes in the positions of the whales in the WOA do not interfere with each other, which means that the components of $\vec{X}(t)$ are updated individually when the population updates to represent the whales' positions.

As the whale circles its prey in a tighter loop, it simultaneously follows a spiral path, emulating its hunting behavior. A 50% probability decides whether the spiral model or the contraction enclosure method will be applied to update the whale's position during the optimization process, thereby replicating this dual behavior.

As demonstrated in the examination conducted in Section 3.4, the WOA often exhibits significant competitiveness compared to algorithms such as the Honey Badger Algorithm (HBA) [46], Sparrow Search Algorithm (SSA) [47], and Osprey Optimization Algorithm (OOA) [48].

2.2. Long Short-Term Memory

Neural network models can be divided into two types: The first one is the Backpropagation Neural Networks, which have simplistic architecture [49].

However, it is likely to trap in overfitting and local minima problems, and it doesn't represent effective utilization of dependency relationship. The remaining models are more advanced and efficient deep neural networks, leading the way in predictive modeling that can fit complicated nonlinear relationships [50]. In conventional neural networks, Recurrent Neural Networks (RNNs) and LSTMs are two famous algorithms that deal with the problem of the shortage of capabilities of memory, thereby enhancing proficient learning and predictive accuracy grounded in past data.

LSTMs, introduced by Sepp Hochreiter and Jürgen Schmidhuber, are built to tackle the issue of vanishing gradients [51] upon RNNs. They excel in long-distance dependencies tasks. While both LSTMs and RNNs share a similar operational framework, LSTMs incorporate more intricate inner processing components that enhance their ability to store and update contextual information. Ai et al. [52] developed an effective tunnel anomaly detection method based on LSTM combined with the Autoregressive Integrated Moving Average strategy. The results of this study demonstrated that LSTM possesses excellent early prediction capabilities and the ability to capture long-term performance trends.

During the development of LSTMs, Hochreiter and his colleagues introduced cells with memory capability and gating mechanisms to retain historical information and manage long-term states effectively. These gates control the flow of information, improving performance. Additionally, researchers such as Graves contributed to the design by integrating a forget gate, which helps mitigate the vanishing and exploding gradient problems often encountered with lengthy sequences of data. LSTM, a key component of the proposed hybrid approach, is structured with three main gates: the input gate, the forget gate, and the output gate. Each gate is a wholly connected layer that enables LSTM to store and update information within itself. These gates rely on gating mechanisms that use the sigmoid function and point-wise multiplication to effectively control data flow and update the internal state.

As is shown in Figure 1, the input gate, the forget gate, and the output gate are represented by the letters i, f, and o, respectively. O is the element-wise multiplication, and the weight matrices of the network are represented by W. b denotes the bias vector, and c represents the memory cell. x and h stand for the LSTM hidden layer's input and output vectors, respectively. The logistic function (σ) and Tanh function (tanh) belong to the sigmoid function.

- The input gate manages the number of current input data (x) that are fed into the memory cell to determine the amount of information that can be stored in cell c. Its value is as in Equations (9)–(11).

$$\sigma(x) = \frac{1}{1+e^{-x}} \tag{9}$$

$$\tanh(x) = \frac{e^x - e^{-x}}{e^x + e^{-x}} \tag{10}$$

$$i_t = \sigma(W_{xi}x_t + W_{hi}h_{t-1} + b_i) = \sigma(W_iV + b_i) \tag{11}$$

- The forget gate contributes to coping with problems of gradient vanishing and explosion that can happen in the framework of the backpropagation process. It effectively manages the data retention process, determining which information to preserve and which to discard. This allows the forget gate to assess the importance of past data and make informed decisions about what should be removed, ensuring that only the most relevant information c_{t-1} is maintained for the new data c_t.

$$f_t = \sigma(W_{xf}x_t + W_{hf}h_{t-1} + b_f) = \sigma(W_fV + b_f) \tag{12}$$

$$\widetilde{c}_t = tanh(W_{xc}x_t + W_{hc}h_{t-1} + b_i) = tanh(W_cV + b_c) \tag{13}$$

$$c_t = f_t \times c_{t-1} + i_t \times \widetilde{c}_t \tag{14}$$

- The output gate is responsible for controlling how c impacts h by selecting the output portion of the memory cell at time step t. The hidden layer's output o_t and the output gate's value h_t are denoted as in Equations (15) and (16).

$$o_t = \sigma(W_{xo}x_t + W_{ho}h_{t-1} + b_o) = \sigma(W_oV + b_o) \tag{15}$$

$$h_t = o_t \times tanh(c_t) \tag{16}$$

- LSTMs still face challenges with hyperparameter settings like iterations, learning rates, and the number of neurons in hidden layers, which can significantly affect the model's accuracy of prediction.

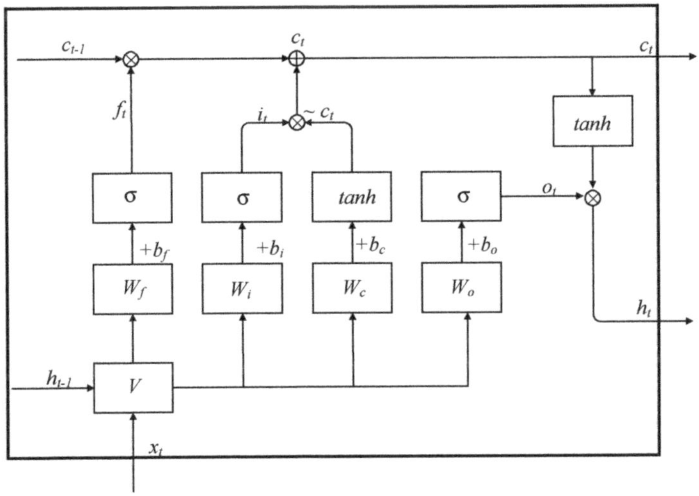

Figure 1. Structure of LSTM.

3. Improved Whale Optimization Algorithm

The WOA is a novel algorithm that distinguishes itself in its new structure and its fewer control parameters when compared to other optimizations [53]. Furthermore, the

WOA converges very quickly, which is quite impressive, and performs better than other intelligent algorithms in many numerical optimization and engineering problems.

However, the WOA still needs to break some barriers. When navigating intricate problems with multiple variables, it searches slowly and is likely to get stuck in local optima, with a poor convergence ability. To this end, this study enhances the filling of the initial population positions of the algorithm through chaotic mapping. Subsequently, it balances the global search capability and local search capability during the convergence process of the algorithm, thereby improving the convergence speed. First, a nonlinear convergence factor is introduced to promote higher global search capability in the early stages and greater local exploitation capability in the later stages of the algorithm. Second, dynamic inertia variables are introduced to further enhance the global search capability of the population in the initial iterations. Finally, the concept of simulated annealing is incorporated to assist the whale population in escaping local optima in the early iterations and to improve the local exploitation capability and convergence rate in the later iterations. Following are the details of the improvements made.

3.1. Chaotic Inverse Learning for Population Initialization

Achieving optimal search performance relies heavily on the proper initialization of swarm algorithms. In the case of the WOA, its random setup can lead to an unequal spread of whales across the search space. Thus, if the fortune does not permit, most of the whales will generate in locations away from the optimal point, which may increase the time to search for the optimal point and slower convergence rates. To achieve diversity in algorithmic searches, we employ chaotic mapping, utilizing the advantages of these two initialization methods.

There are two chaotic perturbation equations: The Logistic map and the Tent map, which are mostly used by people. The Logistic map tends to distribute points more evenly around the middle values, but it is significantly more likely to generate points at the extremes. The Tent map is structurally easier, which still provides better uniform traversal, giving the algorithm a higher search speed. What is more, if we use reverse learning to improve the population initialization, we can greatly enhance the convergence speeds, and the mapping point diagrams of three different methods are shown in Figure 2. Thus, to leverage the benefits of both initialization methods, this paper generates the initial population using reverse learning principles and chaotic mapping.

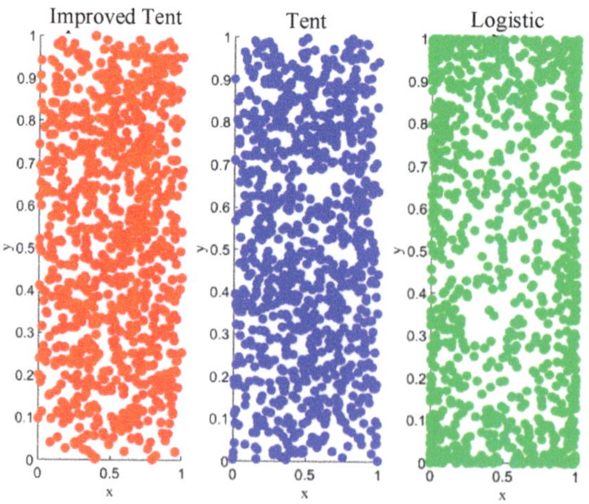

Figure 2. Different maps.

In population optimization algorithms, although a larger N enhances the global search capability of the algorithm, it significantly reduces the convergence speed. The application of chaotic mapping to process the initial whale population in the WOA aims to reduce the correlation among sample individuals, thereby effectively improving the global search capability of the algorithm without adversely affecting the convergence speed. The mathematical model definition is defined as follows:

$$x_{i+1} == \begin{cases} 2x_i + \text{rand}(0,1) \times \frac{1}{N} & 0 \leq x \leq \frac{1}{2} \\ 2(1-x_i) + \text{rand}(0,1) \times \frac{1}{N} & \frac{1}{2} < x \leq 1 \end{cases}, i = 1, \ldots, N \tag{17}$$

where N represents the number of individuals in the population set for the IWOA. x_i represents the individual whale entities in the IWOA. The random variable helps prevent the iterations from settling into unstable or small periodic patterns, which inherited the advantages of the Tent map, which has good ergodicity, regularity, and randomness. The improvement makes a great difference in boosting its robustness and efficiency.

After that, we use the chaotic sequence to generate the corresponding initial population.

$$x_{ij} = x_{\min j} + Z_{kj}(x_{\max j} - x_{\min j}) \tag{18}$$

$$x_{ij}^* = x_{\min j} + x_{\max j} - x_{ij} \tag{19}$$

where x_{ij}^* represents the inverse population. $x_{\min j}$ and $x_{\max j}$ represent the minimum and maximum whale individuals in the j-th column, respectively.

Finally, we compare the inverse population with the initial population, which is made up of the top N individuals chosen according to their best fitness.

3.2. Nonlinear Convergence Factor and Dynamic Inertia Weight

In the WOA, it is universally acknowledged that A and B are the two important parameters. A is mostly dependent on a, while C is mostly influenced by r. For the WOA, A plays a significant part in the WOA's exploration and local exploitation abilities. To enhance its capacities of global exploration, we use three strategies: altering the variation curve of A, introducing a dynamic inertia weight, and combining the WOA with the simulated annealing operation and adaptive mutation perturbation.

3.2.1. Nonlinear Convergence Factor

We employ a nonlinear convergence factor to modify the variation curve. According to Equation (3), as a increases, A also increases. From Equations (5) and (6), it can be observed that as A becomes larger, the iteration step size of the optimization algorithm increases, making it easier for the algorithm to traverse the entire design space, and thus enhancing its global convergence performance. However, as the step size increases, the algorithm's focus on the local region diminishes. Therefore, by reducing the value of a, and consequently decreasing the step size, the local exploitation capability of the algorithm can be enhanced.

Typically, A decreases linearly from 2 to 0 in the WOA, but in some complex optimization problems, this may cause the algorithm to prematurely converge to local exploitation. Then we need a nonlinear convergence factor to keep the A remain at a relatively high rate to keep its good global exploration abilities.

$$\vec{a} = \vec{a}_0 \cdot e^{-\tan\left(\left(1.2 * \frac{t}{T_{\max}}\right)\right)^2} \tag{20}$$

where t represents the current iteration count. $T_{\max}$ represents the maximum iteration count. $\vec{a}_0$ represents the initial control factor, as shown in Equation (3). At the start of the iteration, the value of a is higher than the original, reducing the likelihood of becoming stuck in local optima and enhancing global search capability, as shown in Figure 3. During the later stages of iteration, the curve sharply decreases to a low value, to enhance its local exploitation capabilities, making it convergence quickly. Consequently, when faced with nonlinear complex optimization problems, its performance can be largely enhanced.

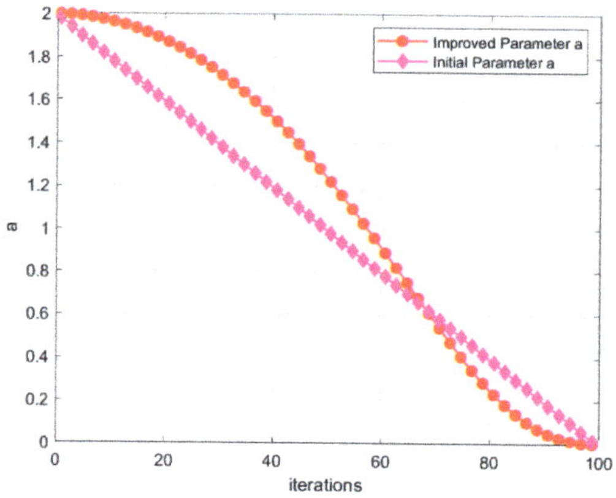

Figure 3. Different nonlinear convergence factors.

3.2.2. Dynamic Inertia Weight

According to document [54], we could use a dynamic inertia weight to update the whales' positions. The formula is as follows:

$$\omega(t) = \omega_{\max} \cdot \left(1 - \sin\left(\frac{\pi t}{2T_{\max}}\right)\right) + \omega_{\min} \cdot \sin\left(\frac{\pi t}{2T_{\max}}\right) \tag{21}$$

where ω represents the dynamic inertia weight. $\omega_{\max}$ and $\omega_{\min}$ represent the maximum and the minimum of the dynamic inertia weight. $T_{\max}$ represents the maximum number of iterations, while t stands for the current iteration count. At last, the formula below represents the adjustment of the spiral position:

$$\overrightarrow{X(t+1)} = \left|\overrightarrow{X_{\text{best}}(t)} - \overrightarrow{X(t)}\right| \cdot e^{bl} \cdot \cos(2\pi l) + \overrightarrow{X_{\text{best}}(t)} \cdot \omega(t) \tag{22}$$

where l is a random value chosen within the range $[-1, 1]$. ω is relatively high at the beginning of the iteration, which makes the algorithm have better capacities in global exploring, preventing early convergence to local optima. As the iteration goes on, it decreases to enhance its local search abilities and to make the convergence quicker.

3.2.3. Simulated Annealing Operation and Adaptive Mutation Perturbation

In 1953, Metropolis introduced the simulated annealing algorithm Metropolis [55]. This algorithm distinguishes itself because of its good capacity to escape local optima. Thus, we can incorporate the principles of simulated annealing into the WOA.

Furthermore, because all individuals are likely to converge towards the optimal solution in the later stages of iteration, this optimal individual may still not be the global optimum. Thus, we use the formula from the literature [54].

$$X_{b_{\text{new}}}^{t} = \frac{t}{\text{Maxiter}} \cdot X_{b_{\text{gaussian}}}^{t} + \left(1 - \frac{t}{\text{Maxiter}}\right) \cdot X_{b_{\text{cauchy}}}^{t} \tag{23}$$

At the beginning of the iteration, we use the Cauchy mutation for large and sharp changes. The weight for Cauchy mutation becomes high when the count t is low, which can help the WOA escape from the local optima. When the iteration goes on, t becomes bigger, making the Gaussian mutation dominant, which can enhance the algorithm's local search ability.

3.3. *Algorithm Diagram*

The improved IWOA computational process is illustrated in Figure 4. The specific computational steps are described as follows:

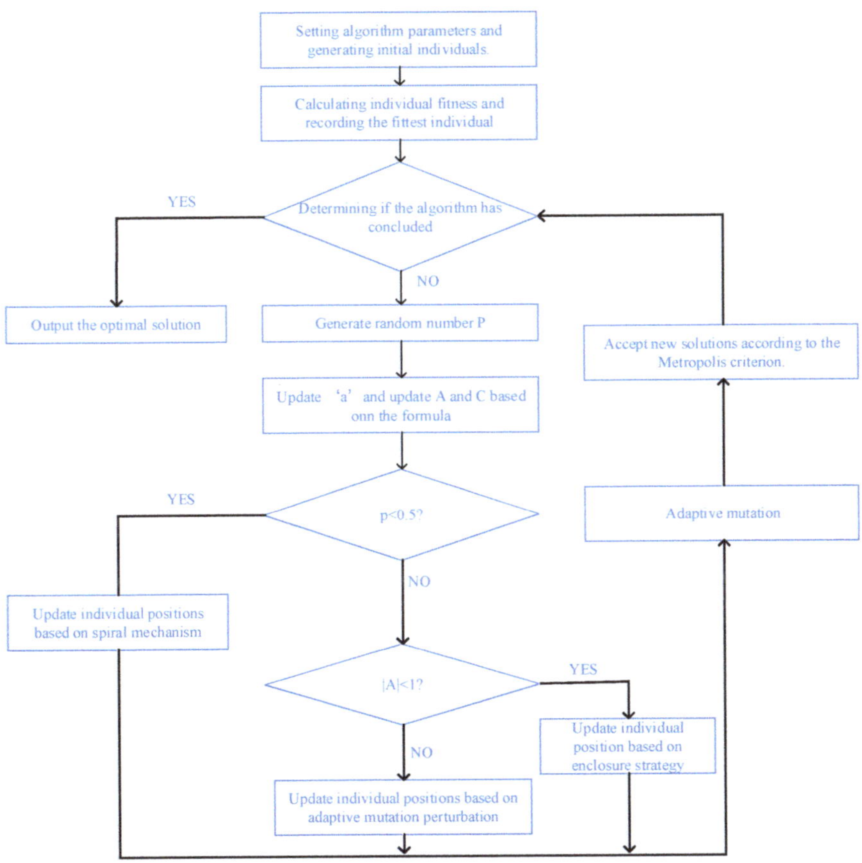

Figure 4. IWOA Structure.

Step 1: Initialize the whale population using a chaotic mapping approach;

Step 2: Select 50% of the individuals from the total whale population and update their positions using the method shown in Equation (22);

Step 3: For the remaining individuals, perform position updates based on the enclosure mechanism as described in Equation (6) or the adaptive mutation perturbation as shown in Equation (23), using the parameters A and C calculated from Equations (3) and (4);

Step 4: Determine whether the maximum number of iterations has been reached. If the maximum iteration count is reached, output the optimal solution; otherwise, proceed to update the positions of the whale population again;

3.4. Test

The study compares some test results from the literature [56] with those of other algorithms. The population size for each heuristic algorithm is set to 20, and the maximum number of iterations is set to 100. A total of 30 repeated experiments were conducted for each algorithm across various test functions to evaluate their robustness.

The relationship of different algorithms between fitness and the number of iterations is shown in Figures 5 and 6. From the average iteration processes of the various heuristic algorithms shown in Figure 5, it can be observed that the IWOA converges to the optimal solution across different test functions, exhibiting the fastest convergence speed in all test cases except for F8 and F9. Figure 6 presents a box plot of the optimal solutions obtained by different heuristic algorithms, using F4 as an example. It is evident from the figure that the IWOA algorithm yields a smaller optimal solution and demonstrates higher stability compared to the other algorithms.

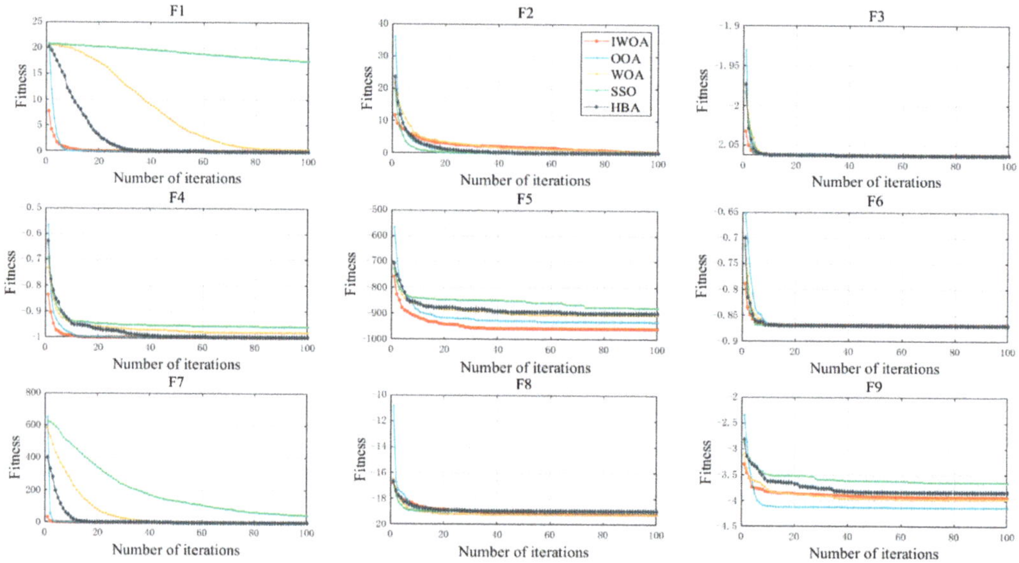

Figure 5. Iteration diagram of some test results.

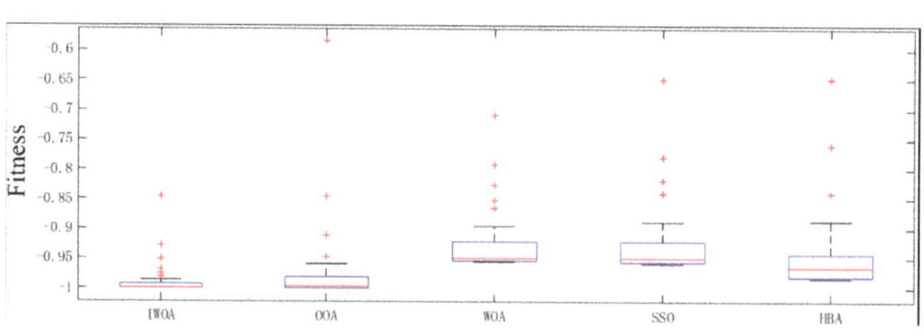

Figure 6. Algorithm Performance Comparison Across F4.

Tables 1 and 2 list the data of the results. These results indicate that the IWOA has strong optimization capabilities compared to other algorithms. Although the IWOA requires a slightly longer time for optimization, the computational results demonstrate higher accuracy and robustness.

Table 1. Data of different algorithms in F4.

F4	Standard Deviation	Mean Value	Optimal Solution	Run Time
HBA	0.029714	−0.98087	−1	0.058833
SSO	0.026751	−0.95073	−1	0.10554
OOA	1.0242×10^{-5}	−1	−1	0.060213
WOA	0.028675	−0.95325	−1	0.02126
IWOA	4.1233×10^{-17}	−1	−1	0.2793

Table 2. Data of different algorithms in F5.

F7	Standard Deviation	Mean Value	Optimal Solution	Run Time
HBA	55.46	−887.57	−959.64	0.063235
SSO	95.003	−866.84	−959.64	0.11575
OOA	58.605	−920.64	−959.64	0.058733
WOA	97.23	−851.37	−959.64	0.022593
IWOA	34.966	−949.03	−959.64	0.29416

4. IWOA-BiLSTM Establishment Strategy

4.1. BiLSTM

Although LSTMs have superior memory capabilities compared to traditional neural networks, they do not consider the future context. To address this limitation, Graves and others developed a new algorithm called BiLSTM, which combines backward feature computation with LSTM [57]. This bidirectional approach allows the algorithm to utilize future information and capture aspects that earlier models might overlook, significantly enhancing both the accuracy and robustness of predictions.

To illustrate how BiLSTM works, we first compare it to traditional LSTM. Since traditional LSTM is unidirectional, it cannot account for the effect of subsequent data on the current data. In contrast, BiLSTM includes a backward-propagating LSTM layer, allowing it to consider both past and future data for forecasting. The architecture of BiLSTM is shown in Figure 7.

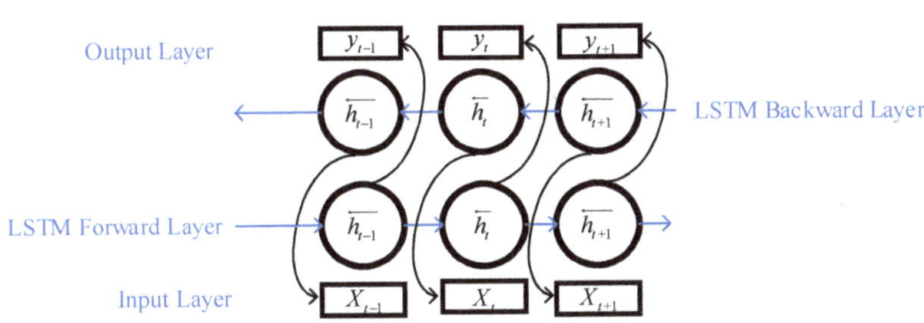

Figure 7. Structure of BiLSTM.

In the architecture of BiLSTM, two distinct LSTM networks process inputs in opposite directions: one forward and one backward. This bidirectional approach allows BiLSTM to learn from the same input sequence in both directions. By combining the outputs of these two networks, BiLSTM effectively takes into account both past and future context, enhancing its predictive capabilities.

In this framework, the forward and backward layers produce their respective outputs X and y, which are then combined to determine the values transmitted to the hidden layer

$\overleftarrow{h}$. This integration of outputs from both directional layers ultimately results in the final BiLSTM output. The mathematical representation of this process is as below:

$$\overrightarrow{h_t} = LSTM(x_t, \overrightarrow{h_{t-1}}) \tag{24}$$

$$\overleftarrow{h_t} = LSTM(x_t, \overrightarrow{h_{t-1}}) \tag{25}$$

$$y_t = \overrightarrow{W}\overrightarrow{h_t} + \overleftarrow{W}\overleftarrow{h_t} + b_y \tag{26}$$

Correspondingly, some hyperparameters can be optimized in the BiLSTM model. Relying exclusively on the trial-and-error method or empirical approaches may result in suboptimal parameter combinations and increased time expenditures. To address this issue, we can employ optimization techniques that utilize random generation as well as iterative refinement of hyperparameter combinations to discover the optimal solutions. The algorithms enhance the speed of finding the optimal solution and improve the overall performance of the BiLSTM, making them a practical choice for adjusting neural networks.

In the BiLSTM, four key hyperparameters can be optimized: dropout rate, learning rate, the number of iterations, and number of neurons. Among these, the learning rate is the most critical, followed closely by the dropout rate and the number of iterations, as demonstrated by Greff in his experiments. Consequently, this article primarily focuses on optimizing these three hyperparameters, which may significantly influence the performance of the BiLSTM by targeting the key parameters. By using the mean squared error of the model on the test set as the optimization objective, the predictive capability of the BiLSTM is enhanced. Compared to traditional methods of establishing BiLSTM, the assistance of the IWOA significantly improves both the efficiency of model construction and its predictive performance. Particularly in the absence of prior information, IWOA-BiLSTM provides a faster and more accurate approach for building surrogate models.

- Neuron count

The number of neurons can significantly impact both the learning ability and speed of the model. A larger number of neurons may lead to increased complexity, substantially extending the training time. Conversely, a smaller number of neurons may result in poor learning capacity, possibly leading to the network failing to optimize a satisfactory solution.

- Amount of iterations

The number of times the model iterates over the whole training data set is reflected by its value.

- Learning rate

The learning rate indicates the speed of parameter updates. A smaller learning rate allows for more precise updates, but it slows down the overall training process. Conversely, a learning rate that is too high can hinder convergence. Therefore, it is essential to select an appropriate learning rate.

4.2. IWOA-BiLSTM

The process flowchart of the algorithm is shown in Figure 8. By combining the IWOA and BiLSTM, we can leverage their respective strengths: the IWOA is used to optimize the hyperparameters, while BiLSTM provides accurate predictions. As shown in Figure 8, during the iterative process, the current trained model is evaluated on the test set based on the data loss. Simultaneously, the IWOA is employed to optimize the hyperparameters of the model, which will be used for parameter settings in the subsequent iteration of model training.

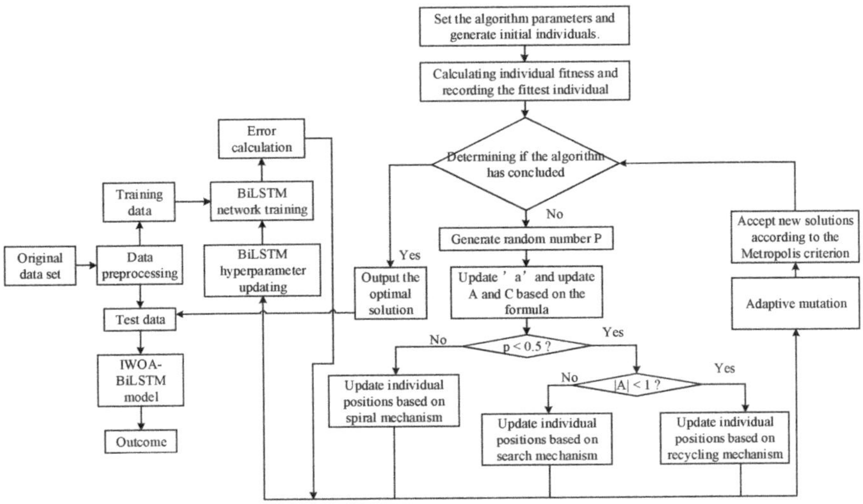

Figure 8. Overall structure of IWOA-BiLSTM.

5. Optimization of Analog Circuit Parameters

The following details the experimental setup for the optimization of simulated circuit parameters based on IWOA-BiLSTM. It is noteworthy that the proposed IWOA-BiLSTM is applicable to this type of simulated circuit experiment, but is not limited to it. Furthermore, IWOA-BiLSTM is also suitable for other types of numerical simulation analyses, such as finite element analysis. It should be noted that the computer used in this study is an Intel (R) Core (TM) i9-9900K CPU @ 3.60GHz, operating on a 64-bit operating system.

5.1. Problems Need to Be Solved

Self-biasing amplifiers are commonly used to enhance the stability and performance of amplifiers, particularly when facing temperature variations or changes in component parameters. Their characteristic feature is the ability to automatically set and maintain the bias point through an internal feedback mechanism, ensuring that the amplifier operates under optimal conditions. Self-biasing amplifiers are widely applied in various electronic devices, especially in scenarios that require high stability and reliability. However, certain specific application environments impose stricter size requirements on such circuits, such as in medical devices used for diagnosing neurological disorders related to epilepsy, where the circuit space must be sufficiently compact.

In these specialized application environments, it is crucial to ensure that the self-biasing amplifier minimizes the potential for reliability issues while guaranteeing the required power output. In the optimization process based on surrogate models, obtaining accurate approximations of simulation results is crucial. For this case study, this research tested the stability and accuracy of the proposed IWOA-BiLSTM. Key circuit parameters to be considered during the experimental process include slew rate, power consumption, load capacitance, minimum and maximum input voltages, reference voltage, and gain-bandwidth product.

5.2. Modified Recycling Folded Cascade Amplifier

In their work, Devi and colleagues introduced an amplifier configuration [58], which is illustrated in Figure 9. The configuration adopts adaptive bias methodologies within an enhanced cyclic folding architecture. Transistors M5 and M6, together with M15 and M16, contribute to the enhancement of input drive capability. To achieve this, we established a cross-coupling between M7-M16 and M6-M15. The transformation into a single-ended configuration is achieved by the incorporation of transistors M17 and M18, enabling $\frac{(k-1)}{10} I_{bias}$ to flow unimpededly through it, where I_{bias} represents the bias current. Within this structure, each component operates in the weak inversion regime. Upon the introduction of a substantial signal V_{ref}, M4 enters the deep triode region of weak inversion when M1 and M2 cease conduction. This biasing current flowing through M3 is redirected first from k and (k − 1) to M9 and M10, then from M17 and M18 towards the load capacitance C_L. In contrast to the conventional structure, this design improves the transition rate by a factor of (2k − 1). Comprehensive improvements are realized in terms of transconductance, gain-bandwidth product, and slew rate. As the value of k increases along with instability, the phase margin of the design contracts. A compensating resistor is positioned at the gate junctions of the current mirrors to mitigate this effect, with transistors Mc 1 and Mc 2 working in the deep triode area, assisting.

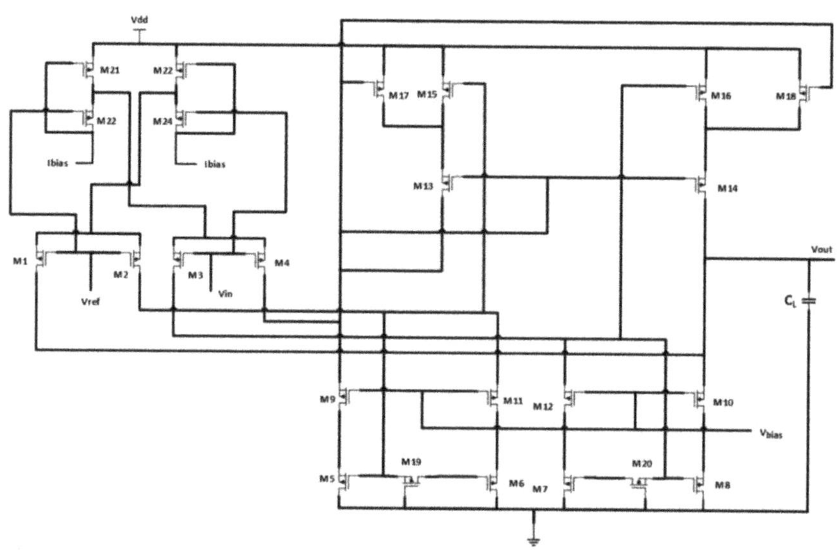

Figure 9. The structure of the circuit.

5.2.1. The Drain Current Equation in Weak Inversion

The weak inversion region enhances both low power consumption and high gain. The particular current (I_S) in the weak inversion region is given by the following expression:

$$I_S = K_\omega \mu C_{ox}(\frac{W}{L})V_T{}^2 = 2\eta\mu C_{ox}(\frac{W}{L})V_T{}^2 \tag{27}$$

The thermal voltage is $V_T = \frac{kT}{q}$, η is the aspect ratio, the mobility is μ, and C_{ox} denotes the oxide capacitance. k represents the Boltzmann constant, T stands for the temperature in

Kelvin, and q shows the elementary charge. W represents the power. As a result, the drain current in the weak inversion conduction can be represented by the following expression:

$$I_D = K_\omega \beta V_T{}^2 e^{\frac{V_G - V_{tho}}{\eta V_T}} [e^{\frac{-V_S}{V_T}} - e^{\frac{-V_D}{V_T}}] = 2\eta\beta V_T{}^2 e^{\frac{V_G - V_{tho}}{\eta V_T}} [e^{\frac{-V_S}{V_T}} - e^{\frac{-V_D}{V_T}}] \quad (28)$$

where η and V_{tho} represent the subthreshold slope factor and threshold voltage respectively; V_D, V_S, and V_G denote the drain, source, and gate voltages respectively. The formula has been modified as follows, following these term changes:

$$I_D = I_S e^{\frac{V_G - V_{tho}}{\eta V_T}} [e^{\frac{-V_S}{V_T}} - e^{\frac{-V_D}{V_T}}] = I_{DO} e^{\frac{V_G}{\eta V_T}} [e^{\frac{-V_S}{V_T}} - e^{\frac{-V_D}{V_T}}] \quad (29)$$

Within the domain of subthreshold studies, $V_{DS} \cong 104$ mV, and $V_{DS} > 4V_T$.

$$e^{\frac{-V_{DS}}{V_T}} = e^{-4} \cong 0.018 < 1, \quad (30)$$

Thus,

$$I_D = I_{DO} e^{\frac{V_{GS}}{\eta V_T}} = I_S e^{\frac{-V_{tho}}{\eta V_T}} e^{\frac{V_{GS}}{\eta V_T}} = 2\eta\mu C_{ox}(\frac{W}{L}) V_T{}^2 e^{\frac{V_{GS} - V_{tho}}{\eta V_T}}. \quad (31)$$

By adopting this method, V_{DS} remains unaffected by V_{GS}, thereby facilitating the maintenance of the MOSFET in its saturated state. The following equation shows the slew rate S_R:

$$S_R = \frac{Biascurrent}{Loadcapacitors} = 2GBW_\eta V_T \quad (32)$$

$$g_{m1} = 2\pi GBWC_L \quad (33)$$

where GB represents the gain bandwidth product.

5.2.2. Adaptive Biasing Technique

To achieve high gain, bandwidth, and slew rate performance, the design incorporates an adaptive biasing circuit within an enhanced cyclic folding cascade. The current flowing through the input transistors M1 to M4 is shown below:

$$I_{b1} = 2I_b e \frac{v_{id}}{\eta V_T} \quad (34)$$

$$I_{b2} = 2I_b e \frac{-v_{id}}{\eta V_T} \quad (35)$$

$$SR = \frac{2I_b(2k-1)}{C_L} (k = 3, C_L \text{ is the load capacitance}) \quad (36)$$

5.2.3. Design Procedure

The load capacitance and the slow rate determine I_b,which represents the bias current.

$$I_b = \frac{SR \times C_L}{2(2k-1)} \quad (37)$$

To avoid a zero-current condition, the transistors' cascade bias current is distributed with a ratio of k:1, making sure that the bias current remains lower than the current flowing through M8 and M5. The current passing through M8 and M5 and the circuit's minimum output voltage can determine the cascade transistors' width. You may use the formulas $W7 = \frac{W8}{k}$ and $W6 = \frac{W5}{k}$ to find M7's and M6's widths. The dimensions of W10 and W9 can be approximated given that the current flowing through M8 is (2k − 1) times lower than that through M10. Transistors M11 and M12 each have a width that is twice that of transistors M11, M10 and M9. To determine the transistors M14 through M16's aspect ratios, one must consider the circuit's maximum output voltage and utilize the equation of transistor drain current. The transistors M15 and M16's aspect ratios are k times those of W17–W20. The formula shows how the input transistors M1–M4's aspect ratios are determined by the load capacitance and gain-bandwidth product.

$$g_{m1} = 2\pi GBWC_L = \frac{I_D}{\eta V_T} \tag{38}$$

where g_{m1} represents the transconductance coefficient of the input transistor. The aspect ratios of cascade and bias transistors are determined by the maximum and minimum input common-mode voltage ranges $V_{in(max)}$ and $V_{in(\min)}$. Use Equation (39) to explore the total area filled by the transistors, where L_i represents the nth transistor's length and i denotes the transistors' maximum number involved.

$$Area = \sum_i W_i L_i \tag{39}$$

Table 3 presents the range of values for the key parameters of the analog circuit. In our study, we explored numerous configurations of metaheuristic optimization techniques and machine learning frameworks to augment the optimization process in applied tests related to this matter. These encompassed, but were not restricted to, Genetic Algorithms, Grey Wolf Optimizers, and Grey Wolf Optimizers in conjunction with BiLSTM and LSTM models. Finally, it was determined that the refined IWOA-BiLSTM model consistently delivered superior outcomes within the given constraints.

Table 3. Design variables ranges.

Parameters	Ranges
Load capacitance C_L (pF)	5–10
Slew rate S_R (V/μs)	1–10
Power consumption in weak inversion region (μW)	1–5
Minimum input voltage $V_{in(\min)}$ (V)	−0.4–0.2
Gain bandwidth product GB (MHz)	1–10
Maximum input voltage $V_{in(max)}$ (V)	0.2–0.4
Reference voltage (mV)	1–2
Input voltage V_{in} (μV)	500–600

In the practical application stage, the IWOA-BiLSTM model provides a variety of parameters that are adjustable to adapt to variable datasets. Through meticulously adjusting these parameters, consistent enhancements in performance can be observed across a variety of datasets. In the specific dataset under investigation, modifying the threshold value for p from 0.5 to 0.4 elevates the likelihood of whales utilizing the tactics of encircling and searching to update their positions, while diminishing the probability of utilizing the mechanism of spiral. Such a refinement makes the model of IWOA-BiLSTM attain superior fitness. Following shows the test results:

$MaxIt$ = 20;

$Popsize$ = 10;

ub = [200 200 200 0.01];

lb = [1 1 10 0.0001];

It can be seen from Figure 10, in almost every evolution generation, the IWOA-BiLSTM shows superior fitness.

Figure 11 presents the performance of the surrogate models established under different strategies on the prediction dataset. Figure 12 provides the evaluation metrics for the various surrogate models, including Root Mean Square Error (RMSE), Mean Absolute Error (MAE), and R_2, among others. We cannot yield satisfactory results if we apply the initial parameters to this dataset, as the predicted outcomes deviated significantly from the actual values. This issue stems from the excessively stringent limits established for the neuron counts in both concealed layers, which hindered effective fitting. Additionally, a bad learning rate and an inadequate iterations amount may have contributed to the suboptimal performance. As a result, in the next round of testing, these parameters would be adjusted.

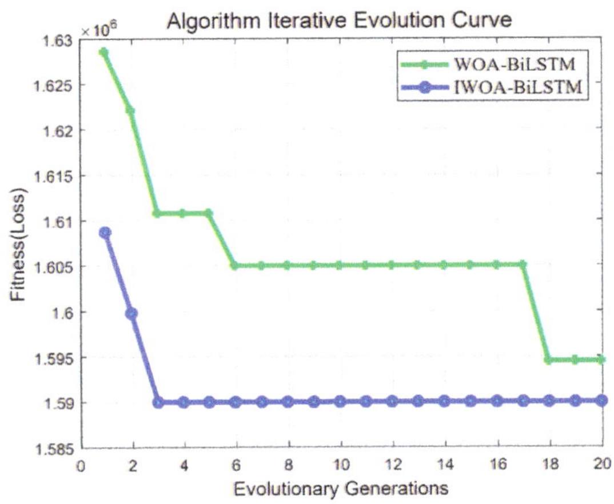

Figure 10. The first test's curve of algorithm iterative evolution.

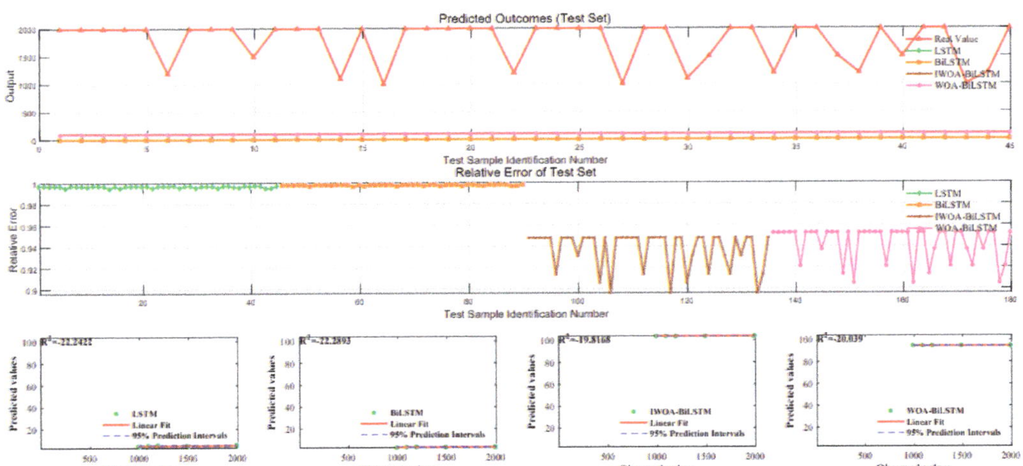

Figure 11. The first test's predicted results.

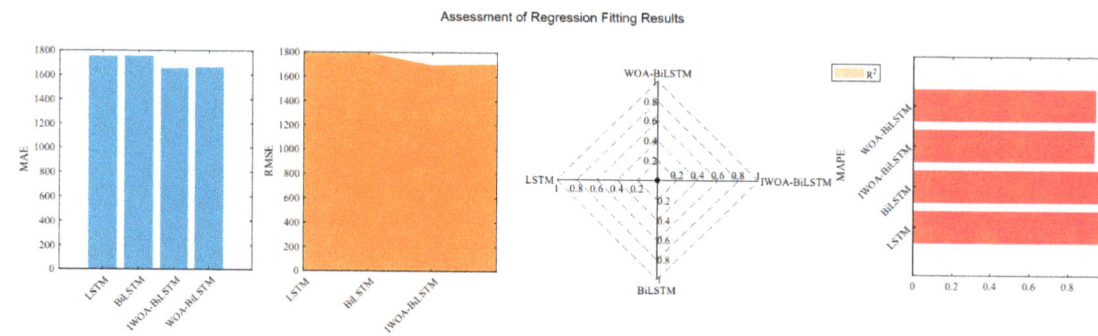

Figure 12. The first test's evaluation.

It is clear that the settings of the initial parameter are not conducive to effectively fitting the dataset, indicating the necessity of a new parameter combination to attain improved results. To expedite testing, the maximum number of iterations was set to 10, and the population size was reduced to 5 in the later tests.

$MaxIt = 10;$

$Popsize = 5;$

$ub = [500\ 500\ 500\ 0.2];$

$lb = [50\ 50\ 50\ 0.05];$

Figure 13 illustrates the variation in data loss during the training process of the BiLSTM model combined with different optimization algorithms. It can be observed from the figure that the convergence speed of IWOA is faster than that of WOA, resulting in better optimization performance.

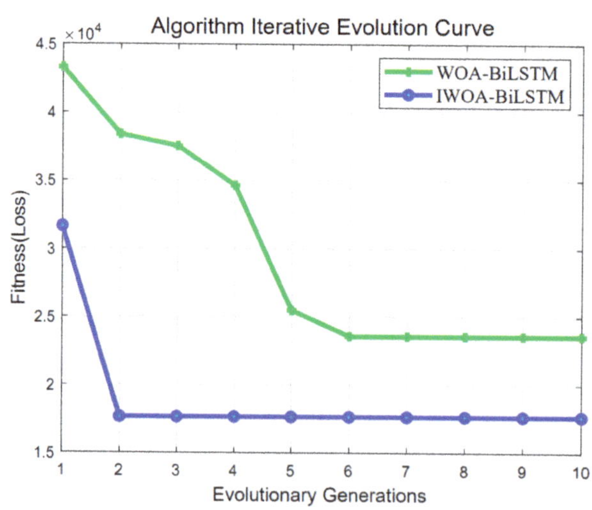

Figure 13. Second test's curve of algorithm iterative evolution.

Figure 14 presents the performance of the surrogate models established under different strategies on the test dataset. As illustrated, both LSTM and BiLSTM models struggle to recognize the features represented by the real data. With the assistance of optimization algorithms, the BiLSTM achieves higher predictive capability, with the effect of IWOA being particularly pronounced, resulting in a more significant reduction in error. Figure 15 provides the evaluation metrics for the models established using various strategies. The results clearly indicate that optimization algorithms have a substantial impact on improving the accuracy of the BiLSTM model.

In the latest test round, the value of p has been adjusted to 0.5. Compared to the previous round, it is clear that not only IWOA-BiLSTM but also WOA-BiLSTM represented improved fitting outcomes. However, with this specific parameter configuration, the WOA outperformed the IWOA.

$MaxIt = 10;$

$Popsize = 5;$

$ub = [500\ 500\ 500\ 0.2];$

$lb = [50\ 50\ 50\ 0.1];$

As shown in Figure 16, the data loss of the BiLSTM model gradually converges during the training process under different optimization algorithms. However, the IWOA demonstrates a higher optimization efficiency.

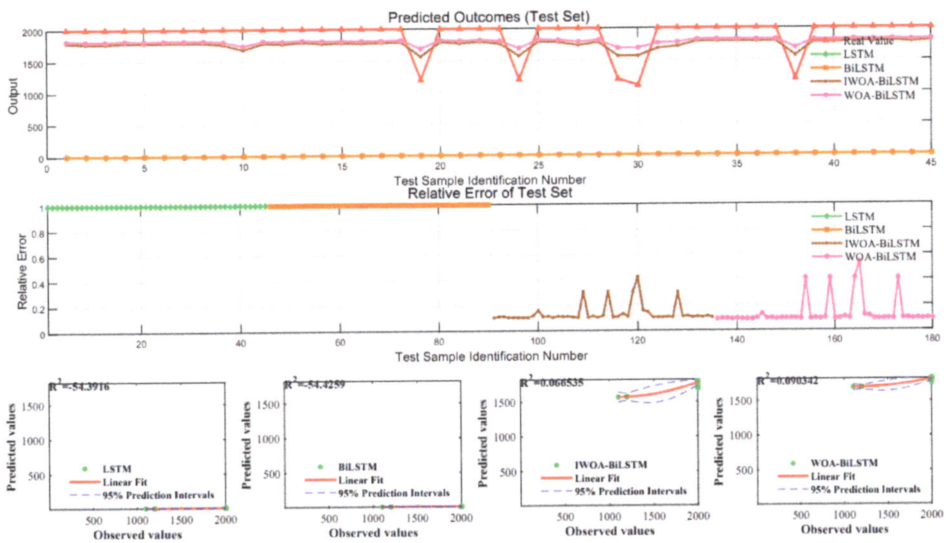

Figure 14. Second test's predicted results.

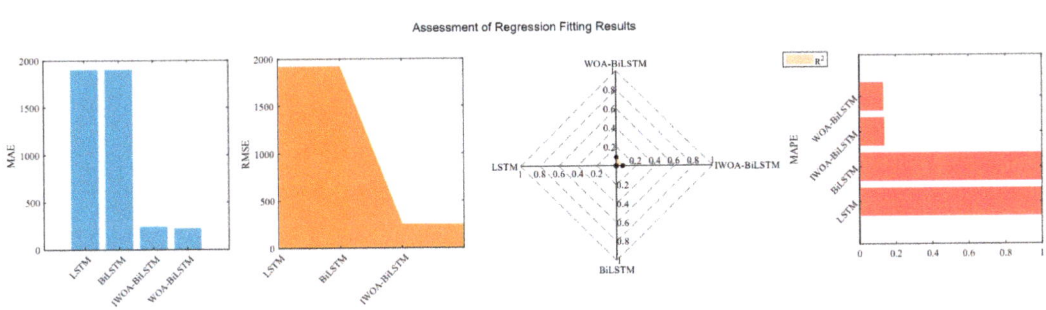

Figure 15. Second test's evaluation.

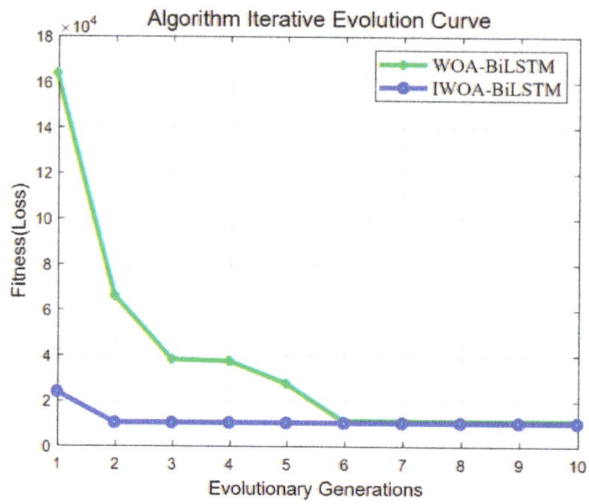

Figure 16. Final test's curve of algorithm iterative evolution.

As shown in Figure 17, the LSTM and BiLSTM models without the assistance of optimization algorithms exhibit significant differences in accuracy compared to the BiLSTM model supported by heuristic algorithms. By comparing the R_2 values, the BiLSTM assisted by IWOA achieved higher accuracy, demonstrating a stronger ability to capture the characteristics of the real data. As illustrated in Figure 18, the IWOA-BiLSTM obtained superior evaluation metrics.

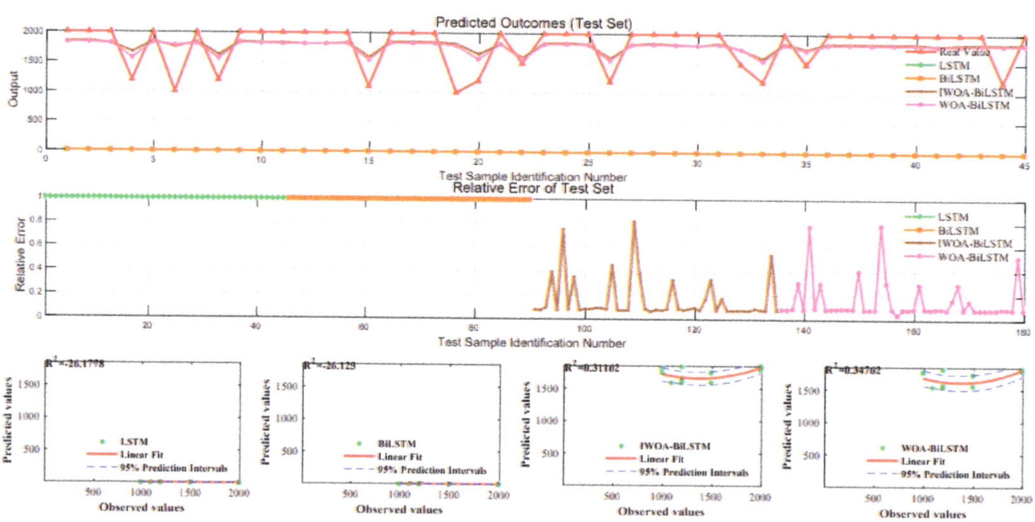

Figure 17. Final test's predicted results.

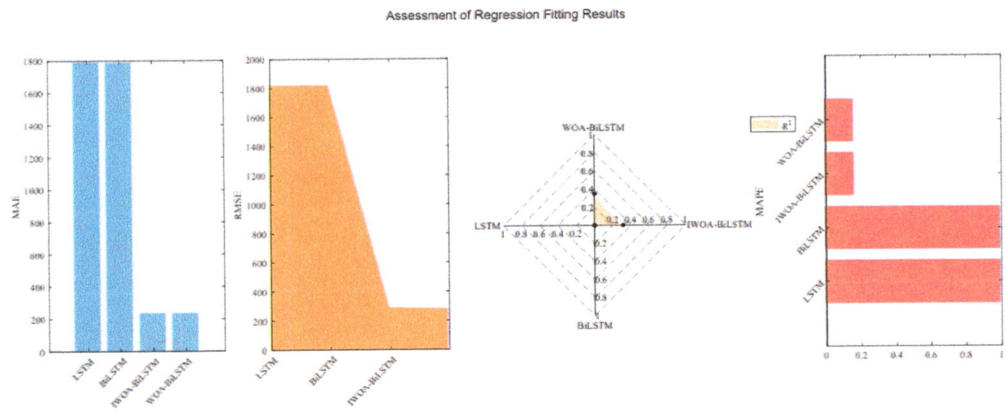

Figure 18. Final test's evaluation.

Although the time consumed by the proposed IWOA-BiLSTM is still influenced by the population size of the heuristic algorithm and the maximum number of iterations, it ensures higher accuracy and stability. Figures 10, 13 and 16 illustrate the iterative process of data loss during the construction of the BiLSTM model assisted by the IWOA and WOA algorithms, respectively. It is evident from the figures that the IWOA algorithm reduces data loss at a faster rate, resulting in models that achieve higher accuracy. Figures 11, 14 and 17 present the relative errors of the BiLSTM models constructed using different methods on the test set, as well as the prediction results at the selected sample points. It can be observed that before employing optimization algorithms to search for the optimal BiLSTM parameters, the model exhibits significant prediction errors. After assistance from either the WOA or IWOA, the accuracy of the model shows a marked improvement. Furthermore, the accuracy of the BiLSTM model assisted by the IWOA outperforms that of the WOA, demonstrating the superiority of the IWOA. Figures 12, 15 and 18 provide metrics such as MAE, RMSE, and prediction variance for the BiLSTM models constructed using different methods on the prediction dataset. These results indicate that optimization algorithms significantly enhance the efficiency of network model construction. Additionally, the figures also reflect a slight advantage in accuracy for IWOA-BiLSTM.

6. Conclusions

The research indicates that the IWOA-BiLSTM model demonstrates excellent performance in the optimization of analog circuit parameters, showing significant improvements in accuracy and efficiency compared to traditional surrogate models. Not only does this hybrid method decrease the time required for design, but it also bolsters robustness by diminishing the likelihood of getting stuck in local optima and by augmenting the optimization process's ability to explore. The combination of deep learning frameworks and metaheuristic algorithms, as evidenced by this study, proves to be a highly effective solution for addressing the growing complexity of circuit design. These findings underscore the potential of this hybrid model as a powerful tool for achieving optimal design parameters, paving the way for further advancements in analog circuit optimization and beyond. Therefore, future work will focus on leveraging more advanced optimization algorithms to unlock the potential of deep learning frameworks, thereby playing a more significant role in the optimization of simulated circuits and other engineering domains.

Author Contributions: Conceptualization, S.Y., D.M., C.H., C.W., B.Y., P.N., H.Y., Y.S. and X.S.; Methodology, S.Y., D.M., C.H., C.W., B.Y., P.N. and H.Y.; Validation, S.Y., D.M., C.H., C.W. and P.N.;

Formal analysis, S.Y., D.M., C.H., C.W. and H.Y.; Resources, S.Y., D.M., C.H., C.W., B.Y., P.N. and Y.S.; Writing—original draft, S.Y., D.M., C.H., C.W. and X.S.; Writing—review and editing, S.Y., D.M., C.H., C.W., B.Y., P.N., H.Y. and Y.S.; Funding acquisition, D.M., C.H., C.W., B.Y., P.N. and Y.S.; All authors have read and agreed to the published version of the manuscript.

Funding: This study was funded by two projects from the China Scholarship Council, No. 202406070025 and 202406070043.

Data Availability Statement: All data that support the findings of this study are included within the article.

Conflicts of Interest: The authors declare no conflicts of interest.

References

1. Bogaerts, W.; Chrostowski, L. Silicon photonics circuit design: Methods, tools and challenges. *Laser Photonics Rev.* **2018**, *12*, 1700237. [CrossRef]
2. Luo, C.; Keshtegar, B.; Zhu, S.P.; Taylan, O.; Niu, X.-P. Hybrid enhanced Monte Carlo simulation coupled with advanced machine learning approach for accurate and efficient structural reliability analysis. *Comput. Methods Appl. Mech. Eng.* **2022**, *388*, 114218. [CrossRef]
3. Chen, L.; Deng, Y. An improved evidential Markov decision making model. *Appl. Intell.* **2022**, *52*, 8008–8017. [CrossRef]
4. Qiang, C.; Deng, Y. A new correlation coefficient of mass function in evidence theory and its application in fault diagnosis. *Appl. Intell.* **2022**, *52*, 7832–7842. [CrossRef]
5. He, J.C.; Zhu, S.P.; Liao, D.; Niu, X.P. Probabilistic fatigue assessment of notched components under size effect using generalized weakest-link model. *Int. J. Fatigue* **2022**, *162*, 107005.
6. Yu, S.; Li, Y. Active learning kriging model with adaptive uniform design for time-dependent reliability analysis. *IEEE Access* **2021**, *9*, 91625–91634. [CrossRef]
7. Huang, J.; Zhang, S.; Tao, C.; Yang, F.; Yan, C.; Zhou, D.; Zeng, X. Bayesian optimization approach for analog circuit design using multi-task Gaussian process. In Proceedings of the 2021 IEEE International Symposium on Circuits and Systems (ISCAS), Daegu, Republic of Korea, 22–28 May 2021; pp. 1–5.
8. Yang, M.; Zhang, D.; Jiang, C.; Han, X.; Li, Q. A hybrid adaptive Kriging-based single loop approach for complex reliability-based design optimization problems. *Reliab. Eng. Syst. Saf.* **2021**, *215*, 107736. [CrossRef]
9. Li, Y.; Garg, A.; Shevya, S.; Li, W.; Gao, L.; Lam, J.S.L. A hybrid convolutional neural network-long short term memory for discharge capacity estimation of lithium-ion batteries. *J. Electrochem. Energy Convers. Storage* **2022**, *19*, 030901. [CrossRef]
10. Song, X.; Xiao, F. Combining time-series evidence: A complex network model based on a visibility graph and belief entropy. *Appl. Intell.* **2022**, *52*, 10706–10715. [CrossRef]
11. Xiong, L.; Su, X.; Qian, H. Conflicting evidence combination from the perspective of networks. *Inf. Sci.* **2021**, *580*, 408–418. [CrossRef]
12. Cherid, D.; Bourahla, N.; Laghoub, M.S.; Mohabeddine, A. Sensor number and placement optimization for detection and localization of damage in a suspension bridge using a hybrid ANN-PCA reduced FRF method. *Int. J. Struct. Integr.* **2022**, *13*, 133–149. [CrossRef]
13. Meng, D.; Yang, S.; He, C.; Wang, H.; Lv, Z.; Guo, Y.; Nie, P. Multidisciplinary design optimization of engineering systems under uncertainty: A review. *Int. J. Struct. Integr.* **2022**, *13*, 565–593. [CrossRef]
14. Yang, S.; He, Z.; Chai, J.; Meng, D.; Macek, W.; Branco, R.; Zhu, S.-P. A novel hybrid adaptive framework for support vector machine-based reliability analysis: A comparative study. *Structures* **2023**, *58*, 105665. [CrossRef]
15. Wang, Y.-H.; Zhang, C.; Su, Y.-Q.; Shang, L.-Y.; Zhang, T. Structure optimization of the frame based on response surface method. *Int. J. Struct. Integr.* **2020**, *11*, 411–425. [CrossRef]
16. Sanabria-Borbón, A.C.; Soto-Aguilar, S.; Estrada-López, J.J.; Allaire, D.; Sánchez-Sinencio, E. Gaussian-process-based surrogate for optimization-aided and process-variations-aware analog circuit design. *Electronics* **2020**, *9*, 685. [CrossRef]
17. Zhang, S.; Lyu, W.; Yang, F.; Yan, C.; Zhou, D.; Zeng, X. Bayesian optimization approach for analog circuit synthesis using neural network. In Proceedings of the 2019 Design, Automation & Test in Europe Conference & Exhibition (DATE), Florence, Italy, 25–29 March 2019; pp. 1463–1468.
18. Budak, A.F.; Gandara, M.; Shi, W.; Pan, D.Z.; Sun, N.; Liu, B. An efficient analog circuit sizing method based on machine learning assisted global optimization. *IEEE Trans. Comput.-Aided Des. Integr. Circuits Syst.* **2021**, *41*, 1209–1221. [CrossRef]
19. Wang, L.; Tian, H.; Zhang, H. Soft fault diagnosis of analog circuits based on semi-supervised support vector machine. *Analog. Integr. Circuits Signal Process.* **2021**, *108*, 305–315. [CrossRef]
20. Binu, D.; Kariyappa, B.S. Rider-deep-LSTM network for hybrid distance score-based fault prediction in analog circuits. *IEEE Trans. Ind. Electron.* **2020**, *68*, 10097–10106. [CrossRef]

21. Liu, X.; Li, T.; Zhou, Z.; Hu, L. An efficient multi-objective reliability-based design optimization method for structure based on probability and interval hybrid model. *Comput. Methods Appl. Mech. Eng.* **2022**, *392*, 114682. [CrossRef]
22. Yang, M.; Zhang, D.; Wang, F.; Han, X. Efficient local adaptive Kriging approximation method with single-loop strategy for reliability-based design optimization. *Comput. Methods Appl. Mech. Eng.* **2022**, *390*, 114462. [CrossRef]
23. Ai, Q.; Yuan, Y.; Shen, S.-L.; Wang, H.; Huang, X. Investigation on inspection scheduling for the maintenance of tunnel with different degradation modes. *Tunn. Undergr. Space Technol.* **2020**, *106*, 103589. [CrossRef]
24. Meng, D.; Yang, S.; de Jesus, A.M.; Zhu, S.-P. A novel Kriging-model-assisted reliability-based multidisciplinary design optimization strategy and its application in the offshore wind turbine tower. *Renew. Energy* **2023**, *203*, 407–420. [CrossRef]
25. Liu, G.; Xiao, F.; Lin, C.-T.; Cao, Z. A fuzzy interval time-series energy and financial forecasting model using network-based multiple time-frequency spaces and the induced-ordered weighted averaging aggregation operation. *IEEE Trans. Fuzzy Syst.* **2020**, *28*, 2677–2690. [CrossRef]
26. Liu, X.; Liu, X.; Zhou, Z.; Hu, L. An efficient multi-objective optimization method based on the adaptive approximation model of the radial basis function. *Struct. Multidiscip. Optim.* **2021**, *63*, 1385–1403. [CrossRef]
27. Wang, Z.; Zhao, D.; Guan, Y. Flexible-constrained time-variant hybrid reliability-based design optimization. *Struct. Multidiscip. Optim.* **2023**, *66*, 89. [CrossRef]
28. Meng, D.; Yang, S.; De Jesus, A.M.; Fazeres-Ferradosa, T.; Zhu, S.-P. A novel hybrid adaptive Kriging and water cycle algorithm for reliability-based design and optimization strategy: Application in offshore wind turbine monopile. *Comput. Methods Appl. Mech. Eng.* **2023**, *412*, 116083. [CrossRef]
29. Yu, S.; Wang, Z. A general decoupling approach for time-and space-variant system reliability-based design optimization. *Comput. Methods Appl. Mech. Eng.* **2019**, *357*, 112608. [CrossRef]
30. Li, Y.; Li, C.; Garg, A.; Gao, L.; Li, W. Heat dissipation analysis and multi-objective optimization of a permanent magnet synchronous motor using surrogate assisted method. *Case Stud. Therm. Eng.* **2021**, *27*, 101203. [CrossRef]
31. Zhu, S.P.; Keshtegar, B.; Seghier, M.E.A.B.; Zio, E.; Taylan, O. Hybrid and enhanced PSO: Novel first order reliability method-based hybrid intelligent approaches. *Comput. Methods Appl. Mech. Eng.* **2022**, *393*, 114730. [CrossRef]
32. Zhu, S.P.; Keshtegar, B.; Tian, K.; Trung, N.T. Optimization of load-carrying hierarchical stiffened shells: Comparative survey and applications of six hybrid heuristic models. *Arch. Comput. Methods Eng.* **2021**, *28*, 4153–4166. [CrossRef]
33. Li, Y.H.; Zhang, C.; Yin, H.; Cao, Y.; Bai, X. Modification optimization-based fatigue life analysis and improvement of EMU gear. *Int. J. Struct. Integr.* **2021**, *12*, 760–772. [CrossRef]
34. Meng, Z.; Li, G.; Wang, X.; Sait, S.M.; Yıldız, A.R. A comparative study of metaheuristic algorithms for reliability-based design optimization problems. *Arch. Comput. Methods Eng.* **2021**, *28*, 1853–1869. [CrossRef]
35. Li, Y.H.; Sheng, Z.; Zhi, P.; Li, D. Multi-objective optimization design of anti-rolling torsion bar based on modified NSGA-III algorithm. *Int. J. Struct. Integr.* **2021**, *12*, 17–30. [CrossRef]
36. Ai, Q.; Huang, J.; Du, S.; Yang, K.; Wang, H. Comprehensive evaluation of very thin asphalt overlays with different aggregate gradations and asphalt materials based on AHP and TOPSIS. *Buildings* **2022**, *12*, 1149. [CrossRef]
37. Viana, C.O.; Carvalho, H.; Correia, J.; Montenegro, P.A.; Heleno, R.P.; Alencar, G.S.; de Jesus, A.M.; Calçada, R. Fatigue assessment based on hot-spot stresses obtained from the global dynamic analysis and local static sub-model. *Int. J. Struct. Integr.* **2019**, *12*, 31–47. [CrossRef]
38. Meng, Z.; Yıldız, A.R.; Mirjalili, S. Efficient decoupling-assisted evolutionary/metaheuristic framework for expensive reliability-based design optimization problems. *Expert Syst. Appl.* **2022**, *205*, 117640. [CrossRef]
39. He, B.; Zhang, S.; Yang, F.; Yan, C.; Zhou, D.; Zeng, X. An efficient bayesian optimization approach for analog circuit synthesis via sparse gaussian process modeling. In Proceedings of the 2020 Design, Automation & Test in Europe Conference & Exhibition (DATE), Grenoble, France, 9–13 March 2020; pp. 67–72.
40. Liu, Y.; Liu, B.; Ur-Rehman, M.; Imran, M.A.; Akinsolu, M.O.; Excell, P.; Hua, Q. An efficient method for antenna design based on a self-adaptive Bayesian neural network-assisted global optimization technique. *IEEE Trans. Antennas Propag.* **2022**, *70*, 11375–11388. [CrossRef]
41. Li, Y.; Wang, Y.; Li, Y.; Zhou, R.; Lin, Z. An artificial neural network assisted optimization system for analog design space exploration. *IEEE Trans. Comput.-Aided Des. Integr. Circuits Syst.* **2019**, *39*, 2640–2653. [CrossRef]
42. Majeed MA, M.; Sreehari Rao, P. Optimal design of CMOS amplifier circuits using whale optimization algorithm. In Proceedings of the Communication, Networks and Computing: First International Conference, Gwalior, India, 22–24 March 2018; pp. 590–605.
43. Mirjalili, S.; Lewis, A. The whale optimization algorithm. *Adv. Eng. Softw.* **2016**, *95*, 51–67. [CrossRef]
44. Wright, L.G.; Onodera, T.; Stein, M.M.; Wang, T.; Schachter, D.T.; Hu, Z.; McMahon, P.L. Deep physical neural networks trained with backpropagation. *Nature* **2022**, *601*, 549–555. [CrossRef]
45. Samek, W.; Montavon, G.; Lapuschkin, S.; Anders, C.J.; Muller, K.-R. Explaining deep neural networks and beyond: A review of methods and applications. *Proc. IEEE* **2021**, *109*, 247–278. [CrossRef]
46. Hashim, F.A.; Houssein, E.H.; Hussain, K.; Mabrouk, M.S.; Al-Atabany, W. Honey Badger Algorithm: New metaheuristic algorithm for solving optimization problems. *Math. Comput. Simul.* **2022**, *192*, 84–110. [CrossRef]

47. Gharehchopogh, F.S.; Namazi, M.; Ebrahimi, L.; Abdollahzadeh, B. Advances in sparrow search algorithm: A comprehensive survey. *Arch. Comput. Methods Eng.* **2023**, *30*, 427–455. [CrossRef]
48. Dehghani, M.; Trojovský, P. Osprey optimization algorithm: A new bio-inspired metaheuristic algorithm for solving engineering optimization problems. *Front. Mech. Eng.* **2023**, *8*, 1126450. [CrossRef]
49. Dampfhoffer, M.; Mesquida, T.; Valentian, A.; Anghel, L. Backpropagation-based learning techniques for deep spiking neural networks: A survey. *IEEE Trans. Neural Netw. Learn. Syst.* **2023**, 11906–11921. [CrossRef]
50. Kiani, A.T.; Nadeem, M.F.; Ahmed, A.; Khan, I.; Elavarasan, R.M.; Das, N. Optimal PV parameter estimation via double exponential function-based dynamic inertia weight particle swarm optimization. *Energies* **2020**, *13*, 4037. [CrossRef]
51. Schmidhuber, J.; Hochreiter, S. Long short-term memory. *Neural Comput.* **1997**, *9*, 1735–1780.
52. Ai, Q.; Tian, H.; Wang, H.; Lang, Q.; Huang, X.; Jiang, X.; Jing, Q. Comparative Analysis of ARIMA and LSTM Model-Based Anomaly Detection for Unannotated Structural Health Monitoring Data in an Immersed Tunnel. *CMES-Comput. Model. Eng. Sci.* **2024**, *139*, 1797–1827. [CrossRef]
53. Gharehchopogh, F.S.; Gholizadeh, H. A comprehensive survey: Whale Optimization Algorithm and its applications. *Swarm Evol. Comput.* **2019**, *48*, 1–24. [CrossRef]
54. Meng, D.; Yang, S.; Zhang, Y.; Zhu, S. Structural reliability analysis and uncertainties-based collaborative design and optimization of turbine blades using surrogate model. *Fatigue Fract. Eng. Mater. Struct.* **2019**, *42*, 1219–1227. [CrossRef]
55. Devi, S.; Guha, K.; Laskar, N.M.; Nath, S.; Baishnab, K.L.; Iannacci, J.; Krishnaswamy, N. Modelling and analysis of a modified preamplifier for seizure detection. *Microsyst. Technol.* **2021**, *27*, 3545–3558. [CrossRef]
56. Surjanovic, S.; Bingham, D. Virtual Library of Simulation Experiments: Test Functions and Datasets. 2013. Available online: http://www.sfu.ca/~ssurjano (accessed on 12 October 2014).
57. Graves, A.; Fernández, S.; Schmidhuber, J. Bidirectional LSTM networks for improved phoneme classification and recognition. In *International Conference on Artificial Neural Networks*; Springer: Berlin/Heidelberg, Germany, 2005; pp. 799–804.
58. Devi, N.; Amritha, G.; Tanniru, K. Effects of nonlinear amplification on differential sensitivity measures in individuals with cochlear hearing impairment. *Indian J. Otol.* **2017**, *23*, 162–167. [CrossRef]

mathematics

MDPI

Article

A New Loss Function for Simultaneous Object Localization and Classification

Ander Sanchez-Chica [1], Beñat Ugartemendia-Telleria [1], Ekaitz Zulueta [1,*], Unai Fernandez-Gamiz [2] and Javier Maria Gomez-Hidalgo [3]

1 System Engineering and Automation Control Department, University of the Basque Country (UPV/EHU), Nieves Cano 12, 01006 Vitoria-Gasteiz, Spain
2 Department of Nuclear and Fluid Mechanics, University of the Basque Country (UPV/EHU), Nieves Cano 12, 01006 Vitoria-Gasteiz, Spain
3 MERCEDES BENZ España, Las arenas 1, 10152 Vitoria-Gasteiz, Spain
* Correspondence: ekaitz.zulueta@ehu.eus

Abstract: Robots play a pivotal role in the manufacturing industry. This has led to the development of computer vision. Since AlexNet won ILSVRC, convolutional neural networks (CNNs) have achieved state-of-the-art status in this area. In this work, a novel method is proposed to simultaneously detect and predict the localization of objects using a custom loop method and a CNN, performing two of the most important tasks in computer vision with a single method. Two different loss functions are proposed to evaluate the method and compare the results. The obtained results show that the network is able to perform both tasks accurately, classifying images correctly and locating objects precisely. Regarding the loss functions, when the target classification values are computed, the network performs better in the localization task. Following this work, improvements are expected to be made in the localization task of networks by refining the training processes of the networks and loss functions.

Keywords: image classification; object detection; deep learning; deep convolutional neural networks; computer vision; custom training loop

MSC: 49J05; 49J15

1. Introduction

Nowadays, robots are essential for the manufacturing industry. The use of robots has helped the manufacturing industry to manufacture products more efficiently, saving both costs and time. Despite the fact that an increasing need for robots has been observed in all industrial sectors in recent years, the electronics industry has been the main customer of industrial robots since 2020, when it overtook the automotive industry. However, the latter still demands 80,000 robots a year; hence, it is still an important sector for robot manufacturers. Industrial robot manufacturers are making every effort to design and develop safe and human-friendly robots. This is spurred on by the fact that small- and medium-sized companies are increasing their use of industrial robots due to the availability of affordable solutions and easy-to-use collaborative robots. Hence, collaborative solutions, where humans and robots work together, are becoming the new frontier in industrial robotics [1,2]. The use of collaborative robots is also supported by the current trend of automation and data exchange in manufacturing industries, also called Industry 4.0 [3].

In the case of the automotive industry, robots are used mainly in the manufacturing process. At the beginning of the 20th century, when chain production was introduced by the Ford Model T, cars were handmade. Nowadays, this process is mainly automatic. However, there are still tasks where humans need to intervene. In this context, collaborative robots can help workers improve the efficiency and reduce the manufacturing faults of production lines [4]. Robots also help in other areas, such as neurosurgery [5]. Since collaborative robots need to be aware of their surroundings, computer vision can help robots to detect their environment and object positions.

Image classification, object detection and semantic segmentation are the main tasks in computer vision. Since LeCun et al. [6] proposed LeNet-5 in 1998 for document recognition, convolutional neural networks (CNNs) have become the state-of-the-art techniques for these tasks. The explosion of deep learning has led to the need for high-quality, diverse and structured image datasets. In 2010, ImageNet [7] was presented as a solution to this problem. Following the path that started LeNet-5, in 2012, AlexNet [8] won the ImageNet Large-Scale Visual Recognition Challenge (ILSVRC) [9] by outperforming previous image-classifying state-of-the-art techniques. This success led researchers to improve the performance of CNNs. Following this trend of making deeper and larger networks, Zeiler et al. [10] proposed ZFNet to understand and improve the results obtained by Krizhevsky et al. [8]. In 2014, Simonyan et al. [11] proposed a CNN with very small convolution filters to evaluate the effect of the convolutional network depth on its accuracy in the large-scale image recognition setting.

To tackle the difficulty of training very deep neural networks, He et al. [12] presented a residual learning framework called Residual Network (ResNet), which allows for an increase in the depth, while maintaining the complexity of the network. ResNet cross-layer connections try to solve the gradient diffusion problem that very deep convolutional networks, such as VGGNet and ZFNet, have. However, training very deep residual networks is extremely costly. Thus, Zagoruyko et al. [13] conducted an experimental study on the architecture of ResNet blocks. Based on this study, they proposed a novel architecture, where they decreased the depth and increased the width of residual networks. The resulting network structures, called wide residual networks (WRNs), overperformed their thin and very deep counterparts.

GoogLeNet [14], also called Inception-v1, combines inception modules with conventional convolution modules to improve the utilization of the computing resources inside the network, hence increasing the depth and width of the network, while keeping the computational budget constant by varying the sizes of the convolution filters. Inception-v4 [15] aggregates residual connections to the inception architecture to accelerate training, while maintaining the accuracy of similarly expensive inception networks. Huang G. et al. [16] proposed the Dense Convolutional Network (DenseNet), which connects each layer to every other layer downstream, reusing the features of all previous layers to strengthen feature propagation and reduce the vanishing gradient problem. Following the trend of dense connectivity, with CondenseNetV2, Yang et al. [17] ensured that each layer simultaneously learned to carry out the following:

1. Selectively reuse the set of the most important features from preceding layers;
2. Actively update the set of preceding features to increase their utility for later layers, achieving promising performance in image classification (ImageNet) and object detection (MS COCO) in terms of both theoretical efficiency and practical speed.

In recent years, large advancements have been made in image classification tasks [18]. Therefore, CNNs have great value when there is a need to identify images. However, normally, this feature is not useful when it is used alone. It can be combined with a region proposal network (RPN) and perform traditional object detection.

The traditional object detection method consists of generating region proposals first using an RPN and then classifying each proposal into different object categories [19]. This is the case of R-CNN [20]. Nevertheless, this process is normally very computationally costly. In order to tackle this issue, different iterations of R-CNN have been proposed. Girshick et al. [21] improved their original R-CNN to be faster and more accurate. Ren et al. [22] improved this by introducing an RPN that shares full-image convolutional features with the detection network, thus enabling nearly cost-free region proposals. The Faster R-CNN architecture has achieved good results in object detection tasks. For example,

Fu et al. [23] and Song et al. [24] used the Faster R-CNN based on ZFNet and VGG16, respectively, to detect kiwifruits in order to enable robots to pick them up.

The other object detection method with regard to the task of regression or the classification problem adopts a unified framework to achieve the final results (categories and locations) directly. Redmon et al. [25] predicted bounding boxes and their associated class probabilities directly from full images in one evaluation. They called this new approach to object detection You Only Look Once (YOLO). The Single-Shot Multibox Detector (SSD) [26] discretizes the output space of bounding boxes into a set of default boxes, adjusting them by the scores generated for the presence of each object category in each default box in order to better match the object shape. CenterNet, proposed by Duan et al. [27], presents an efficient solution based on the detection of each object as a triplet of key points rather than a pair, improving both precision and recall.

However, each of these methods has its own issues: the traditional object detection techniques require a high computational power, whereas the single-stage methods do not have the same level of accuracy as the traditional techniques. In 2017, Li et al. [28] proposed a two-stage object detector based on ResNet-101 [12] to address the shortcomings of these types of detectors, that is, the slow speed of these networks due to their heavy-head designs. In 2018, Zhang et al. [29] proposed a novel single-shot-based detector that achieves a better accuracy than the two-stage methods and maintains an efficiency comparable to that of the one-stage methods. Examples of the advancements that have been made in object detection tasks in recent years are in reference [30].

In 2019, EfficientDet [31] proposed a new family of object detectors based on EfficientNet backbones and optimized the weighted bi-directional feature pyramid network (BiFPN) and the compound scaling method. In particular, the model EfficientDet-D7 achieved state-of-the-art results at MS COCO. Another example of this appeared in 2022, when Liu et al. [32] presented a network called ConvNeXts, constructed entirely from standard ConvNet modules. These modules are ResNet modules modernized towards the design of a vision transformer, and they compete favorably with transformers in terms of accuracy and scalability.

Additionally, the networks observed in the literature focus on single-task problems: image classification, object detection, image recognition, etc. To the best of our knowledge, there are no or very few examples of CNNs that have been used to simultaneously perform different tasks. Therefore, we see the need for exploring image classification and object localization tasks using the same CNN. The objective of this article is to determine whether both tasks can be performed accurately with a single CNN. Therefore, we propose a custom evaluation loop that merges the cross-entropy loss (Ex) for the classification task and the half mean square error (mse) for the regression task (object localization). We also compare two different loss functions using different Ex and mse loss proportions and determine which method is the best.

2. Materials and Methods

2.1. Convolutional Neural Network

A CNN is a type of deep neural network that uses convolutional layers to extract feature maps from the input image. Usually, the network consists of one input layer, one or more convolutional layers, one fully connected layer and one output layer [33]. In this case, the network has two fully connected layers at the end of the convolutional layers, separating each one from the main branch. This allows the network to perform two different tasks using the same convolutional layers. At the end of one fully connected layer, a softmax layer is connected. This branch performs the classification task, while the other performs the detection task. In Figure 1, the structure of the network can be seen.

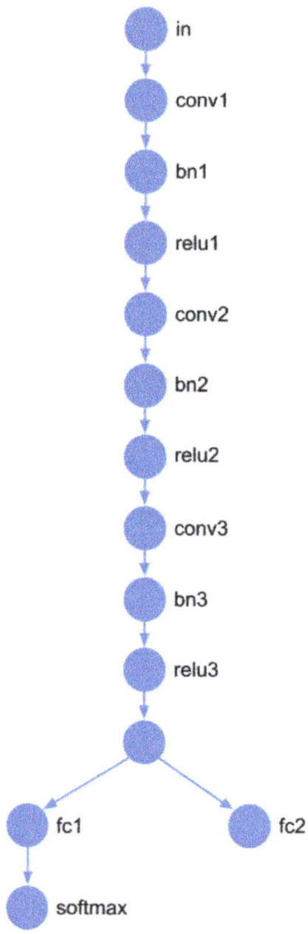

Figure 1. Structure of the proposed CNN.

The input layer in has a dimension of 100 × 100 × 1. Therefore, the input data consist of a single matrix with dimensions of 100 × 100, which contain the value of each pixel in gray-scale from 0 (black) to 255 (white).

The convolutional layer is the specific layer of the CNN. The convolutional equation used is that shown in Equation (1):

$$y_j = \sum(w_{ij} \cdot x_j) + b_j \tag{1}$$

where y_j is the result, w_{ij} is the filter matrix, x_j is the input of the convolutional layer, and b_j is the bias term. In this case, the network features three convolutional layers. The first one has 16 filters with a 5 × 5 size. The second one has 32 filters with a 3 × 3 size. Finally, the third one also has 32 filters with a 3 × 3 size, although it has a stride of one, instead of two like the second layer. Furthermore, the output of this network uses a nonlinear activation function (ReLU), as shown in Equation (2):

$$f(x) = \begin{cases} x, & x \geq 0 \\ 0, & x < 0 \end{cases} \tag{2}$$

In order to speed up the training and reduce the sensitivity to network initialization, a batch normalization layer is included between each convolutional layer and the ReLU layer. This is achieved by normalizing a mini-batch of data across all observations for each channel independently. The parameters of the model are listed in detail in Table 1.

Table 1. Parameters and output shapes of the proposed CNN model.

Layer Name	Previous Layer	Function	Weight Filter Size /Kernels	Padding	Stride	Output Tensor Size	Learnable Parameters
in	-	-		-	-	$100 \times 100 \times 1$	-
conv1	in	conv2d	$5 \times 5 \times 1/16$	same	1	$100 \times 100 \times 16$	416
bn1	conv1	-		-	-	$100 \times 100 \times 16$	32
relu1	bn1	ReLU		-	-	$100 \times 100 \times 16$	-
conv2	relu1	conv2d	$3 \times 3 \times 16/32$	same	2	$50 \times 50 \times 32$	4608
bn2	conv2	-		-	-	$50 \times 50 \times 32$	64
relu2	bn2	ReLU		-	-	$50 \times 50 \times 32$	-
conv3	relu2	conv2d	$3 \times 3 \times 32/32$	same	1	$50 \times 50 \times 32$	9216
bn3	conv3	-		-	-	$50 \times 50 \times 32$	64
relu3	bn3	ReLU		-	-	$50 \times 50 \times 32$	-
fc1	relu3	-		-	-	$1 \times 1 \times 2$	160 k
softmax	fc1	softmax		-	-	$1 \times 1 \times 2$	-
fc2	relu3	-		-	-	$1 \times 1 \times 2$	160 k

The proposed neural network contains 334.4 k parameters and has a model size of 1.22 MB after training. This network was used because it showed good results in similar tasks. It was considered valuable to use other types of convolutional neural networks, such as VGG-16 and ZFNet, but these networks had too many parameters for this application, and, thus, training would take too long to evaluate the performance of the proposed custom training loop with a custom loss function.

We analyzed the basic structure of the proposed convolutional neural network; in the next subsection, the learning process of the network is discussed.

2.2. Learning Process

The learning process of a deep learning network consists of three steps: data acquisition, data preparation and model training. In the current work, the first step consists of capturing images of the surroundings of the pin. The images are taken using a camera that captures images of 612×512 pixels. The images are in gray-scale and are saved as a tiff file.

The second step consists of preparing the data to train the network. The first task is to label the images. After manually identifying the pin in each image, the data are used to generate images starting from the seed images. The identification is made by drawing a rectangle surrounding the pin. The center pixel of the marked rectangle is taken as the location of the pin, which is then used in the training process as the target value. Then, from each seed image, 5 images are obtained. In these images, the position of the pin is the same, but the contrast and the brightness of the images are randomly modified using Equations (3)–(5):

$$\text{Contrast factor}: \; Cf = 1 - 0.2 \cdot rand, \tag{3}$$

$$\text{Brightness factor}: Bf = 0.3 \cdot (rand - 0.5), \tag{4}$$

$$I_{ij} = Cf \cdot Is_{ij} + Bf \tag{5}$$

where $rand$ is a random value between 0 and 1, I_{sij} is the seed pixel value, and I_{ij} is the resulting pixel value. This is applied to all seed images to obtain 1620 images.

These images, however, still have a size of 612×512. In order to train the network, the images need to be transformed so that their size is 100×100. Therefore, each image receives a random transformation, where a 100×100 size region is chosen from each image. This is carried out by randomly selecting whether the image has a pin, the chance of which is 50/50. At the end of the transformation, there are 810 images with a pin and 810 without a pin.

The final step of the training consists of the model training itself. In this case, a custom training loop is used. MATLAB is the software chosen to develop the different algorithms that are involved in this work. This software has different tools to develop and train deep neural networks. One of these functionalities is to train custom training loops, updating the learnable parameters of the network using different solvers. In this case, the Adam (adaptative moment estimation) solver is used [34].

In this process, each mini-batch of data is evaluated using the modeloGradients function. The modeloGradients function takes the following as inputs: the network and a mini-batch of input data, with the corresponding targets T1 and T2 containing the labels and positions, respectively. Then, it returns the gradients of the loss with respect to the learnable parameters, the updated network state and the corresponding loss.

The loss for each mini-batch θ is calculated by adding the cross-entropy loss of the classification task and the half mean squared error, with the latter multiplied by factor $\lambda = 0.1$, following Equation (6):

$$loss_{\theta} = loss_{Ex,\theta} + \lambda \cdot loss_{mse,\theta} \tag{6}$$

The cross-entropy loss (Ex) for each mini-batch θ is calculated using Equation (7):

$$loss_{Ex,\theta} = -\frac{1}{N}\sum_{n=1}^{N}\sum_{i=1}^{K} t_{ni} \ln y_{ni} \tag{7}$$

where N is the number of samples, K is the number of classes, t_{ni} is the indicator showing that the nth sample belongs to the ith class, and y_{ni} is the output for sample n for class i. That is, y_{ni} is the probability that the network associates the nth input with class i.

The half mean squared error (mse) operation computes the half mean squared error loss between the network predictions and target values for regression tasks. The loss for each mini-batch θ is calculated using the following Equation (8):

$$loss_{mse,\theta} = \frac{1}{2N}\sum_{i=1}^{M}(X_i - T_i)^2 \tag{8}$$

where X_i is the network prediction, T_i is the target value, M is the total number of responses in X (across all observations), and N is the total number of observations in X.

Afterwards, the calculated gradients are used to update the learnable parameters of the network. This process continues until the training ends, which is when the training reaches 200 epochs. Each mini-batch consists of 60 elements. Therefore, 5400 iterations are performed. The parameters of the Adam solver are listed in Table 2.

Table 2. Parameter values of the Adam solver.

Parameter	Value
Learn rate	0.001
Gradient decay factor	0.9
Squared gradient decay factor	0.999
Epsilon *	10^{-8}

* Small constant for preventing divide-by-zero errors.

During the training, a validation evaluation is performed. This is carried out to ensure that the training is performing well and that the results are converging. To perform this task, a new dataset is created following the same steps as those used for the training data. In this case, 3 images are obtained from each seed image in order to speed up the validation process. This dataset is evaluated as the training dataset in groups of 60 data samples. At the end of each training epoch, all the validation data are evaluated, and the average loss value is returned by the algorithm.

The first loss function is based on a constant ratio between the two different losses. Regarding the second loss function, we only want to perform the localization task when the network detects an object in order to evaluate whether this approach improves the effectiveness of the network. This new loss function is also based on the cross-entropy loss of the classification task and the half mean square error of the regression task. However, the combination of both is not a simple constant ratio, as with the first loss function. At first, we thought that the loss function only needed to take into account the cross-entropy loss when the classification was not performed correctly, because trying to locate a pin in an image that does not have one would not be correct. Therefore, the loss function that was proposed included the target values of the classification task, as well as the network prediction. However, the use of the predictions to calculate the loss led the network to classify all images in one group due to the learnable parameters being related to the predictions. Because of this, it was decided that the network predictions should not be used. Consequently, only the target values of the classification task are used. In the images where there is no pin, only the cross-entropy loss is used to calculate the overall loss. In the other case, the half mean squared error is also computed. This is carried out with the objective of only taking into account the localization task when there is a pin to locate. All this is performed in each image μ of the mini-batch θ using Equation (9):

$$loss_{\theta} = loss_{Ex,\theta} + \frac{1}{N}\sum t^{\mu}_{pc1} \cdot loss_{mse,\mu} \quad (9)$$

where t^{μ}_{pc1} is the target probability that image μ contains a pin, $loss_{Ex,\theta}$ is the cross-entropy loss of the mini-batch θ (Equation (7)), $loss_{mse,\mu}$ is the half mean square error loss of the image μ (Equation (8)), and N is the number of images in the mini-batch θ.

As with the first proposed loss in this article, this loss is used to calculate the gradients of the loss with respect to the learnable parameters in order to update the latter to improve the predictions of the network. The same base network is used to compare the obtained results.

After finalizing the training, the same validation data are used to evaluate the training. At this point, 10 randomly selected images are chosen to evaluate the network performance. The same images are used to evaluate the training of the second loss function. Therefore, both results are directly comparable and allow one to conclude whether the proposed method is effective and which loss function has the best performance.

3. Results

In this section, the results of the investigation are presented. First, the network is trained using the presented loss function. The loss during the training and the average validation loss are presented in Figure 2. The quick drop that appears in the first iterations suggests that the classification of the images is optimized early in the training. The values obtained at the end of the training are collected in Table 3.

Table 3. Training properties values.

Property	Value
Epoch	200
Iteration	5400
Training time	54 min 37 sec
Loss	2.11
Classification loss	0
Regression loss	21.087
Validation loss	1.87
Validation classification loss	2×10^{-4}
Validation regression loss	18.699

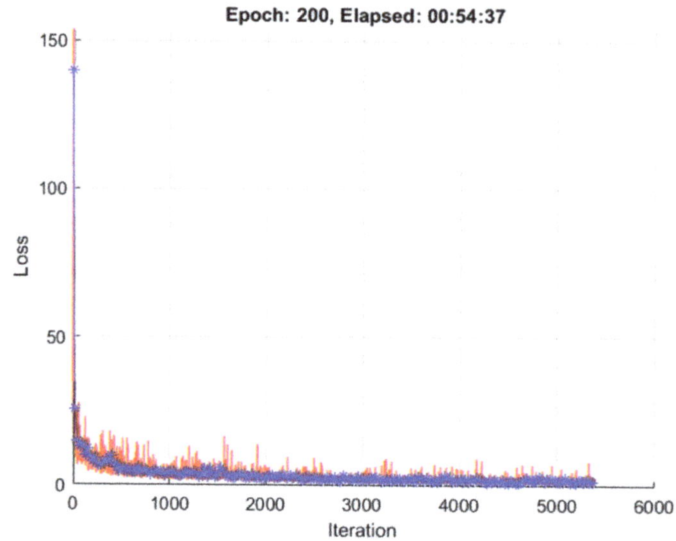

Figure 2. The loss during the training process (red) and the average validation error obtained for each epoch of the training data (blue) of the first proposed loss function. In this figure, the downward trend of the loss value can be seen. The loss value continues to drop at a low but constant rate after the quick drop of the early iterations.

Looking at the results in Table 4, it can be seen that the network achieves very good results in the classification task, labeling most of the images correctly. After analyzing all the images in the validation dataset, 10 images were randomly selected to expose the training results. Regarding the pin localization, the results can be improved. Most of the time, the network is able to locate the pin with decent precision. However, the localization task fails when there is no pin in the image, for example, as shown in images 816, 165 and 836 in Figure 3. It can also be noted that image 357 is not classified correctly, although the localization task is performed accurately.

Table 4. The values of the analyzed validation images.

Image Index	T1		Y1		T2		Y2		Loss	Classification	Regression
	No Pin	Pin	No Pin	Pin	x	y	x	y			
774	0	1	0	1	47	25	44.19	26.49	0.505	0	5.053
34	1	0	1	0	0	0	−0.40	−2.47	0.314	0	3.142
816	1	0	1	0	0	0	29.24	33.41	98.58	0	985.8
869	0	1	0	1	43	55	37.63	47.26	4.438	0	44.384
11	0	1	0	1	60	66	55.52	64.16	1.173	0	11.728
165	1	0	1	0	0	0	10.94	15.25	17.624	0	176.24
836	1	0	1	0	0	0	10.53	7.06	8.036	0	80.364
357	0	1	1	0	31	25	21.04	16.74	44.416	36.044	83.724
697	0	1	0	1	28	31	33.59	40.84	6.401	0	64.014
827	0	1	0	1	28	29	21.69	22.37	4.193	1.59×10^{-4}	41.93

T1 and T2 are the target values of each image. Y1 and Y2 are the predictions made by the network. Loss is the total loss; Classification is the cross-entropy error; Regression is the half mean square error. All the values smaller than 10^{-4} are considered null.

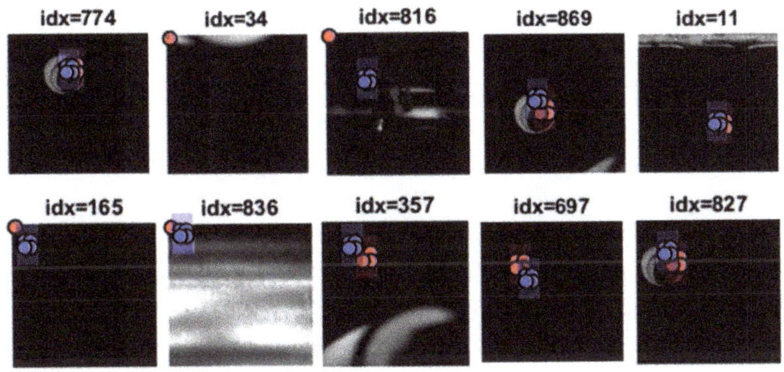

Figure 3. Images used to analyze the performance of the network. The red marking shows the real position of the pin (manually labeled), whereas the blue marking shows the prediction of the network.

The same observation can be made with the second proposed loss. In Figure 4, the loss during the training and the average validation loss are presented.

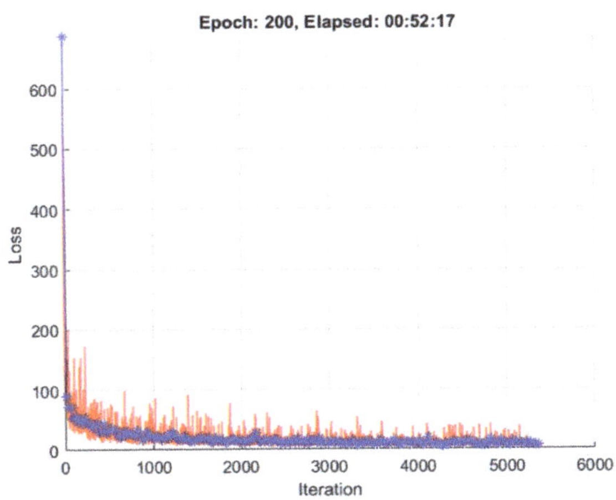

Figure 4. The loss during the training process (red) and the average validation error obtained for each epoch of the training data (blue) of the second proposed loss function. In this figure, the downward trend of the loss value can be seen. Comparing the values with those in Figure 2, the loss value is higher at the beginning, although at the end of the training process, the values converge, as can be seen in Table 5.

Table 5. Training properties values.

Property	Value
Epoch	200
Iteration	5400
Training time	52 min 17 sec
Loss	4.497
Classification loss	0
Regression loss	8.431
Validation loss	6.461
Validation classification loss	0
Validation regression loss	12.922

After analyzing all the images in the validation dataset, 10 images were randomly selected to present the training results. Looking at the results in Table 6, as well as those of the first network, this network performs well on the classification task, thus improving its performance in the location task. In images 816 and 836 in Figure 5, it can be seen that the network predicts the positions of the pins, although they are not in the images. However, in the other images, the network predicts the positions of the pins more accurately than the previous network. This can be the result of giving the regression task more influence when there is a pin. This can also provide an explanation for the overall *loss* values being higher than those in the first network.

Table 6. The values of the analyzed validation images.

Image Index	T1		Y1		T2		Y2		Loss	Classification	Regression
	No Pin	Pin	No Pin	Pin	x	y	x	y			
774	0	1	0	1	47	25	41.62	23.61	15.414	0	15.414
34	1	0	1	0	0	0	3.35	1.84	0	0	7.295
816	1	0	1	0	0	0	17.07	21.18	0	0	370.07
869	0	1	0	1	43	55	40.28	45.80	46.019	0	46.019
11	0	1	0	1	60	66	59.09	65.53	0.521	0	0.521
165	1	0	1	0	0	0	−2.39	3.31	0	0	8.315
836	1	0	1	0	0	0	10.77	4.42	0	0	67.727
357	0	1	0.991	0.009	31	25	17.13	13.61	196.74	35.736	161
697	0	1	0	1	28	31	25.48	28.55	6.170	0	6.170
827	0	1	0	1	28	29	25.91	29.84	2.533	0	2.533

T1 and T2 are the target values of each image. Y1 and Y2 are the predictions made by the network. Loss is the total loss; Classification is the cross-entropy error; Regression is the half mean square error. All the values smaller than 10^{-4} are considered null.

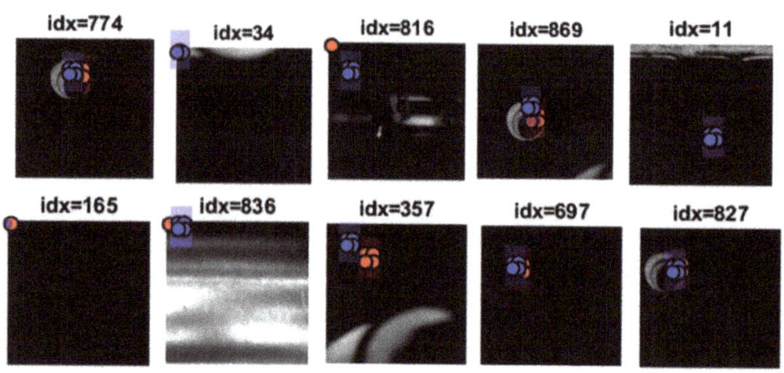

Figure 5. Images used to analyze the performance of the network. The red marking shows the real position of the pin (manually labeled), whereas the blue marking shows the prediction of the network.

4. Discussion

The improvements of convolutional neural networks in image classification [18] and object detection [19,30] have positioned CNNs as the best solution to perform these tasks. Most of the reviewed literature suggests that a single task is performed by each network. Although single-stage object detectors, such as YOLO [25] and SSD [26], perform both the region proposal task and the detection task as a single task, they do not classify the input image. In this work, the objective was to first classify the input image into two groups, namely, images that contain a pin and images that do not contain a pin, and to then position the pin inside the image, all while using the same simple network.

In this work, we proposed two different approaches to perform a custom training loop. The two approaches differ from each other in the loss function that is used in each case. After analyzing the results, we could see that the classification task was performed accurately in both trained networks. Regarding the localization of the pin, the second network achieved better results. The differences in the approaches of the two methods led us to think that the second network performed better in the localization task because it gives more weight to the half mean squared error when it needs to perform the localization task. However, both networks underperformed in the localization task when there was no pin in the image. Therefore, in following iterations of this network, we will attempt to improve the localization task of the network by refining the training processes of the network and the loss function.

5. Conclusions

The objective of this research is to determine whether image classification and object localization tasks can be performed using a single CNN. In this work, two new loss functions are added to a custom training loop. Both loss functions combine the cross-entropy loss (Ex) for the classification task and the half mean square error (mse) for the regression task (object localization). The main differences in both networks are as follows:

1. The first network always computes the loss by adding the classification task loss and the localization task loss (Equation (6)), whereas the second only takes into account the localization task loss when there is a pin in the image (Equation (8)).
2. In the first network, the localization task loss is multiplied by factor λ (Equation (6)), reducing the importance that this loss has in the overall loss of the network.

The first loss function is very simple, allowing for the results to be more easily analyzed and for the network to be finetuned more accurately. However, the second loss function introduces differentiation between the two types of losses that computes the total loss depending on the image localization task. By doing this, only the half mean square error is computed when an object is detected in the image. This is the key aspect of this second loss, because the first loss does not make any differentiation in the computing of the total loss, which, in our humble opinion, is the biggest contribution of this work. Based on the results, this approach shows better performance than the first loss function, paving the way forward for future research.

These results show that computer vision can benefit the manufacturing industry. The tasks that require some type of visual recognition, detection or classification can now be performed efficiently using neural networks. This can lead to more automated manufacturing processes. Therefore, workers can focus less on automatic tasks and more on their efforts in other tasks, such as problem solving and organizational tasks.

Author Contributions: Conceptualization, E.Z., A.S.-C. and J.M.G.-H.; methodology, B.U.-T. and E.Z.; software, E.Z., A.S.-C. and B.U.-T.; validation, B.U.-T., E.Z. and U.F.-G.; formal analysis, B.U.-T., E.Z.; investigation, B.U.-T. and E.Z.; resources, B.U.-T. and E.Z.; writing—original draft preparation, B.U.-T.; writing—review and editing, B.U-T. All authors have read and agreed to the published version of the manuscript.

Funding: The current study was sponsored by the Government of the Basque Country-ELKARTEK21/10 KK-2021/00014 ("Estudio de nuevas técnicas de inteligencia artificial basadas en Deep Learning dirigidas a la optimización de procesos industriales") research program.

Institutional Review Board Statement: Not applicable.

Informed Consent Statement: Not applicable.

Acknowledgments: The authors want to thank the technical support provided by Javier Loredo.

Conflicts of Interest: The authors declare no conflict of interest.

References

1. International Federation of Robotics. Available online: https://ifr.org/img/worldrobotics/Executive_Summary_WR_Industrial_Robots_2021.pdf (accessed on 10 December 2022).
2. Probst, L.; Frideres, L.; Pedersen, B.; Caputi, C.; Luxembourg, P. *Service Innovation for Smart Industry Human-Robot Collaboration Business Innovation Observatory Contract No 190/PP/ENT/CIP/12/C/N03C01*; European Commission: Brussels, Belgium, 2015.
3. Forschungsunion. *Recommendations for Implementing the Strategic Initiative INDUSTRIE 4.0 April 2013 Securing the Future of German Manufacturing Industry Final Report of the Industrie 4.0 Working Group*; Forschungsunion: Berlin, Germany, 2012.
4. Villani, V.; Pini, F.; Leali, F.; Secchi, C. Survey on Human–Robot Collaboration in Industrial Settings: Safety, Intuitive Interfaces and Applications. *Mechatronics* **2018**, *55*, 248–266. [CrossRef]
5. Inziarte-Hidalgo, I.; Uriarte, I.; Fernandez-Gamiz, U.; Sorrosal, G.; Zulueta, E. Robotic-Arm-Based Force Control in Neurosurgical Practice. *Mathematics* **2023**, *11*, 828. [CrossRef]
6. LeCun, Y.; Bottou, L.; Bengio, Y.; Haffner, P. Gradient-Based Learning Applied to Document Recognition. *Proc. IEEE* **1998**, *86*, 2278–2323. [CrossRef]
7. Deng, J.; Dong, W.; Socher, R.; Li, L.-J.; Kai, L.; Li, F.-F. *ImageNet: A Large-Scale Hierarchical Image Database*; Institute of Electrical and Electronics Engineers (IEEE): New York, NY, USA, 2010; pp. 248–255.
8. Krizhevsky, A.; Sutskever, I.; Hinton, G.E. ImageNet Classification with Deep Convolutional Neural Networks. *Commun. ACM* **2017**, *60*, 84–90. [CrossRef]
9. Russakovsky, O.; Deng, J.; Su, H.; Krause, J.; Satheesh, S.; Ma, S.; Huang, Z.; Karpathy, A.; Khosla, A.; Bernstein, M.; et al. ImageNet Large Scale Visual Recognition Challenge. *Int. J. Comput. Vis.* **2015**, *115*, 211–252. [CrossRef]
10. Zeiler, M.D.; Fergus, R. Visualizing and Understanding Convolutional Networks. In Proceedings of the Computer Vision–ECCV 2014 13th European Conference, Zurich, Switzerland, 6–12 September 2014; Springer International Publishing: New York, NY, USA, 2014; pp. 818–833.
11. Simonyan, K.; Zisserman, A. Very Deep Convolutional Networks for Large-Scale Image Recognition. *arXiv* **2014**, arXiv:1409.1556.
12. He, K.; Zhang, X.; Ren, S.; Sun, J. Deep Residual Learning for Image Recognition. In Proceedings of the IEEE Conference on Computer Vision and Pattern Recognition, Las Vegas, NV, USA, 27–30 June 2016.
13. Zagoruyko, S.; Komodakis, N. Wide Residual Networks. *arXiv* **2016**, arXiv:1605.07146.
14. Szegedy, C.; Liu, W.; Jia, Y.; Sermanet, P.; Reed, S.; Anguelov, D.; Erhan, D.; Vanhoucke, V.; Rabinovich, A. Going Deeper with Convolutions. In Proceedings of the IEEE Computer Society Conference on Computer Vision and Pattern Recognition, Boston, MA, USA, 7–12 June 2015; IEEE Computer Society: Washington, DC, USA, 2015; pp. 1–9.
15. Szegedy, C.; Ioffe, S.; Vanhoucke, V.; Alemi, A. Inception-v4, Inception-ResNet and the Impact of Residual Connections on Learning. In Proceedings of the AAAI Conference on Artificial Intelligence, Phoenix, AZ, USA, 12–17 February 2016.
16. Huang, G.; Liu, Z.; van der Maaten, L.; Weinberger, K.Q. Densely Connected Convolutional Networks. In Proceedings of the IEEE Conference on Computer Vision and Pattern Recognition, Las Vegas, NV, USA, 27–30 June 2016.
17. Yang, L.; Jiang, H.; Cai, R.; Wang, Y.; Song, S.; Huang, G.; Tian, Q. CondenseNet V2: Sparse Feature Reactivation for Deep Networks. In Proceedings of the IEEE/CVF Conference on Computer Vision and Pattern Recognition, Nashville, TN, USA, 20–25 June 2021.
18. Sultana, F.; Sufian, A.; Dutta, P. Advancements in Image Classification Using Convolutional Neural Network. In Proceedings of the 2018 Fourth International Conference on Research in Computational Intelligence and Communication Networks (ICRCICN), Kolkata, India, 22–23 November 2018. [CrossRef]
19. Zhao, Z.Q.; Zheng, P.; Xu, S.T.; Wu, X. Object Detection with Deep Learning: A Review. *IEEE Trans. Neural Netw. Learn. Syst.* **2019**, *30*, 3212–3232. [CrossRef] [PubMed]
20. Girshick, R.; Donahue, J.; Darrell, T.; Malik, J. Rich Feature Hierarchies for Accurate Object Detection and Semantic Segmentation. In Proceedings of the IEEE Computer Society Conference on Computer Vision and Pattern Recognition, Columbus, OH, USA, 23–28 June 2014; IEEE Computer Society: Washington, DC, USA, 2014; pp. 580–587.
21. Girshick, R. Fast R-CNN. In Proceedings of the 2015 IEEE International Conference on Computer Vision (ICCV), Santiago, Chile, 7–13 December 2015; IEEE: Washington, DC, USA, 2015; pp. 1440–1448.
22. Ren, S.; He, K.; Girshick, R.; Sun, J. Faster R-CNN: Towards Real-Time Object Detection with Region Proposal Networks. *IEEE Trans. Pattern Anal. Mach. Intell.* **2017**, *39*, 1137–1149. [CrossRef] [PubMed]
23. Fu, L.; Feng, Y.; Majeed, Y.; Zhang, X.; Zhang, J.; Karkee, M.; Zhang, Q. *Kiwifruit Detection in Field Images Using Faster R-CNN with ZFNet*; Elsevier B.V.: Amsterdam, The Netherlands, 2018; Volume 51, pp. 45–50.
24. Song, Z.; Fu, L.; Wu, J.; Liu, Z.; Li, R.; Cui, Y. Kiwifruit Detection in Field Images Using Faster R-CNN with VGG16. *IFAC Pap.* **2019**, *52*, 76–81. [CrossRef]
25. Redmon, J.; Divvala, S.; Girshick, R.; Farhadi, A. You Only Look Once: Unified, Real-Time Object Detection. In Proceedings of the IEEE Conference on Computer Vision and Pattern Recognition, Las Vegas, NV, USA, 27–30 June 2016.
26. Liu, W.; Anguelov, D.; Erhan, D.; Szegedy, C.; Reed, S.; Fu, C.-Y.; Berg, A.C. SSD: Single Shot MultiBox Detector. In Proceedings of the Computer Vision–ECCV 2016 14th European Conference, Amsterdam, The Netherlands, 11–14 October 2016.
27. Duan, K.; Bai, S.; Xie, L.; Qi, H.; Huang, Q.; Tian, Q. CenterNet: Keypoint Triplets for Object Detection. In Proceedings of the IEEE/CVF International Conference on Computer Vision, Seoul, Republic of Korea, 27 October–2 November 2019.

28. Li, Z.; Peng, C.; Yu, G.; Zhang, X.; Deng, Y.; Sun, J. Light-Head R-CNN: In Defense of Two-Stage Object Detector. *arXiv* **2017**, arXiv:1711.07264.
29. Zhang, S.; Wen, L.; Bian, X.; Lei, Z.; Li, S.Z. Single-Shot Refinement Neural Network for Object Detection. In Proceedings of the Proceedings of the IEEE Computer Society Conference on Computer Vision and Pattern Recognition, Salt Lake City, UT, USA, 18–22 June 2018; IEEE Computer Society: Washington, DC, USA, 2018; pp. 4203–4212.
30. Wu, X.; Sahoo, D.; Hoi, S.C.H. Recent Advances in Deep Learning for Object Detection. *Neurocomputing* **2020**, *396*, 39–64. [CrossRef]
31. Tan, M.; Pang, R.; Le, Q.V. EfficientDet: Scalable and Efficient Object Detection. In Proceedings of the IEEE/CVF Conference on Computer Vision and Pattern Recognition, Seattle, WA, USA, 13–19 June 2020.
32. Liu, Z.; Mao, H.; Wu, C.-Y.; Feichtenhofer, C.; Darrell, T.; Xie, S. A ConvNet for the 2020s. In Proceedings of the IEEE/CVF Conference on Computer Vision and Pattern Recognition, New Orleans, LA, USA, 18–24 June 2022.
33. Teso-Fz-Betoño, D.; Zulueta, E.; Sánchez-Chica, A.; Fernandez-Gamiz, U.; Saenz-Aguirre, A. Semantic Segmentation to Develop an Indoor Navigation System for an Autonomous Mobile Robot. *Mathematics* **2020**, *8*, 855. [CrossRef]
34. Kingma, D.P.; Ba, J. Adam: A Method for Stochastic Optimization. *arXiv* **2014**, arXiv:1412.6980.

Σ mathematics

MDPI

Article

Anomaly Detection on Laminated Composite Plate Using Self-Attention Autoencoder and Gaussian Mixture Model

Olivier Munyaneza [1] and Jung Woo Sohn [2,*]

[1] Department of Aeronautics, Mechanical and Electronic Convergence Engineering, Graduated School, Kumoh National Institute of Technology, Daehak-ro 61, Gumi 39177, Republic of Korea; olivis@kumoh.ac.kr

[2] School of Mechanical Engineering, Kumoh National Institute of Technology, Daehak-ro 61, Gumi 39177, Republic of Korea

* Correspondence: jwsohn@kumoh.ac.kr

Abstract

Composite laminates are widely used in aerospace, automotive, construction, and luxury industries, owing to their superior mechanical properties and design flexibility. However, detecting manufacturing defects and in-service damage remains a vital challenge for structural safety. While traditional unsupervised machine learning methods have been used in structural health monitoring (SHM), their high false positive rates limit their reliability in real-world applications. This issue is mostly inherited from their limited ability to capture small temporal variations in Lamb wave signals and their dependence on shallow architectures that suffer with complex signal distributions, causing the misclassification of damaged signals as healthy data. To address this, we suggested an unsupervised anomaly detection framework that integrates a self-attention autoencoder with a Gaussian mixture model (SAE-GMM). The model is solely trained on healthy Lamb wave signals, including high-quality synthetic data generated via a generative adversarial network (GAN). Damages are detected through reconstruction errors and probabilistic clustering in the latent space. The self-attention mechanism enhances feature representation by capturing subtle temporal dependencies, while the GMM enables a solid separation among signals. Experimental results demonstrated that the proposed model (SAE-GMM) achieves high detection accuracy, a low false positive rate, and strong generalization under varying noise conditions, outperforming traditional and deep learning baselines.

Keywords: composite laminates; unsupervised machine learning; structural healthy monitoring; self-attention; Gaussian mixture model; generative adversarial network; Lamb waves

MSC: 68T01

1. Introduction

The need for composite laminates has gradually increased in the automotive, aerospace, naval, and energy fields due to their unique properties, such as high specific strength, high toughness, high flexibility, and low density [1,2]. Composite materials are prone to intricate flaws during manufacturing and assembly processes. Moreover, they are subjected to harsh environmental conditions and various cyclic loadings, which adversely affect their performance and can lead to structural integrity failure [3,4]. To detect flaws in composite materials, nondestructive testing using ultrasonic guided waves, also known as Lamb waves, has been used in the past decades because of their ability to propagate over

https://doi.org/10.3390/math13152445

long distances with minimal attenuation, a larger inspection range, and high sensitivity to small damages [5].

The basic principle of NDT-based structural health monitoring (SHM) is to assess the condition of a structure by collecting signal responses from multiple sensor networks, analyzing them, and determining whether the structure is healthy or damaged, using either a physics-based (model-driven) or data-driven approach. Physics-based models typically rely on mathematical formulations and physical principles to define structural characteristics and predict damage. However, owing to their computational intensity, reliance on accurate material properties and boundary conditions, and limited adaptability to real-world uncertainties, the quantitative analysis of the physical behavior of guided waves remains challenging [6]. On the contrary, data-driven approaches utilize machine learning and artificial intelligence to learn complex patterns from collected time-series data without requiring expert knowledge or exact structural information [2,7]. Supervised data-driven approaches have been extensively used for Lamb wave-based damage detection in SHM, achieving good performance for both image and time-series datasets. However, supervised learning relies on labeled data from both healthy and damaged states of a structure, which can be time-consuming, labor-intensive, and sometimes impractical to obtain in real-life scenarios. To tackle this problem, unsupervised approaches have been successful in detecting abnormalities at an early stage before catastrophic failure occurs. Unsupervised anomaly detection for SHM does not require damaged data to train the model. Instead, the model only requires normal data, and it solely uses a small portion of the damaged data for testing [8]. Khan et al. [9] proposed the processing of guided waves using a sparse autoencoder to extract unsupervised autonomous damage features. The unsupervised features, when applied in supervised learning, demonstrated that the sparse autoencoder (SAE) could distinguish between pristine and damaged conditions with 99% accuracy. Abbassi et al. [10] evaluated four unsupervised dimensionality reduction methods (PCA, KPCA, t-SNE, and AE) for detecting and localizing damage under varying temperature conditions. Through the dimensionality reduction strategy, the AE outperformed the other models in detecting and localizing damage, whereas the others succeeded in detecting damage at low temperatures. Additionally, using the strategy involving the Q and T^2 indices, all the methods successfully detected damage across all temperature ranges. The effectiveness of the unsupervised autoencoder was also highlighted in [11], as it eliminated the use of labeled data by proposing a CNN autoencoder for damage localization. They validated their method using numerical and experimental datasets. The proposed method demonstrated excellent results compared to the tomography method.

Guided-wave-based SHM presents significant complexities and heterogeneity, which primarily affect models' ability to extract meaningful features. To address this challenge, various deep learning models have been proposed for feature differentiation; however, these approaches require a substantial number of learning parameters in addition to the computational complexity of the task. Sawant et al. [4] utilized raw Lamb wave time-series data to identify and localize damage through unsupervised transfer learning using a convolutional autoencoder (TL-CAE). The proposed unsupervised model outperformed its supervised counterpart trained on the same dataset. In SHM, gathering a sufficient dataset to train deep learning models can be challenging, costly, and time-consuming, particularly for damage-related data. To minimize the negative impact of an imbalanced dataset on anomaly detection, Zhao et al. [12] proposed an SGAD-GAN model to perform data augmentation and anomaly detection simultaneously. The issue of data scarcity in SHM was also addressed by Furkan et al. [13] by employing a generative adversarial network with a gradient penalty to generate synthetic labeled acceleration data. The data generated were augmented using varying ratios and were used to train a 1D-CNN. Training GANs is not an effortless task, and it often produces misleading samples or fails to capture the important patterns in the signals. To identify and filter such low-quality samples, different clustering-based techniques have been employed, including DBSCAN [14], K-means [15], and discriminative fuzzy K-means [16].

In this study, a self-attention autoencoder combined with a Gaussian mixture model (SAE-GMM) for unsupervised anomaly detection in laminated composite plates was proposed. The model was trained exclusively on the original healthy data and synthetic data generated using a GAN. A deep autoencoder was employed to extract the low-dimensional latent features and compute the reconstruction errors for each input signal. Additionally, a self-attention mechanism was integrated to enhance the performance of the deep autoencoder by dynamically prioritizing the most relevant parts of the input signal. Finally, the extracted latent features and reconstruction error outputs from the AE were input into the estimation network for density estimation via a GMM. This combination provides a full anomaly detection model, capable of detecting damage with high accuracy and inference time compared to conventional models. The key contributions of this study are summarized as follows:

- The developed SAE-GMM architecture was trained solely on healthy Lamb wave data, enabling reliable damage detection without requiring labeled damage samples.
- The proposed unsupervised framework was specifically designed to minimize false positive rates, thereby improving the robustness and reliability of damage detection.
- A GAN was employed to generate high-fidelity synthetic signals, filtered via K-means clustering, to enrich healthy training data and overcome data shortage issue in SHM.
- The self-attention mechanism was integrated into the encoded network, enhancing sensitivity to subtle signal distortions, improving representation quality and reconstruction fidelity.
- Leveraged Gaussian mixture modeling combined latent features and reconstruction errors to effectively separate healthy and damaged signals.
- We achieved state-of-the-art anomaly detection performance on an experimental composite plate, with validated generalization under varied Gaussian noise levels.

2. The Proposed Framework

2.1. Overview

The proposed framework comprises of three main components: (1) an experimental setup and data acquisition, (2) a GAN for generating synthetic data, and (3) a self-attention autoencoder (SAE) with a Gaussian Mixture Model (GMM) for anomaly detection. Figure 1 shows the architecture of the SAE-GMM framework. First, a composite plate was fabricated, and Lamb wave-based experiments were conducted to collect both healthy and damaged signals. The GAN model was employed to generate synthetic healthy data that closely resembled the original healthy signals. To ensure data quality, the K-means algorithm was applied to filter out the most realistic synthetic samples before incorporating them into the dataset for augmentation. The autoencoder was trained exclusively on healthy data using a self-attention module integrated into the encoder to enhance feature extraction. The reconstruction error and latent vector were then combined to form a new input vector for density estimation using the GMM, enabling effective anomaly detection.

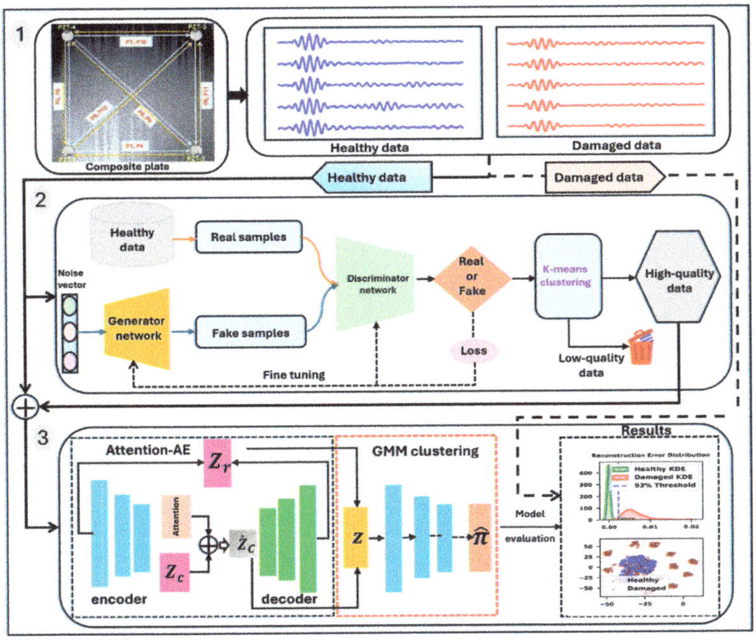

Figure 1. The flowchart of the proposed model, SAE-GMM. The proposed framework comprises of three main components: (1) an experimental setup and data acquisition, (2) a GAN for generating synthetic data, and (3) a self-attention autoencoder (SAE) with a Gaussian Mixture Model (GMM) for anomaly detection.

2.2. GAN Model for Data Augmentation

The GAN consists of two key components: a generator network (G) and a discriminator network (D). As shown in Step 2 of Figure 1, the generator network converts Gaussian noise into synthetic data that closely resembles the original data distribution, aiming to deceive the discriminator. The discriminator network is responsible for distinguishing between fake and real data. Through an adversarial process, the two networks engage in a competitive game: the generator continuously improves to produce more realistic data, whereas the discriminator enhances its ability to detect fake data. During training, the objective function follows a minimax strategy [17,18]:

$$V(D,G) = \mathbb{E}_{x\sim P(x)}[logD(x)] + \mathbb{E}_{x\sim P(Z)}[log(1 - D(G(Z)))] \quad (1)$$

where $P(x)$ represents the distribution of the original data and $P(Z)$ denotes the distribution of the synthetic data generated by the model. The first term, $\mathbb{E}_{x\sim P(x)}[\log D(x)]$, represents the discriminator's goal of maximizing its ability to classify real samples. Simultaneously, the generator minimizes the discriminator's success in distinguishing fake data through the second term, $\mathbb{E}_{x\sim P(Z)}[\log(1 - D(G(Z)))]$. This process continues until the generator reaches the stage of generating samples that are closely related to real data, and the discriminator's accuracy can no longer be improved further.

The generator maps a 150-dimensional latent vector to a 1500-point time-domain signal. Both the generator and discriminator consist of three fully connected layers with 64, 128, and 256 neurons, each followed by LeakyReLU activation functions. To improve training stability, batch normalization and dropout were applied. The models were optimized using the Adam optimizer with a learning rate of 2×10^{-4} and a momentum coefficient β_1

= 0.5. Binary cross-entropy was used as the loss function. The training process was carried out over 5000 epochs with a batch size of 32 to ensure stable convergence.

After training the model, 5000 synthetic data samples were generated. However, some of the synthetic signals were of poor quality. To ensure the quality of the samples generated, K-means clustering was used to distinguish between high- and low-quality signals. Additionally, this algorithm is simple to implement and efficient for large datasets. First, the mean square error (MSE) was calculated and stored for each synthetic signal in comparison with all the original data as follows:

$$MSE\left(d_{syn}, d_{real}\right) = \frac{1}{n}\sum_{i=1}^{n}\left(d_{syn,i} - d_{real,i}\right)^2 \tag{2}$$

where d_{syn} and d_{real} are synthetic data and real data, respectively.

After storing all the MSE values as $\{n_1, n_2, n_3, \ldots, n_n\}$, K-means clustering was initialized with two clusters, and the two centroids (C_1, C_2) were assigned randomly. Each value in the MSE set was assigned to the closest centroid as follows:

$$K_j = \left\{m_i \middle| argmin_j \middle| n_i - C_j \middle| \right\} \tag{3}$$

where K_j is the cluster set, and the updated centroid C_j is calculated as $C_j = \frac{1}{|K_j|}\sum_{ni \in K_j}(n_i)$. The centroids are continuously updated until convergence is achieved. To select the highest-quality synthetic signals, the threshold was determined as $Threshold = min\ (C_1, C_2)$. Finally, only 3270 quality signals fell below the threshold.

2.3. Self-Attention Autoencoder with GMM

The self-attention autoencoder with Gaussian mixture model (SAE-GMM) consists of two main components, as shown in Figure 1. The first is a self-attention autoencoder, which functions as a compression network to reduce input dimensionality into a lower-dimensional representation while simultaneously computing reconstruction errors. In the second stage, both the low-dimensional latent features and their corresponding reconstruction errors are concatenated and fed into an estimation network, which performs density estimation and maximizes the likelihood of the input samples using a Gaussian mixture model.

2.3.1. The Encoder

One key component of the compression network is the encoder, which transforms a sequence of input data $(X \in \mathbb{R}^n)$ from a high-dimensional space into a lower-dimensional latent representation $(Z_c \in \mathbb{R}^t,\ t < n)$. This compression process is accomplished by extracting and encoding essential features from the input data. In the proposed model, the encoder consists of two stacked layers with 128 and 64 neurons. Each layer employs a Rectified Linear Unit (ReLu) activation function. The encoding process that maps the input data X to the low-dimensional latent space Z_c is formulated as follows:

$$Z_c = f_\theta(X) \tag{4}$$

where f_θ represents the fully connected layers of the encoder part.

$$Z_c = \rho(W_3 * \delta(W_2 * \delta(W_1 * X + b_1) + b_2) + b_3) \tag{5}$$

where X is the input data, W_i and b_i are weight and bias, respectively, and ρ is the activation function.

2.3.2. The Attention Mechanism

The attention block in the autoencoder enhances the encoder's ability to focus on the most salient features of the input data while suppressing less important features. The mechanism computes attention weights by evaluating the relative importance of each input element, measuring their similarities, and normalizing these values to form a weighted representation [19]. The self-attention mechanism computes three matrices, namely query (Q), key (K), and value (V) from the hidden states, and they are calculated as follows:

$$Q_i = X_c W_Q \tag{6}$$

$$K_i = X_c W_K \tag{7}$$

$$V_i = X_c W_V \tag{8}$$

where X_c denotes the ith feature sliding window matrix of a low-dimensional latent space. W_Q, W_K, and W_V are the weight matrices corresponding to query, key, and value, respectively. The attention function is calculated as follows [20]:

$$A_i = \text{Softmax}\left(Q_i K_i^T \Big/ \sqrt{d} \right) . V_i \tag{9}$$

where A_i is the attention coefficient of matrix X_c, and d represents the scaling factor. The output from the attention layer is obtained by applying attention weights to the input sequences.

$$Z_c' = Z_c \bigodot A_i \tag{10}$$

During implementation, the attention module was constructed using the Dot-product attention layer from TensorFlow-Keras. The encoded feature tensor is passed simultaneously as both the query and value inputs to this layer, enabling self-attention across all steps. The resulting attention scores highlight interdependence within the sequence and are used to compute a weighted representation of the input. This attention-enhanced output is combined with the original encoded features via elementwise multiplication before further transformation through dense layers.

2.3.3. The Decoder

The decoder typically consists of hidden layers with an increasing number of nodes and gradually decompresses the low-dimensional features from the encoder. Its primary goal is to reconstruct X from the latent features z_c', with minimal loss. The last layer of the decoder network can be mathematically expressed as follows:

$$\hat{X} = \rho(W_c * \delta(W_b * \delta(W_a * Z_C' + b_a) + b_b) + b_c) \tag{11}$$

where $\hat{X}$ is the reconstructed output from the decoder and W and b are the weight and bias of the decoder network, respectively. The reconstruction loss of the compression network is computed as follows:

$$\mathcal{L}_{rec} = \frac{1}{N} \sum_{i=1}^{N} ||X_i - \hat{X}_i||^2 \tag{12}$$

2.4. Estimation Network and Anomaly Score

The estimation network computes density estimation of the input data (Z) by leveraging concatenation of the reconstruction error (Z_r) and low-dimension latent vector (z_c').

This enables the model to estimate the likelihood of a sample belonging to either the healthy or damaged class. The process was performed within the framework of the Gaussian mixture model (GMM). In this study, a multilayer perceptron (MLP) with three hidden layers consisting of 16, 8, and 4 neurons was employed to estimate the parameters of the GMM. This classifier can learn efficiently the complex relationships between construction error, latent features, and output probabilities [21]. The mathematical formulation of this process is as follows [22]:

$$h = [Z, |X - \hat{X}|] \tag{13}$$

The final layer of the MLP is obtained as follows:

$$h^{(3)} = \rho\left(W^{(3)} * \rho\left(W^{(2)} * \rho\left(W^{(1)} * h + b^{(1)}\right) + b^{(2)}\right) + b^{(3)}\right) \tag{14}$$

where $h^{(3)}$ represents the output feature vector of the MLP, ρ is the activation function (ReLU), and $W^{(i)}$ and $b^{(i)}$ represent the weight matrices and bias for the ith layer, respectively. To estimate the probabilities of each GMM component, the last layer of the MLP passes through SoftMax activation and is expressed as follows:

$$\gamma_k = \frac{exp\left(h_k^{(3)}\right)}{\sum_{j=1}^{K} exp\left(h_j^{(3)}\right)} \tag{15}$$

Here, γ_k represents the probability of data belonging to the kth Gaussian component, K is the total number of Gaussian components, and $h_k^{(3)}$ is the output of the final MLP layer corresponding to the kth component. Furthermore, to maximize the likelihood of the input samples, the mean (μ_k) and variance $(\sum_k)$ parameters of the GMM can be estimated as follows [23]:

$$\mu_k = \frac{\sum_{i=1}^{N} \gamma_{ik} Z_i}{\sum_{i=1}^{N} \gamma_{ik}} \tag{16}$$

$$\sum\nolimits_k = \frac{\sum_{i=1}^{N} \gamma_{ik} (Z_i - \mu_k)(Z_i - \mu_k)^T}{\sum_{i=1}^{N} \gamma_{ik}} \tag{17}$$

where N denotes the total number of samples. With the estimated parameters, the likelihood of each sample being computed using the energy function is as follows:

$$E(Z) = -\log \sum\nolimits_{k=1}^{K} \pi_k \frac{exp\left(-\frac{1}{2}(Z - \mu_k)^T \sum_k^{-1} (Z - \mu_k)\right)}{\sqrt{|2\pi \sum_k|}} \tag{18}$$

where π_k is the mixture probability of the kth component and $|.|$ represents the matrix determinant. Based on Equation (18), samples with higher energy values are more likely to correspond to the damaged cases. In this study, the threshold was set at the 95th percentile of the healthy samples, meaning that any sample exceeding this threshold was classified as damaged.

3. Experiments and Analysis

3.1. Experimental Verification on Laminated Composite Plate

To validate the proposed model, a laminated composite plate with dimensions of 300 mm × 300 mm × 1mm was fabricated using an epoxy-based carbon fiber prepreg with a cross-ply orientation of $[0/90/0/90]_S$. The composite laminates were manufactured using a hot-press machine and carefully cured to achieve the desired mechanical properties: a tensile strength of 4900 MPa, tensile modulus of 230 GPa, thermal conductivity of 9.4 W/m.k, and density of 1.8 g/cm^3. After trimming the composite plate to its final dimensions, four piezoelectric transducers (PZTs) from the PI ceramics were mounted diagonally at the four corners of the laminate plate using Loctite 401 adhesive to monitor the structure. Each PZT had a diameter of 10 mm and thickness of 0.5 mm.

3.2. Data Acquisition

The configuration consisting of four piezoelectric transducers, each with the dual functions of actuation and sensing, attached to a laminated plate is presented in Figure 2a. Twelve sensing paths (P1–P12) were used for data acquisition. The composite plate was segmented into nine grid zones, each measuring 90 mm $\times$ 90 mm. To simulate varying damage severity levels, as presented in Figure 2b, three distinct masses (13 g, 16 g, and 20 g) were simultaneously placed at the center of each grid zone. A disk magnet was chosen to simulate the damage because it was non-destructive, easy to position, and capable of altering the local stiffness and acoustic impedance of the laminate, thereby affecting the propagation of Lamb waves. This approach also allowed for a reversible process that enabled the collection of both healthy and damaged data under controlled conditions. The experimental setup, as shown in Figure 2c, comprised an NI-USB 6341 series data acquisition system, a dual-channel PZT amplifier, and a LabVIEW-controlled PC for signal generation and data acquisition.

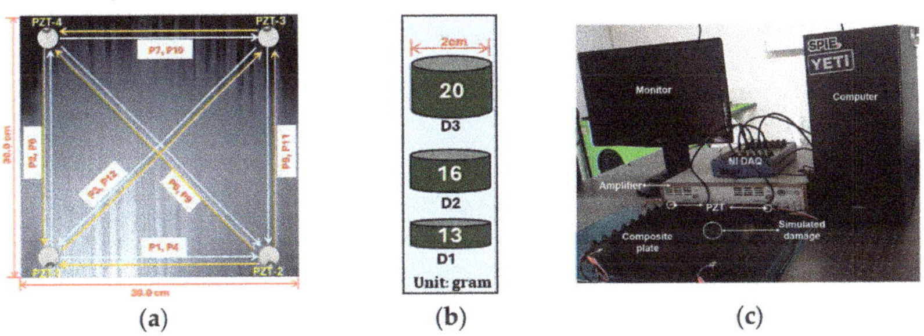

Figure 2. Data acquisition setup: (**a**) laminated composite with PZT layout and sensing paths; (**b**) different masses used to simulate artificial damage; (**c**) experimental setup.

The excitation signal and measured Lamb wave signals are presented in Figure 3. As shown in Figure 3a, a five-cycle sinusoidal tone burst, modulated by a Hanning window and centered at 150 kHz, was employed as the excitation signal. Signals were transmitted and recorded at a sampling rate of 500 kHz per sample. As shown in Figure 3b–f, healthy and damaged responses (D1–D3) were acquired sequentially using the pitch–catch method. The signals were collected along path 3 between PZT-1 and PZT-3, with all damage cases introduced simultaneously at the center of the plate. The influence of the damage was evident in the direct-wave packet region (index 0–400), where noticeable amplitude reductions and signal distortions were observed in the damaged signal compared to the healthy one (see Figure 3c–e). The damaged responses exhibited reduced amplitudes owing to the scattering effects induced by the defects. Subtle differences were observed among the three damage cases. As shown in Figure 3f, damage case D3 resulted in greater energy loss than D1 and D2, indicating more severe disruptions.

To ensure experimental repeatability, each test cycle was repeated ten times. A total of 3240 damaged signals (12 paths $\times$ 10 repetitions $\times$ 9 locations $\times$ 3 damage levels) and 600 healthy signals (12 paths $\times$ 10 repetitions $\times$ 5 trials) were collected. Due to the limited quantity of healthy signals and the risk of overfitting, a generative adversarial network (GAN), described in Section 2.2, was employed to generate new high-fidelity samples rather than simply replicating the existing data patterns. Moreover, to ensure the quality of the generated signals, K-means clustering was used to distinguish between high- and low-quality synthetic samples.

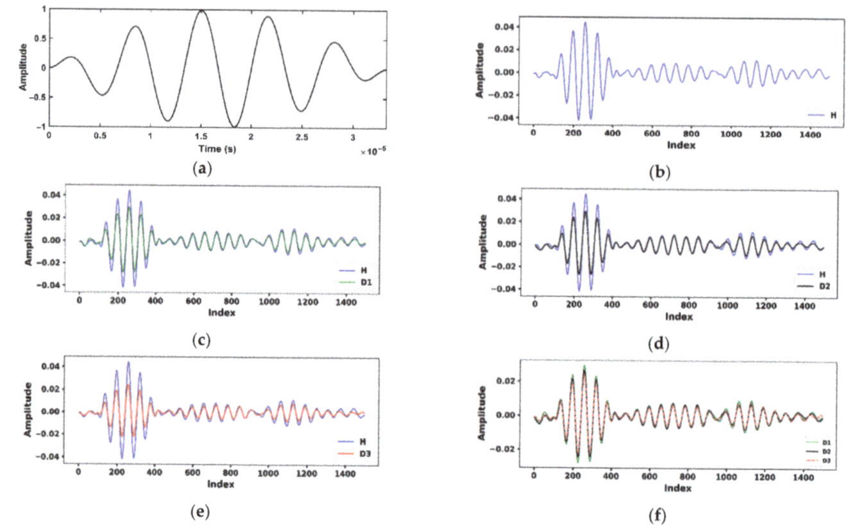

Figure 3. Measured Lamb wave signals along path 3: (**a**) excitation signal; (**b**) response under healthy conditions; (**c**) comparison between healthy and damaged case D1; (**d**) comparison between healthy and damaged case D2; (**e**) comparison between healthy and damaged case D3; (**f**) comparison of all damage cases (D1–D3).

Specifically, the root mean square (RMS) of each generated signal was compared with that of the original healthy signal. A threshold was established based on the minimum distance between the centroids of two clusters. Synthetic signals with mean squared error (MSE) values below this threshold were classified as high-quality, as shown in Figure 4a. A representative comparison between a generated signal and an original healthy signal is shown in Figure 4b, demonstrating a close resemblance in both amplitude and temporal structure, with only minor deviations observed in the second-wave packet. In total, 3270 high-quality synthetic signals were generated and combined with the original healthy data, yielding a final dataset comprising 3870 samples.

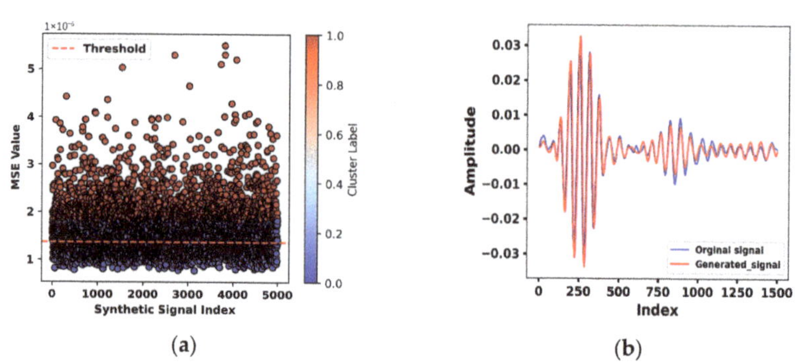

Figure 4. Augmented Lamb wave data: (**a**) K-means clustering of synthetic signals based on mean squared error (MSE) values; (**b**) comparison between the original and the generated healthy Lamb wave signals.

3.3. Baseline Methods and Evaluation Metrics

To demonstrate the effectiveness of our model, we compared it with various state-of-the-art models that are widely used for anomaly detection. These include shallow machine learning and deep learning approaches. Some of the models evaluated were the One-Class Support Vector Machine (Oc-SVM) [24], IsoForest [25], Local Outlier Factor (LOF) [26], and K-nearest neighbor (KNN) [27]. To ensure a fair comparison, latent features from the pretrained autoencoder were extracted and used to train the selected shallow models. Although shallow machine learning algorithms have demonstrated effectiveness in certain tasks, they often struggle with complex datasets. Therefore, in this study, we considered several deep learning models as the baseline for our proposed approach. These deep models include the Variational Autoencoder (VAE) [28], Invariant Representation Anomaly Detection (IRAD) [29], Deep support vector data description (Deep-SVDD) [30], and the transformer autoencoder (TAE) [31].

3.4. Implementation Details

To ensure a fair comparison between shallow machine learning and deep learning models, features were extracted using an autoencoder to train the KNN, IsoForest, Oc-SVM, and LOF models. The autoencoder, with an input shape of 1500 and a 64-dimensional latent representation, was trained exclusively on healthy data. All experiments were conducted on a workstation equipped with an NVIDIA GeForce RTX 3060 GPU, an Intel Core i7-10700F CPU, and 32 GB of RAM. All models were trained using the same hyperparameters: the Adam optimizer, a batch size of 32, and 50 training epochs. For KNN and LOF, the neighborhood size was set to five based on trial-and-error experimentation. In contrast, the number of estimators for IsoForest was set to 30, and the radial basis function (RBF) kernel was selected for Oc-SVM. Fully connected layers were used to construct deep learning-based models such as VAE, IRAD, and Deep-SVDD, all trained exclusively on healthy data with identical training parameters. Anomaly detection in both the VAE and IRAD models is based on reconstruction errors, which serve as the anomaly score via the mean squared error (MSE). In the case of VAE, Kullback–Leibler (KL) divergence is added to the loss function to enforce a standard normal distribution in the latent space, whereas Deep-SVDD initializes its center point based on features extracted from healthy data. The transformer autoencoder model was constructed with a dense layer of 64 units, two attention heads, a feed-forward network with a hidden size of 128 and dropout rate of 0.25.

The proposed model, summarized in Table 1, identified abnormalities by initially training an attention-enhanced autoencoder solely on healthy data. This allowed the model to learn a compact latent representation and accurately reconstruct normal signal patterns. Subsequently, a Gaussian mixture model (GMM) with four components was then fitted to the latent features extracted from the healthy data. The number of components was selected based on a trial-and-error approach rather than exhaustive parameter optimization. Anomaly scores were then computed using the negative log-likelihood of each sample under the GMM. Samples with scores exceeding 95th percentile of the healthy data were classified as having anomalies, indicating potential damage.

To assess the contribution of the attention mechanism to our proposed model, we conducted a comparative experiment by retraining the SAE-GMM model with the attention module excluding from the encoder section. The modified model (AE-GMM) was evaluated under similar conditions, and its performance metrics were compared to those of the original architecture.

Table 1. Detailed architecture of the proposed SAE-GMM model.

Layers	Output Shape	Parameters	Hyperparameters
Input layer	(None, 1500)	0	input shape = 1500
Dense	(None, 128)	192,128	units = 128; activation = ReLu
Dense	(None, 64)	8256	units = 64; activation = ReLu
Attention (encoder)	(None, 64)	0	self-attention over 64-d latent space.
Multiply	(None, 64)	0	encoded ⊙ attention output
Dense (latent)	(None, 32)	2080	units = 32; activation = ReLu
Dense	(None, 64)	2112	units = 64; activation = ReLu
Dense	(None, 128)	8320	units = 128; activation = ReLu
Dense (reconstruction)	(None, 1500)	193,500	units = 1500; activation = sigmoid
Concatenate	(None, 1532)	0	combined latent (32) + abs (1500)
Dense	(None, 16)	24,528	units = 16; activation = ReLu
Dense	(None, 8)	136	units = 8; activation = ReLu
Dense (GMM output)	(None, 4)	36	units = 4; activation = SoftMax
Total params: 431,096			

3.5. Evaluation Metrics

To evaluate the performance of the proposed model, four key metrics were selected: the F1-score, recall (R), the false positive rate (FPR), and inference time. According to [25], recall indicates the proportion of correctly classified damaged instances, whereas the FPR assesses the model's reliability by measuring how often healthy data are misclassified as damaged. Inference time tells how long it takes for a trained model to analyze new data.

4. Experimental Results

4.1. Influence of Synthetic GAN Data on Proposed Model's Performance

To evaluate the influence of synthetic data on our model's performance, we designed four different scenarios, as summarized in Table 2. The first scenario is composed exclusively of real data (100% real samples). The second scenario includes a balanced mix of real and synthetic samples, consisting of 100% real and 20% synthetic data. The third scenario features a complete mix of real and synthetic data. Lastly, the fourth scenario consists solely of synthetic data (100% synthetic samples). Each scenario was evaluated using the same set of 1080 damaged samples.

Table 2. Performance of SAE-GMM under various real–synthetic data configurations.

Scenario	Real Samples	Synthetic Samples	Accuracy	Precision	Recall	F1-Score	FPR
1	600	0	0.92	0.97	0.93	0.95	9.50
2	600	654	0.97	0.96	1.0	0.96	5.06
3	600	3270	0.97	0.98	1.0	0.97	5.02
4	0	3270	0.97	0.94	1.0	0.96	6.40

From Table 2, it is clearly seen that the model trained solely on real data achieved low accuracy and a high false positive rate. This suggests that the model struggles to generalize well to unseen datasets due to the scarcity of real samples.

In contrast, the inclusion of synthetic data on real samples (scenario 3) demonstrated the best F1-score and the lowest false positive rate, highlighting the quality of the synthetic signals filtered by K-means clustering. Finally, the fourth scenario showed also strong anomaly detection; however, it suffered from low precision and an increased FPR, likely due to the absence of real data during training. Overall, the results indicate that synthetic data enhanced our model's performance, with scenario 3 exhibiting optimal performance.

4.2. Anomaly Detection Results

To train the proposed and baseline models, 5-fold cross-validation was employed to split the healthy data into training and validation sets. For each damage category, 35% of the corresponding data were randomly selected to minimize imbalances during the testing phase. The selected samples from the three damage severities were concatenated to construct the damage dataset. Subsequently, the damaged dataset was combined with validation healthy dataset to form the testing dataset.

Table 3 lists the average performance metrics of the proposed and baseline models. For each metric, the highest score is indicated in bold, and the second-highest score is underlined. Among traditional models, Isolation Forest delivered the best performance with an F1-score of 91.4% and a recall of 93.8%, though it suffered from a relatively high false positive rate (FPR) of 11.3%. The K-nearest neighbor (KNN) model achieved an almost perfect recall (99.4%) but was undermined by the highest FPR (31.8%), indicating poor discrimination of healthy signals. Both One-Class SVM and Local Outlier Factor (LOF) performed poorly across all metrics. These findings suggest that while traditional machine learning models offer faster inference, they lack the feature extraction capacity required for complex signals such as Lamb waves. In contrast, deep learning models demonstrated superior feature extraction capabilities. The Variational Autoencoder (VAE) stood out among the baselines, achieving an F1-score of 96.1%, a recall of 98.3%, and a moderate FPR of 5.16%. However, its inference time (0.75 s)—nearly double that of the proposed model—limits its practicality in real-time settings. The transformer autoencoder (TAE) attained a moderate F1-score of 90.0% and a recall of 94.0% but exhibited the longest inference time (5.56 s), reflecting high computational demand despite decent detection performance. Both Deep-SVDD and IRAD failed to strike a balance across metrics. Deep-SVDD achieved the lowest FPR (0.8%) but suffered from extremely low recall (44.0%) and a corresponding F1-score of 60.6%, indicating severe overfitting and poor anomaly detection capability.

Table 3. Anomaly detection performance for baselines and our proposed model. For each metric, the highest score is indicated in bold, and the second-highest score is underlined.

Models	F1-Score	Recall	False Positive Rate	Inference Time (s)
Oc-SVM	60.0 ± 0.1	51.1 ± 0.22	11.0 ± 18	0.09
IsoForest	91.4 ± 0.1	93.8 ± 0.03	11.3 ± 21	0.01
KNN	83.8 ± 0.2	99.4 ± 0.01	31.8 ± 15	0.03
LOF	78.8 ± 0.3	80.1 ± 0.34	8.5 ± 0.01	0.02
IRAD	88.7 ± 0.1	88.7 ± 0.09	8.2 ± 0.04	2.3×10^{-3}
Deep-SVDD	60.6 ± 0.0	44.0 ± 0.01	**0.8 ± 0.33**	0.93
TAE	90.0 ± 0.4	94.0 ± 0.06	10.0 ± 0.03	5.56
VAE	**$\underline{96.1 \pm 0.1}$**	98.3 ± 0.03	5.16 ± 0.09	0.75
AE-GMM	95.8 ± 0.3	**100 ± 0.0**	7.01 ± 0.01	**0.32**
SAE-GMM	**97.1 ± 0.0**	$\underline{99.9 \pm 0.05}$	$\underline{4.99 \pm 0.03}$	$\underline{0.37}$

The proposed SAE-GMM model outperformed all baselines, achieving the highest F1-score (97.1%), nearly perfect recall (99.9%), and the lowest FPR (4.99%). Additionally, it maintained a fast inference time of 0.37 s, offering an ideal balance between speed and accuracy. The trained model without the self-attention module (AE-GMM) achieved perfect recall but suffered from a higher FPR (7.01%). In addition, SAE-GMM provides a clear balance between recall and false alarms. These results clearly demonstrate that integrating self-attention improves robustness and reduces false positives, with only a slight increase in runtime.

Figure 5 shows the confusion matrices for all baseline models and the proposed model, highlighting the effectiveness of each in distinguishing between healthy and damaged samples. The Oc-SVM and Deep-SVDD models exhibited limited capabilities, misclassifying nearly half of the damaged samples. Although Deep-SVDD achieved the lowest FPR, its overall detection performance was inadequate for practical applications. Models such as IsoForest, LOF, and IRAD demonstrated moderate performance in detecting true positives.

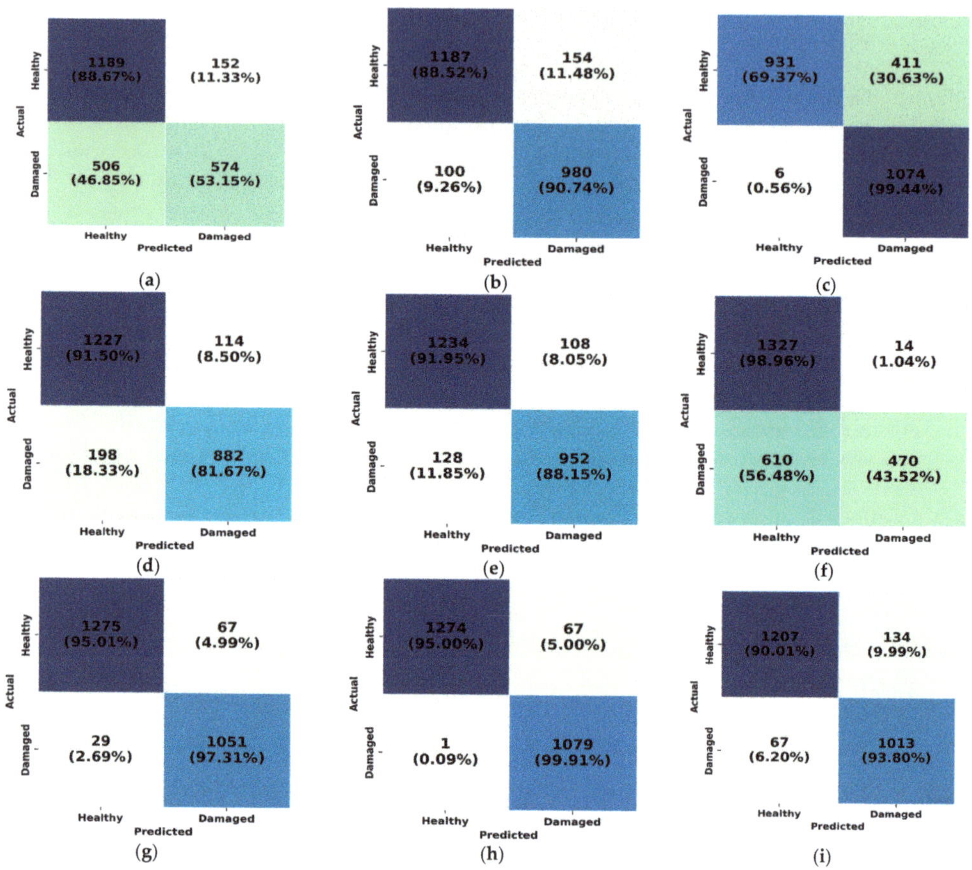

Figure 5. Confusion matrices for baselines and proposed model: (**a**) Oc-SVM; (**b**) IsoForest; (**c**) KNN; (**d**) LOF; (**e**) IRAD; (**f**) Deep-SVDD; (**g**) VAE; (**h**) SAE-GMM; (**i**) TAE.

The KNN model achieved the second-highest number of true positives, correctly identifying 1074 out of 1080 damaged samples; however, it suffered from a high false positive rate, misclassifying 33.6% of the healthy signals. The VAE also performed well, misclassifying only 29 damaged samples and yielding a low FPR of 5.04%. The transformer autoencoder (TAE) achieved decent classification performance, correctly identifying 1013 damaged samples (93.8% recall) and 1207 healthy samples (90.01%). However, it misclassified 67 damaged and 134 healthy instances, indicating a moderate trade-off between detection and precision.

In contrast, the proposed SAE-GMM model outperformed all baselines, achieving the highest number of true positives—correctly classifying 1079 out of 1080 damaged samples and misclassifying only one sample. This highlights its robustness in differentiating between healthy and damaged signals. These results demonstrate that the superior performance of the proposed model stems from its ability to effectively capture the underlying structure of healthy data through a combination of deep representation learning, self-attention mechanisms, and GMM-based clustering in the latent space.

4.3. Visualization of the Results

To further evaluate the separation capabilities of the proposed model relative to baseline approaches, we employed t-distributed Stochastic Neighbor Embedding (t-SNE) and Kernel Density Estimation (KDE) visualizations. As shown on the left side of Figure 6, the t-SNE results indicate that both Deep-SVDD and Oc-SVM exhibited a limited ability to discriminate between healthy (blue) and damaged (red) samples in the latent space. A significant portion of the damaged samples were incorrectly clustered with healthy samples, reflecting suboptimal separation. In contrast, the KNN model tended to misclassify a large number of healthy samples as damaged. Deep learning-based models, including the VAE, IRAD, and LOF demonstrated improved class separation with reduced overlap between healthy and damaged sample distributions compared with shallow machine learning methods. Among these, the proposed model achieved the most distinct separation, followed by the VAE model. In the t-SNE plot, the healthy samples form a compact cluster, whereas the damaged samples are more widely distributed and separated. This clear delineation suggests that the proposed model is more effective in learning discriminative features, thereby enhancing its capacity for reliable and accurate damage detection. Additionally, the KDE plots shown on the right side of Figure 6 are used to illustrate the distribution of anomaly scores and reconstruction errors for the two classes. Note that the Oc-SVM achieved the worst separation between healthy and damaged samples, whereas the proposed model exhibited the best separation. The healthy (green) and damaged samples (red) show a clearer overlap around the decision threshold at zero, suggesting the limited ability of the Oc-SVM model to separate false positives and false negatives.

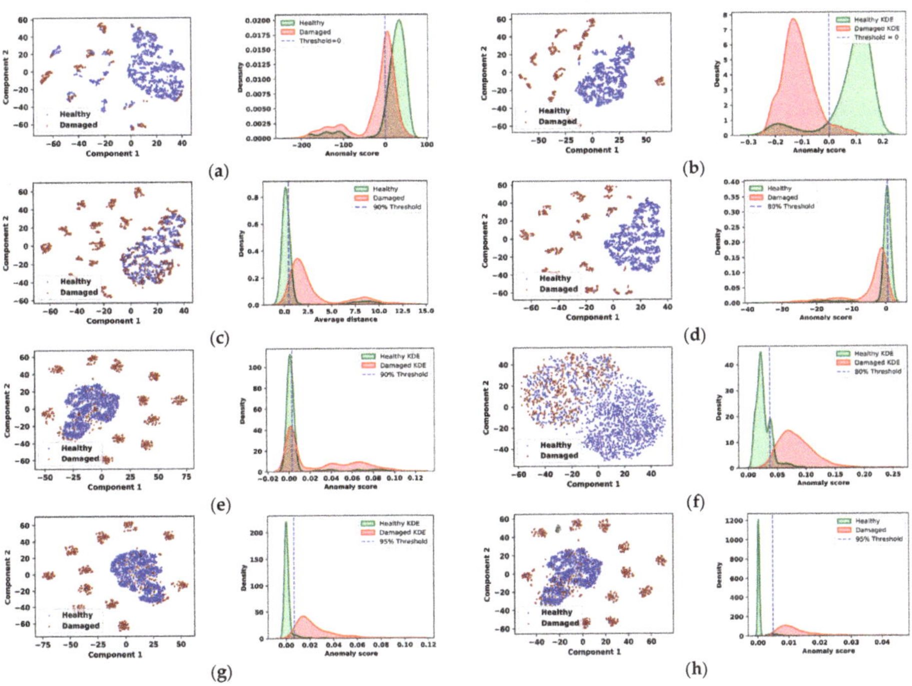

Figure 6. t-SNE visualizations and KDE plots: **(a)** Oc-SVM; **(b)** IsoForest; **(c)** KNN; **(d)** LOF; **(e)** IRAD; **(f)** Deep-SVDD; **(g)** VAE; **(h)** SAE-GMM.

To highlight the impact of the attention mechanism on the proposed model, the feature distributions before and after applying attention are shown in Figure 7. Figure 7a shows the t-SNE plot of the features before the implementation of the attention mechanism, where a significant overlap between healthy and damaged samples is observed, indicating a poor class distribution. By contrast, Figure 7b shows the feature distribution after applying attention, demonstrating an improved separation between the two classes with a distinct gap. This indicates that the attention mechanism effectively enhances the feature representation for the proposed SAE-GMM model, resulting in better class separation compared to other models that do not utilize attention.

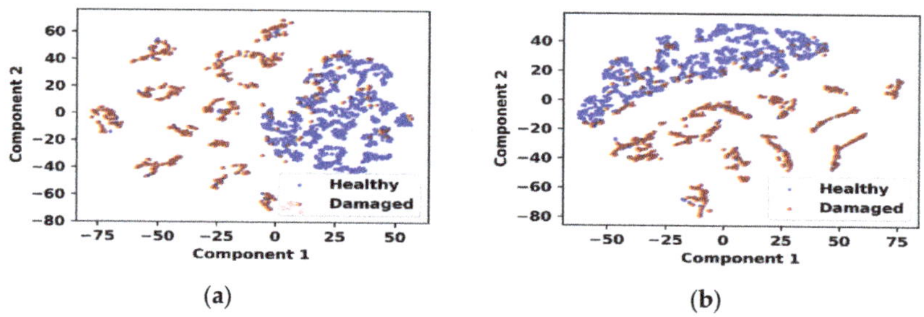

Figure 7. Comparison of feature distribution using t-SNE plots: (**a**) pre-attention; (**b**) post-attention.

The proposed model outperformed all baseline models, with a much more distinct separation between the samples. It is evident that the healthy samples were concentrated near very low anomaly scores, whereas the damaged samples were spread over a broader range of high anomaly scores. The 95% threshold determined from healthy samples cleanly separated the most damaged samples with a small overlap. Overall, the SAE-GMM model achieved superior class separability and a more reliable threshold margin for identifying structural damage.

4.4. Robust Analysis Under Varying Gaussian Noise Levels

To evaluate the generalization capability of the proposed SAE-GMM model under noisy conditions, Gaussian noise with three standard deviations ($\sigma = 0.05, 0.075, 0.1$) was added to training data. Rather than augmenting the dataset with additional noisy samples, 50% of the original training data were perturbed to mitigate computational overhead. The model's performance under each noise condition was evaluated and compared to its baseline performance on clean data, as summarized in Table 4. Under moderate noise levels ($\sigma = 0.05$ and $\sigma = 0.075$), the model retained stable F-1 scores of 0.97 and 0.96 with strong recall values of 97% and 95%, respectively. At the highest noise level ($\sigma = 0.1$), the model demonstrated notable resilience, achieving an F1-score of 0.93 and recall of 90%, highlighting its effectiveness in anomaly detection. The false positive rate (FPR) experienced a steady increase with noise level, from 4.99% (clean data) to 6.10% ($\sigma = 0.1$), yet remained within an acceptable range. These results validate the robustness of the proposed model under realistic signal perturbations.

Table 4. Proposed model performance under varying noise levels.

	Noise Level	Accuracy	Precision	Recall	F1-Score	FPR
SAE-GMM	clean	0.97	0.96	99.9	0.97	4.99%
	$\sigma = 0.05$	0.95	0.94	0.97	0.97	5.15%
	$\sigma = 0.075$	0.95	0.94	0.95	0.96	5.54%
	$\sigma = 0.1$	0.92	0.94	0.90	0.93	6.10%

5. Conclusions

This study presents a robust unsupervised anomaly detection framework for laminated composite plates, combining GAN-based data augmentation, a self-attention autoencoder, and Gaussian mixture modeling. The proposed model successfully captures complex signal patterns and separates damaged signals with high metric scores. Compared to traditional and deep learning baseline models, SAE-GMM achieves high detection accuracy, low false positive rates, low computational time, and strong generalization under noisy conditions. The attention mechanism enriches the model's capability of separating features, while the Gaussian mixture model (GMM) provides a reliable decision boundary. These obtained results emphasize the proposed model's potential for real-world structural health monitoring applications. For the future, we plan to explore cross-plate validation and real-time deployment further to evaluate scalability and adaptability across diverse composite structures.

Author Contributions: Conceptualization, J.W.S.; methodology, O.M.; writing—original draft preparation, O.M.; writing—review and editing, O.M. and J.W.S.; supervision, J.W.S. All authors have read and agreed to the published version of the manuscript.

Funding: This work was supported by a National Research Foundation of Korea (NRF) grant funded by the Korean Government (Ministry of Science and ICT, MSIT) (No. RS-2023-NR076925, 50%). This work was partly supported by the Institute of Information & Communications Technology Planning & Evaluation (IITP)'s Innovative Human Resource Development for Local Intellectualization program grant funded by the Korea government (MSIT) (IITP-2025-RS-2020-II201612, 50%).

Data Availability Statement: The original contributions presented in this study are included in the article. Further inquiries can be directed to the corresponding author.

Conflicts of Interest: The authors declare no conflicts of interest.

References

1. Liew, K.M.; Pan, Z.Z.; Zhang, L.W. An overview of layerwise theories for composite laminates and structures: Development, numerical implementation and application. *Compos. Struct.* **2019**, *216*, 240–259. [CrossRef]
2. Munyaneza, O.; Yuk, D.-G.; Sohn, J.W. A State-of-art on Damage Detection of Composite Structure Using Lamb Wave and Deep Learning Techniques. *Int. J. Precis. Eng. Manuf.-Smart Technol.* **2025**, *3*, 65–82. [CrossRef]
3. Ahmed, O.; Wang, X.; Tran, M.-V.; Ismadi, M.-Z. Advancements in fiber-reinforced polymer composite materials damage detection methods: Towards achieving energy-efficient SHM systems. *Compos. Part B Eng.* **2021**, *223*, 109136. [CrossRef]
4. Sawant, S.; Sethi, A.; Banerjee, S.; Tallur, S. Unsupervised learning framework for temperature compensated damage identification and localization in ultrasonic guided wave SHM with transfer learning. *Ultrasonics* **2023**, *130*, 106931. [CrossRef] [PubMed]
5. Yang, Z.; Zhang, J.; Xu, H.; Yang, L.; Ma, S.; Wu, Z. Phased Array System for Damage Detection in Plate-Like Structures Based on Single Lamb Wave Mode Extraction. *J. Aerosp. Eng.* **2023**, *36*, 04023004. [CrossRef]
6. Mariani, S.; Kalantari, A.; Kromanis, R.; Marzani, A. Data-driven modeling of long temperature time-series to capture the thermal behavior of bridges for SHM purposes. *Mech. Syst. Signal Process.* **2024**, *206*, 110934. [CrossRef]
7. Yang, Z.; Yang, H.; Tian, T.; Deng, D.; Hu, M.; Ma, J.; Gao, D.; Zhang, J.; Ma, S.; Yang, L.; et al. A review on guided-ultrasonic-wave-based structural health monitoring: From fundamental theory to machine learning techniques. *Ultrasonics* **2023**, *133*, 107014. [CrossRef]
8. Eltouny, K.; Gomaa, M.; Liang, X. Unsupervised Learning Methods for Data-Driven Vibration-Based Structural Health Monitoring: A Review. *Sensors* **2023**, *23*, 3290. [CrossRef]
9. Khan, A.; Kim, H.S. Damage assessment of laminated composites using unsupervised autonomous features. *J. Thermoplast. Compos. Mater.* **2024**, *37*, 2123–2148. [CrossRef]
10. Abbassi, A.; Römgens, N.; Tritschel, F.F.; Penner, N.; Rolfes, R. Evaluation of machine learning techniques for structural health monitoring using ultrasonic guided waves under varying temperature conditions. *Struct. Health Monit.* **2023**, *22*, 1308–1325. [CrossRef]
11. Junges, R.; Rastin, Z.; Lomazzi, L.; Giglio, M.; Cadini, F. Convolutional autoencoders and CGANs for unsupervised structural damage localization. *Mech. Syst. Signal Process.* **2024**, *220*, 111645. [CrossRef]

12. Zhao, P.; Ding, Z.; Li, Y.; Zhang, X.; Zhao, Y.; Wang, H.; Yang, Y. SGAD-GAN: Simultaneous Generation and Anomaly Detection for time-series sensor data with Generative Adversarial Networks. *Mech. Syst. Signal Process.* **2024**, *210*, 111141. [CrossRef]
13. Luleci, F.; Catbas, F.N.; Avci, O. Generative adversarial networks for labeled acceleration data augmentation for structural damage detection. *J. Civ. Struct. Health Monit.* **2023**, *13*, 181–198. [CrossRef]
14. Msigwa, G.; Ntambala, E.; Yun, J. Enhancing atrial fibrillation classification from single-lead electrocardiogram signals using attention-based networks and generative adversarial networks with density-based clustering. *Eng. Appl. Artif. Intell.* **2024**, *133*, 108607. [CrossRef]
15. Dreher, N.R.; Storti, G.C.; Machado, T.H. Machado. Vibration Signal Evaluation Based on K-Means Clustering as a Pre-Stage of Operational Modal Analysis for Structural Health Monitoring of Rotating Machines. *Energies* **2023**, *16*, 7848. [CrossRef]
16. Yu, Y.-F.; Wei, P.; Wu, X.; Feng, Q.; Zhang, C. Discriminative fuzzy K-means clustering with local structure preservation for high-dimensional data. *Knowl.-Based Syst.* **2024**, *304*, 112537. [CrossRef]
17. He, Y.; Chen, X.; Miao, D.; Zhang, H.; Qin, X.; Du, S.; Lu, P. Graph-enhanced anomaly detection framework in multivariate time series using Graph Attention and Enhanced Generative Adversarial Networks. *Expert Syst. Appl.* **2025**, *271*, 126667. [CrossRef]
18. Chen, L.; Jiang, H.; Wang, L.; Li, J.; Yu, M.; Shen, Y.; Du, X. Generative adversarial synthetic neighbors-based unsupervised anomaly detection. *Sci. Rep.* **2025**, *15*, 16. [CrossRef] [PubMed]
19. Ma, C.; Wang, Y.; Li, F.; Zhang, H.; Zhang, Y.; Edalatpanah, S.A. Constructing Attention-LSTM-VAE Power Load Model Based on Multiple Features. *Adv. Math. Phys.* **2024**, *2024*, 1041791. [CrossRef]
20. Roy, M.; Halder, A.; Majumder, S.; Biswas, U. AttentivECGRU: GRU based autoencoder with attention mechanism and automated fuzzy thresholding for ECG arrhythmia detection. *Appl. Soft Comput.* **2024**, *167*, 112337. [CrossRef]
21. Zong, B.; Song, Q.; Min, M.R.; Cheng, W.; Lumezanu, C.; Cho, D.; Chen, H. Deep autoencoding gaussian mixture model for unsupervised anomaly detection. In Proceedings of the 6th International Conference on Learning Representations (ICLR 2018), Vancouver, BC, Canada, 30 April–3 May 2018.
22. Khan, W.; Khan, A.N.; Hasan, M.K.; Khan, A.; Mokhtar, U.A.; Islam, S. DVAEGMM: Dual Variational Autoencoder with Gaussian Mixture Model for Anomaly Detection on Attributed Networks. *IEEE Access* **2022**, *10*, 91160–91176. [CrossRef]
23. Zhou, Y.-C.; Li, M.-Q.; Ji, L.-B. Denoising Deep Autoencoder Gaussian Mixture Model and Its Application for Robust Nonlinear Industrial Process Monitoring. In Proceedings of the 2021 International Conference on Computer Information Science and Artificial Intelligence (CISAI), Kunming, China, 17–19 September 2021; IEEE: New York, NY, USA; pp. 67–73. [CrossRef]
24. Bigoni, C.; Hesthaven, J.S. Simulation-based Anomaly Detection and Damage Localization: An application to Structural Health Monitoring. *Comput. Methods Appl. Mech. Eng.* **2020**, *363*, 112896. [CrossRef]
25. Li, C.; Guo, L.; Gao, H.; Li, Y. Similarity-Measured Isolation Forest: Anomaly Detection Method for Machine Monitoring Data. *IEEE Trans. Instrum. Meas.* **2021**, *70*, 1–12. [CrossRef]
26. Swana, E.F.; Bokoro, P.; Doorsamy, W. Isolation Forest and Local Outlier Factor-Based Anomaly Detection on an Induction Machine. In Proceedings of the 2024 IEEE PES/IAS PowerAfrica, Johannesburg, South Africa, 7–11 October 2024; IEEE: New York, NY, USA; pp. 1–5. [CrossRef]
27. Nizan, O.; Tal, A. k-NNN: Nearest Neighbors of Neighbors for Anomaly Detection. *arXiv* **2023**, arXiv:2305.17695.
28. Komorska, I.; Puchalski, A. Condition Monitoring Using a Latent Space of Variational Autoencoder Trained Only on a Healthy Machine. *Sensors* **2024**, *24*, 6825. [CrossRef]
29. Yang, Z.; Bozchalooi, I.S.; Darve, E. Anomaly Detection with Domain Adaptation. *arXiv* **2020**, arXiv:2006.03689.
30. Ruff, L.; Vandermeulen, R.; Goernitz, N.; Deecke, L.; Siddiqui, S.A.; Binder, A.; Müller, E.; Kloft, M. Deep One-Class Classification. In Proceedings of the 35th International Conference on Machine Learning, Stockholm, Sweden, 10–15 July 2018; Dy, J., Krause, A., Eds.; Volume 80, pp. 4393–4402. Available online: https://proceedings.mlr.press/v80/ruff18a.html (accessed on 5 February 2025).
31. Tuli, S.; Casale, G.; Jennings, N.R. TranAD: Deep Transformer Networks for Anomaly Detection in Multivariate Time Series Data. *arXiv* **2022**, arXiv:2201.07284. [CrossRef]

Σ mathematics

MDPI

Article

Residual Strength Modeling and Reliability Analysis of Wind Turbine Gear under Different Random Loadings

Jianxiong Gao *, Yuanyuan Liu, Yiping Yuan and Fei Heng

School of Mechanical Engineering, Xinjiang University, Urumqi 830046, China
* Correspondence: jianxionggao@xju.edu.cn

Abstract: A novel method is proposed to investigate the pattern of variation in the residual strength and reliability of wind turbine gear. First, the interaction between loads and the effect of the loading sequence is considered based on the fatigue damage accumulation theory, and a residual strength degradation model with few parameters is established. Experimental data from two materials are used to verify the predictive performance of the proposed model. Secondly, the modeling and simulation of the wind turbine gear is conducted to analyze the types of fatigue failures and obtain their fatigue life curves. Due to the randomness of the load on the gear, the rain flow counting method and the Goodman method are employed. Thirdly, considering the seasonal variation of load, the decreasing trend of gear fatigue strength under multistage random load is calculated. Finally, the dynamic failure rate and reliability of gear fatigue failure under multistage random loads are analyzed. The results demonstrate that the randomness of residual strength increases with increasing service time. The seasonality of load causes fluctuations in the reliability of gear, providing a new idea for evaluating the reliability of the wind turbine gear.

Keywords: wind turbine gear; residual strength; reliability; multistage random loads

MSC: 62N05

1. Introduction

The energy resource of wind power generation is green and environmentally friendly, and the reliability of wind turbines has become a hot research topic in recent years. Pérez et al. [1] focused on the failure rate of the wind turbine components and found that the gearbox and blades were the most likely locations to cause faults, and they proposed that state detection can improve the reliability of wind turbines. Kusiak and Li [2] predicted the fault situation of the wind turbine based on data from state detection to ensure its reliability. Chen et al. [3] proposed a transfer condition monitoring based on feature alignment and parameter fine-tuning for more accurate monitoring, which can more accurately identify the status of wind turbines. Dui et al. [4] proposed a resilience optimization model of a multi-component system to determine the degree of influence of components on the reliability of the wind turbine system, thus improving the reliability of the wind turbine system. Su et al. [5] established a stochastic differential equation state model to describe the degradation of wind turbines, preventing wind turbine failure. Research has shown that focusing on the faults and reliability of wind turbine components is necessary to increase the reliability of wind turbines.

Wind turbine gears are one of the core components of the wind turbine system, which transfer power and adjust the wind speed and output torque. If the gear fails, it will directly affect the operating efficiency and output power of the wind turbine, causing the production line to stagnate and resulting in significant losses [6]. Therefore, the reliability of the gear directly affects the reliability of the wind turbine system. The reliability evaluation of wind turbine gears can predict the probability of gear failure and possible failure modes.

It provides necessary information for preventive maintenance of the wind turbine, ensures safe and stable operation of the wind turbine, and can reduce shutdown costs. Reliability-based design optimization methods and control methods to improve the reliability of wind power systems have also been widely recognized and studied in recent years [7–10]. In conclusion, the calculation and analysis of gear reliability are very important.

In order to evaluate the reliability of gears more accurately, it is necessary to fully and realistically consider influencing factors such as gear load cycling and material quality. Wind turbine gears subjected to random load changes will experience fatigue damage, resulting in reduced fatigue strength. The decrease in gear strength will cause the problem of tooth surface wear or fatigue fracture during operation, which will affect the reliability of the gears [11]. The ability of a gear to resist external loads after a certain degree of fatigue damage is defined as the residual strength.

Researchers have proposed a variety of residual strength models. For instance, Schaff and Davidson [12] proposed a general residual strength model of materials, and its key parameters need to be fitted by the experimental data of materials. Based on the hypothesis of Hahn and Kim [13], Chou and Croman [14] established the residual strength model of time by the relationship between strength and life. Ganesan and Joanna [15] considered the effect of the stress ratio of the continuous load on the component and proposed a two-parameter residual strength model of glass-fiber-reinforced polymer. Cheng and Hwu [16] obtained the residual strength degradation trajectory of the composite material based on Schaff's model.

Some researchers have also developed residual strength models for metals, in addition to the residual strength model for composite materials. For instance, in the aspect of damage development, Li et al. [17] established the residual strength degradation model of the material based on a large number of experimental data of 35CrMo. Gao and An [18] developed a residual strength model that requires a small amount of data and takes into account the dispersion of residual strength based on the stress interference theory. Based on the fatigue damage theory and the interval theory, Jiang et al. [19] established a two-parameter residual strength model using experimental data and obtained fuzzy dynamic reliability. In recent years, many researchers have used data-driven methods to predict the degradation of residual strength. For instance, Yang et al. [20] used an artificial neural network to predict the residual strength of composites after impact. Lu et al. [21] used principal component analysis combined with a multi-objective optimization vector machine to predict the residual strength of the pipeline. Miao and Zhao [22] proposed a method of deep extreme machine learning to predict the residual strength of defective pipes. Meng et al. [23] proposed an adaptive Kriging model to improve the efficiency of optimal design for offshore wind turbines.

In summary, most of the residual strength models are used to describe composite materials. Significantly, there is no consistent residual strength model for both composite materials and metal materials. Furthermore, most of the existing residual strength models require a large amount of experimental data to predict. However, many materials or parts require long experimental cycles and high costs. For this, a simple model based on the fatigue damage accumulation theory is proposed, which requires a small number of parameters. The effect of the loading condition, loading sequence, and interaction between loads on strength degradation is fully considered. Moreover, the degradation trajectory of fatigue strength can only be predicted by understanding the fatigue life data of materials or mechanical parts.

Wind energy is an unstable energy source, with variable wind speeds and directions. Variations in wind speed will impact the load on the gear directly. Furthermore, changes in the operational status of the wind turbine will also affect the gear load. From this point of view, the load on the wind turbine gear shows obvious randomness. Actually, the wind load is not completely irregular. The wind speed in different regions varies seasonally, such as in southeastern China, where the wind speed is usually higher during the winter and summer but weaker in autumn [24]. In addition, the wind loads vary in different seasons due to the seasonal nature of the loads applied to the gears of wind turbines. As mentioned above, in order to more closely characterize the residual strength of wind turbine gears and more accurately predict their reliability, the stochastic and seasonal nature of the loads to which they are subjected needs to be fully taken into account.

The remainder of the paper is organized as follows. In Section 2, the boundary conditions of the residual strength model are described, and the existing nonlinear fatigue damage accumulation model is introduced. Based on this model, a residual strength model considering the loading sequence and load interaction is established. The experimental data of two materials are used to validate the proposed residual strength model and compare it with Schaff's model. In Section 3, the main fatigue failure modes of the wind turbine gear are analyzed, and the fatigue life curve of the gear is obtained by modeling and simulation. Then, the statistical analysis of the four-season wind load on the gear is carried out, and the degradation trend of the residual strength of the gear is obtained. In Section 4, the reliability of wind turbine gear is obtained by the Monte Carlo simulation method based on the random stress-residual strength interference theory. Section 5 summarizes some main conclusions and proposes some further study directions.

2. Residual Strength Model of Multistage Loading Based on the Fatigue Damage Accumulation Theory

The strength degradation of materials has always been a hot topic in the field of reliability. The gear will suffer fatigue damage under the continuous action of cyclic loads. From a macro perspective, the fatigue damage of materials can be evaluated by measuring the residual strength changes of the material [25]. Thus, it can be considered that the strength degradation is closely related to the degree of fatigue damage accumulation. Conversely, the trend of residual strength degradation can also be measured by fatigue damage. Based on these theories, the existing nonlinear fatigue cumulative damage theories are introduced. We then explain the boundary conditions of the residual strength model. Finally, a residual strength model for multistage loading is proposed from the perspective of cumulative fatigue damage, and the proposed model is validated.

2.1. Nonlinear Fatigue Damage Accumulation Model

To date, the linear damage accumulation theory proposed by Miner is widely used in engineering, since its form is concise and simple for calculation [26]. With the development of damage theory, it is found that damage is not only related to the size of the load but also to the loading sequence and the interaction between the loads. Due to the fact that fatigue damage of gears is a complex nonlinear process in practical engineering, establishing a nonlinear damage model is more practical. Many researchers have established nonlinear damage accumulation models from different perspectives. Manson and Halford [27] used the damage curve method to establish a nonlinear damage accumulation model. Freudenthal and Heller [28] developed a fatigue damage model considering the interaction between variable amplitude loads. Zhu and Huang [29] established a damage model based on the law of creep. Zhu et al. [30] introduced the energy damage parameter to define uncertain fatigue damage. Risitano et al. [31] quantified fatigue damage accumulation based on the relationship between temperature and loads.

Considering the loading sequence effect, Peng et al. [32] proposed a nonlinear damage accumulation model based on the energy method, which can be formulated as

$$\frac{dD}{dn} = \frac{1}{\ln N_f} \cdot \left(\frac{1}{N_f}\right)^{1-D} \tag{1}$$

where D is fatigue damage, n is the number of load cycles, and N_f is the fatigue life of parts or materials.

The model is verified by 45 steel, 16 Mn steel, and Al-2024 aluminum alloy. It is found that the damage prediction has good accuracy.

By integrating Equation (1), the following expression can be obtained:

$$D = -\frac{\ln\left(1 - \frac{n}{N_f}\right)}{\ln N_f} \tag{2}$$

From the above equation, it can be seen that when $n = 0$, the cumulative damage $D = 0$. When $n = N_f - 1$, the total cumulative damage D reaches 1. If the load is applied once more, the material will fail. Therefore, the material fails when the number of load cycles is N_f [26,33].

2.2. Boundary Conditions of the Residual Strength Model

In general, the residual strength of the material is related to the initial strength of the material, the quality of processing and manufacturing, the loading method of the load, and the size of the load. According to the existing residual strength model [34,35], it can be found that the formula generally satisfies the following two conditions:

(1) The initial residual strength is the static strength of the material.

$$r(0) = \sigma_b \tag{3}$$

where $r(0)$ is the residual strength of the load 0 times and σ_b is the static strength.

(2) When the material or part fails, the residual strength is equal to the peak value of the load.

$$r\left(N_f - 1\right) = S_{\max} \tag{4}$$

where $S_{\max}$ is the maximum value of the load on the part or material.

Among numerous residual strength models, the model proposed by Schaff is quite consistent with various practical situations. Due to the fewer parameters required to determine and its relatively high accuracy, this model is widely used in practical engineering applications. Schaff's model contains two parameters: The initial residual strength and the maximum value of the load, which also meet the boundary conditions of Equations (3) and (4) mentioned above. Therefore, a residual strength model based on Schaff's model [12] is proposed, which can be formulated as

$$r(n) = r(0) - [r(0) - S_{\max}] \cdot Y \tag{5}$$

where Y should make the residual strength expression satisfy the above two boundary conditions, which can be formulated as

$$Y = \begin{cases} 0, & n = 0 \\ 1, & n = N_f - 1 \end{cases} \tag{6}$$

The decrease in residual strength is related to the degree of fatigue damage accumulation. It is also found that D satisfies the condition of Y. Thus, let $D = Y$. We substitute Equation (2) into Equation (5) to obtain the residual strength model considering the loading sequence effect, which can be formulated as

$$r(n) = r(0) - [r(0) - S_{\max}] \cdot \left[-\frac{\ln\left(1 - \frac{n}{N_f}\right)}{\ln N_f} \right] \tag{7}$$

From Equation (7), it can be seen that the proposed residual strength model satisfies the initial state of static strength, and the load on the material at failure is equal to the maximum load. With the increase in loading times n, the residual strength $r(n)$ decreases monotonously. Using this model, the residual strength degradation law of the material under the load can be obtained.

2.3. Residual Strength Model under Multistage Loading

In engineering practice, mechanical components are usually subjected to constantly changing loads. Therefore, it is necessary to consider how to characterize residual strength when loading multistage loads. If the residual strength model of the two-level load is known, then the residual strength model of the multistage load only needs to be analogized on this basis. Therefore, in this paper, we derive the residual strength model expression of two levels for load.

If the first-level loads and the second-level loads are applied separately to the same material, the rate of decline of the two residual strengths will necessarily be different. In other words, there are two different curves. According to the equivalent theory of fatigue damage accumulation, it is necessary to equalize the residual strength of the first-level loads to the residual strength curve of the second-level loads. Therefore, a suitable equivalence formula needs to be established to perform the equivalence of the residual strength under different levels of loading. The equal percentage reduction in residual strength under different loads is defined as the equivalent basis. The percentage expression of the decrease in residual strength can be formulated as

$$P = \frac{r(0) - r(n)}{r(0) - S_{\max}} \tag{8}$$

The percentage of residual strength reduction after the first-level loads is equal to the percentage of residual strength reduction after the second-level loads, which can be formulated as

$$P_1 = P_2 \tag{9}$$

In the theory of fatigue damage accumulation, some researchers considered the interaction between loads [33,36]. The ratio of the two-level load is introduced into the expression of damage equivalence to characterize this influencing factor. In this paper, this theory is also applied to the residual strength equivalent theory, and the load ratio factor is introduced into the equivalent expression. Then, the equivalent residual strength can be formulated as

$$P_1 = P_2^{\frac{\sigma_2}{\sigma_1}} \tag{10}$$

$$\frac{r_1(0) - r_1(n_1)}{r_1(0) - S_{1\max}} = \left[\frac{r_2(0) - r_2(n_2')}{r_2(0) - S_{2\max}}\right]^{\frac{\sigma_2}{\sigma_1}} \tag{11}$$

where n_1 is the number of first-level actions to load, n_2' is the number of times that the residual strength after the first level of loads is equivalent to the second level of loads, and the second level of loads need to be applied. σ_1 is the mean stress of the first level of loads and σ_2 is the mean stress of the second level of loads.

Based on the concept of fatigue damage theory, the residual strength of two levels of load is equivalent. The equivalent loading number n_2' of the second-level load can be obtained and added to the original loading number n_2 of the second-level load to obtain the remaining strength after the second-level load is loaded. Therefore, it is necessary to derive the equivalent loading number n_2' of the second-level load. Substituting the residual strength formula (7) into formula (11) can obtain

$$\frac{r_1(0) - \left\{r_1(0) - [r_1(0) - S_{1\max}] \cdot \left[-\frac{\ln\left(1 - \frac{n_1}{N_{f1}}\right)}{\ln N_{f1}}\right]\right\}}{r_1(0) - S_{1\max}} = \left\{\frac{r_2(0) - \left\{r_2(0) - [r_2(0) - S_{2\max}] \cdot \left[-\frac{\ln\left(1 - \frac{n_2'}{N_{f2}}\right)}{\ln N_{f2}}\right]\right\}}{r_2(0) - S_{2\max}}\right\}^{\frac{\sigma_2}{\sigma_1}} \tag{12}$$

By simplifying Equation (12), the equivalent number of actions $n_2{}'$ can be obtained, which can be formulated as

$$n_2{}' = N_{f2} - N_{f2}^{1+[-\frac{\ln(1-\frac{n_1}{N_{f1}})}{\ln N_{f1}}]^{-\frac{\sigma_1}{\sigma_2}}} \tag{13}$$

The first level of loads are n_1 times, and the residual strength after n_2 times of the second level of loads are equivalent to $n_2{}' + n_2$ times of the second level of loads. The residual strength after two levels of loads can be obtained, which can be formulated as

$$r(n) = r(0) - [r(0) - S_{\max}] \cdot \left\{ -\frac{\ln\left\{1 - \frac{n_2 + N_{f2} - N_{f2}^{1+[-\frac{\ln(1-\frac{n_1}{N_{f1}})}{\ln N_{f1}}]^{-\frac{\sigma_1}{\sigma_2}}}}{N_f}\right\}}{\ln N_f} \right\} \tag{14}$$

In summary, when the material is subjected to the multistage load, the calculation is performed according to the above ideas based on the residual strength equivalent theory.

2.4. Verification of Residual Strength Model

At present, the typical residual strength model is Schaff's model. Due to its few parameters and high precision, it is widely used in practical engineering. The degradation model described by Schaff's model is generally consistent with the actual degradation situation. Therefore, the proposed model is compared with the typical Schaff's model in this section. The materials used to verify model performance include the residual strength data of 45 steel under first-level loading and the experimental data of 30CrMnSiA steel under second-level loading from the published literature [32].

2.4.1. One-Level Loading

45 steel was subjected to a constant amplitude load of 310.37 MPa. The number of load cycles, the experimental residual strength data, the residual strength predicted by Schaff's model, and the residual strength predicted by the proposed model are shown in Table 1.

Table 1. Test results and model prediction of residual strength of 45 steel.

Stress/MPa	Cycle Ratio	Cycles	Experimental Residual Strength/MPa	Schaff's Model/MPa	Proposed Model/MPa
310.37	0	0	1183.26	1183.26	1183.26
	0.2	6970	1180.94	1183.22	1164.65
	0.4	13,940	1179.38	1180.49	1140.65
	0.6	20,970	1067.8	1147.35	1106.49
	0.8	27,900	998.20	967.76	1048.86
	1	34,866	310.37	310.37	310.37

The calculation results of the two models are compared, as shown in Figure 1.

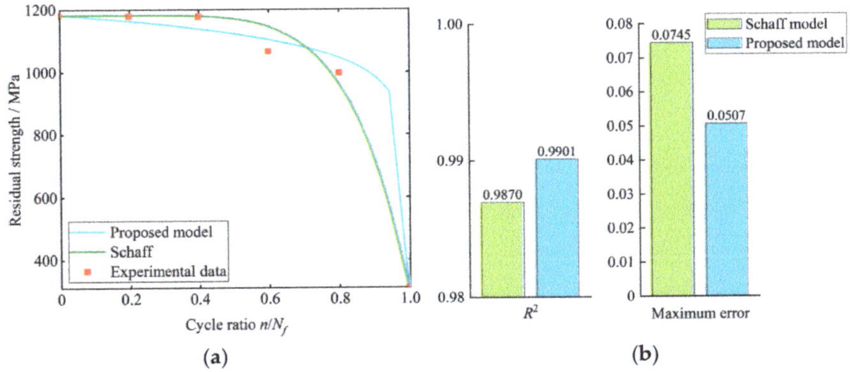

Figure 1. Residual strength prediction results of the proposed model and Schaff's model comparison. (**a**) Residual strength of 45 steel under one-level constant amplitude load; (**b**) goodness of fit and the maximum error of the results predicted by the two models.

In Table 1, it can be seen that the calculation results of Schaff's model are closer to the second and third points of the experiment. However, the overall results of the proposed model perform better predictive performance. In Figure 1, it can be seen that the maximum error of Schaff's model is 7.45% and the maximum error of the proposed model is 5.07%, indicating that the error of the proposed model is closer to the true value. The R^2 of Schaff's model is 0.9870, while the R^2 of the proposed model is 0.9901, indicating that the predicted residual strength of the proposed model fits better with the actual value. Both Schaff's model and the proposed model show a decreasing pattern of strength in their residual strength curves. The residual strength decays slowly in the early stages and decreases abruptly in the later stages, leading to sudden failure of the material.

2.4.2. Two-Level Loading

The experimental data of 30CrMnSiA and aluminum alloy Al-2024 is also used to validate the proposed model [32]. Both materials are subjected to two levels of horizontal loading, and the experimental data of the two materials in different load sequences are shown in Tables 2 and 3.

Table 2. Experimental data of residual life of 30CrMnSiA under two-level loading.

Stress/MPa	Loading Sequence	n_1	$\frac{n_1}{N_{f1}}$	n_2	$\frac{n_2}{N_{f2}}$
732→836	Low→High	13,000	0.233	6602	0.917
		15,000	0.269	6501	0.903
		25,000	0.448	5400	0.750
		35,000	0.628	4428	0.615
		45,000	0.807	3254	0.425
836→732	High→Low	1200	0.167	36,911	0.833
		1800	0.208	32,450	0.792
		3000	0.417	16,002	0.583
		5000	0.694	6969	0.306

Table 3. Experimental data of residual life of aluminum alloy Al-2024 under two-level loading.

Stress/MPa	Loading Sequence	n_1	$\frac{n_1}{N_{f1}}$	n_2	$\frac{n_2}{N_{f2}}$
150→200	Low→High	86,000	0.2	144,500	0.9633
		172,000	0.4	133,500	0.8900
		258,000	0.6	81,700	0.5447
200→150	High→Low	30,000	0.2	28,700	0.5319
		60,000	0.4	101,050	0.2350
		90,000	0.6	76,050	0.1769

Schaff's model and the proposed model are used to calculate the residual strength degradation curve of the material under two levels of sequential loading, as shown in Figures 2 and 3.

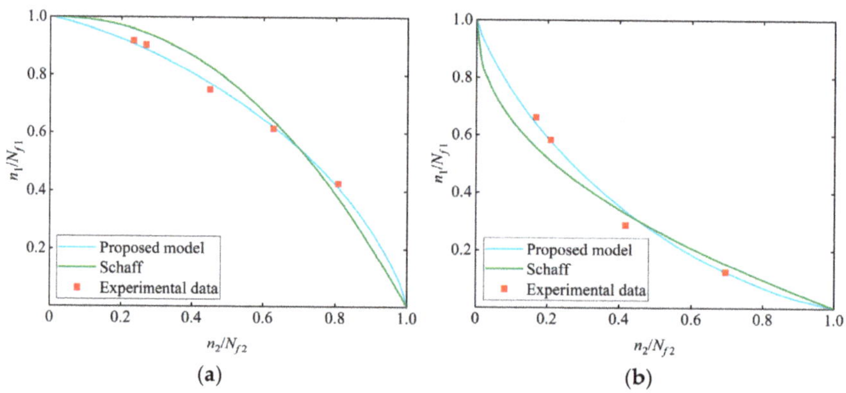

Figure 2. Residual strength of 30CrMnSiA steel with different loading levels. (**a**) Residual strength of 30CrMnSiA steel under low→high loading sequence; (**b**) residual strength of 30CrMnSiA steel under high→low loading sequence.

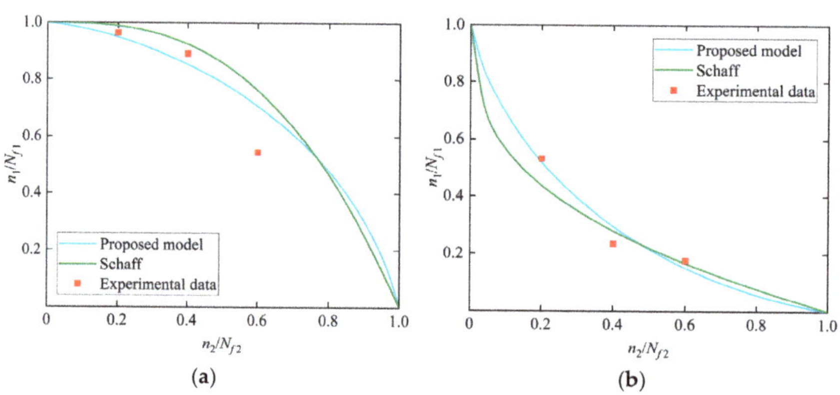

Figure 3. Residual strength of aluminum alloy Al-2024 with different loading levels. (**a**) Residual strength of aluminum alloy Al-2024 under low→high loading sequence; (**b**) residual strength of aluminum alloy Al-2024 under high→low loading sequence.

In order to evaluate the predictive performance of the model, the maximum error and the goodness of fit between the predicted and true values are calculated, as shown in Figures 4 and 5.

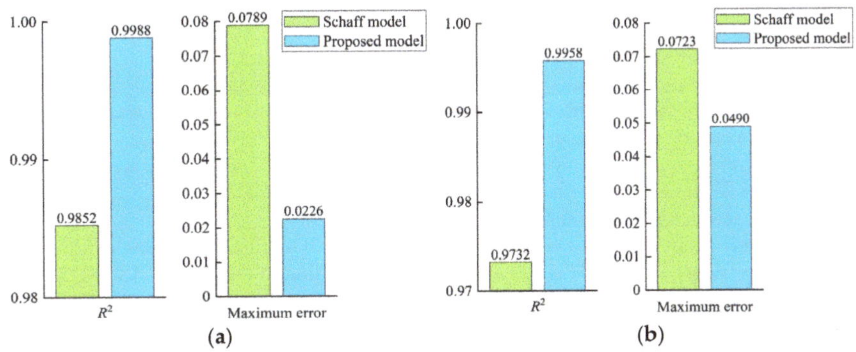

Figure 4. Maximum error and goodness of fit between model predictions and experimental values of 30CrMnSiA. (**a**) low→high loading sequence; (**b**) high→low loading sequence.

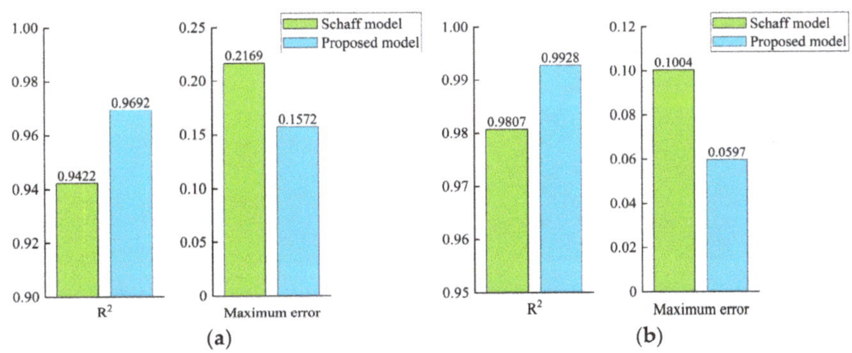

Figure 5. Maximum error and goodness of fit between model predictions and experimental values of aluminum alloy Al-2024. (**a**) low→high loading sequence; (**b**) high→low loading sequence.

From Figures 4 and 5, it can be clearly seen that the R^2 of the proposed model is higher than that of Schaff's model for both materials, regardless of the high-to-low loading order or the low-to-high loading order. The maximum error of the proposed model is smaller than that of Schaff's model. Therefore, it can be considered that the proposed residual strength model has high accuracy for both high-to-low loading and low-to-high loading. Moreover, in Figures 2 and 3, it can be seen that the loading sequence has an impact on the strength degradation trend of the load. Therefore, it is necessary to consider the loading sequence of the load in predicting the trend of strength degradation. The proposed model reflects this influencing factor well, which indicates that it is suitable for residual strength prediction.

3. Modeling of Residual Strength of Wind Turbine Gears

The forms of fatigue failure of gears with different materials and parameters are also different, due to tooth root bending fatigue failure or tooth surface contact fatigue failure [37]. Therefore, it is necessary to analyze whether the maximum stress on the gear occurs at the bending of the tooth root or at the contact of the tooth surface. In addition, the proposed residual strength model requires the S-N curve of the gear, and the S-N curve of the material is different from the S-N curve of the part. If the S-N curve of the gear material is used directly for the calculation of the residual strength, there will be a greater deviation in the calculation results. Therefore, it is necessary to obtain the force analysis and S-N curve of the gear by experimental or simulation methods.

3.1. Fatigue Failure Mode Analysis of Gears and Fatigue Life Curve Fitting

It is a common research method to analyze the force on machine parts by software simulation. Some researchers compared the simulation results of fatigue analysis software or finite element software with experimental results [38,39]. It is proven that software simulation tools can quickly obtain the stress and fatigue life results of components, which have certain reference significance. Furthermore, it significantly reduces the analysis cycle time and cost. Thus, computer simulation technology can be used to efficiently and quickly complete the stress analysis and fatigue life analysis of gears.

The working principle of the gear fatigue testing machine is simulated, and the Workbench software is used for static simulation. The version of the Workbench is 2022 R1. The first step is to simplify the model appropriately, and single-tooth loading is adopted. In order to eliminate the impact of non-critical components on the simulation results, the model is simplified based on the working principle of the fatigue testing machine. Moreover, only a portion of the gear and support heads are retained, as shown in Figure 6.

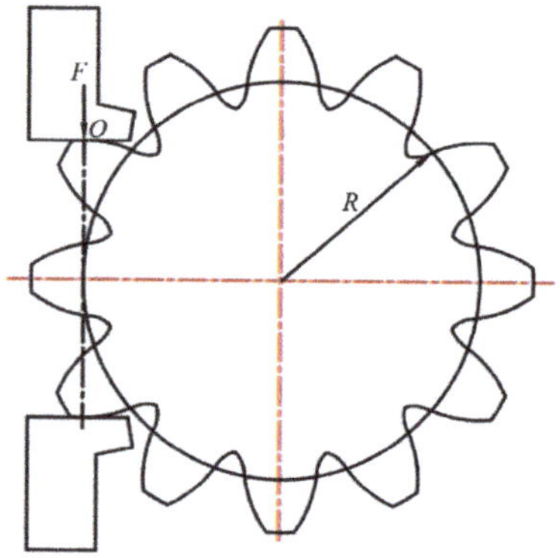

Figure 6. Simplified structure diagram of gear fatigue testing machine.

According to experimental principles, the position of the load action is set at the intersection point O between the tangent line of the gear base circle and the tooth profile. The loading direction F of the load is the perpendicular downward direction of the normal tooth profile passing through point O.

The simulation analysis process is as follows:

(1) Establish a three-dimensional model as shown in Figure 7.
(2) Set the material parameters. The elastic modulus of the material 20CrMnTi is 207 GPa, Poisson's ratio is 0.25, the hardness is 40 HB, and the tensile strength is 2747 MPa. Considering the influence of the deformation of the contact head on the simulation results, it is set as a rigid body.
(3) Mesh generation. Firstly, the whole mesh is divided by a multi-zone. Then, the contact surface between the gear and the upper and lower support heads is densified locally, and the mesh of the tooth root part is refined.
(4) Set the contact type. In the part of the contact between the support head and the tooth surface, the contact is not separated.
(5) Set loads and boundary conditions. The upper support head only retains the movement of the z-axis. Fully fixed constraints are applied to the lower support head. The inner hole of the gear only retains the rotational freedom of the y-axis. A vertical downward load is applied to the upper end of the upper support head. Five groups of loads are set up, which are 200 KN, 400 KN, and 600 KN, respectively. In this study, the simulation results of 400 KN are employed to illustrate the results.

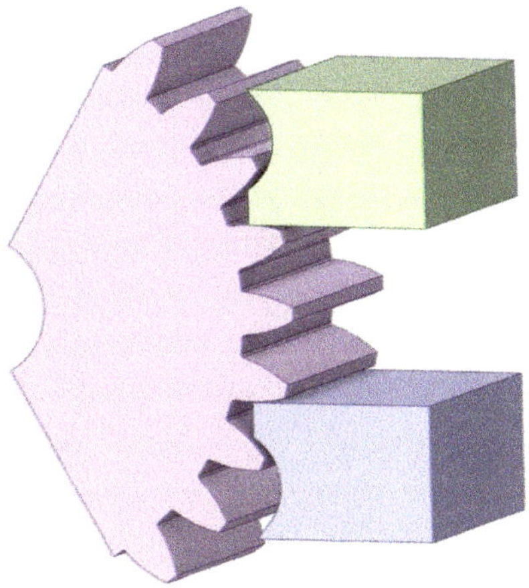

Figure 7. Results of the three-dimensional model establishment.

The equivalent stress cloud diagram of the gear obtained by the software is shown in Figure 8.

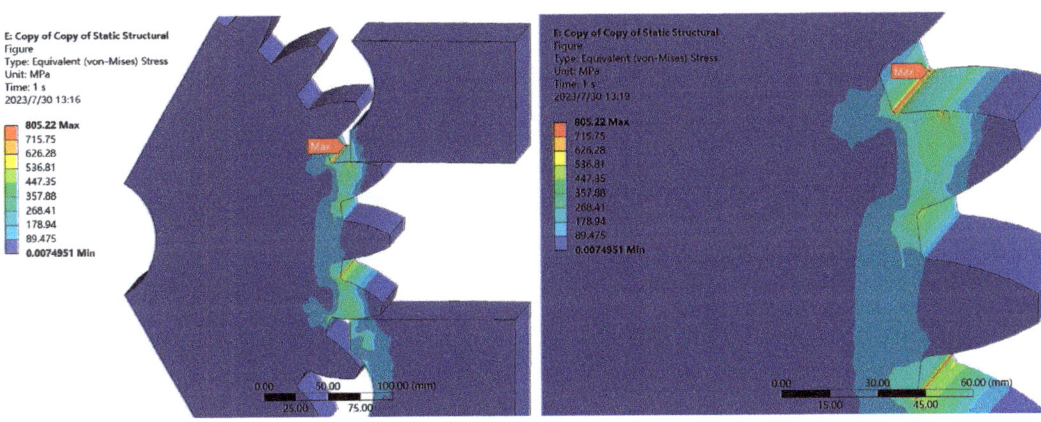

Figure 8. Equivalent stress cloud map of gear.

The static analysis shows that the maximum equivalent stress of the gear is 805.22 Mpa on the side of the tooth root. From the results of modeling and simulation, it can be concluded that the main failure form of the gear is tooth root bending fatigue failure. The accuracy of the model is evaluated by theoretical calculation. According to the calculation formula of tooth root bending fatigue stress in the published literature [40], when the gear is subjected to the tangential load of 400 KN, the bending stress of the tooth root is 809.47 Mpa. The theoretical calculation value is close to the simulation value, so it can be considered that the model is reasonable and can be used for subsequent life analysis. Finally, using Ncode (2022 R1) software analysis and setting the load as symmetric cyclic stress loading, the stress ratio is -1. Then the life values of each point at the tooth root can be obtained. The cloud diagram is illustrated in Figure 9.

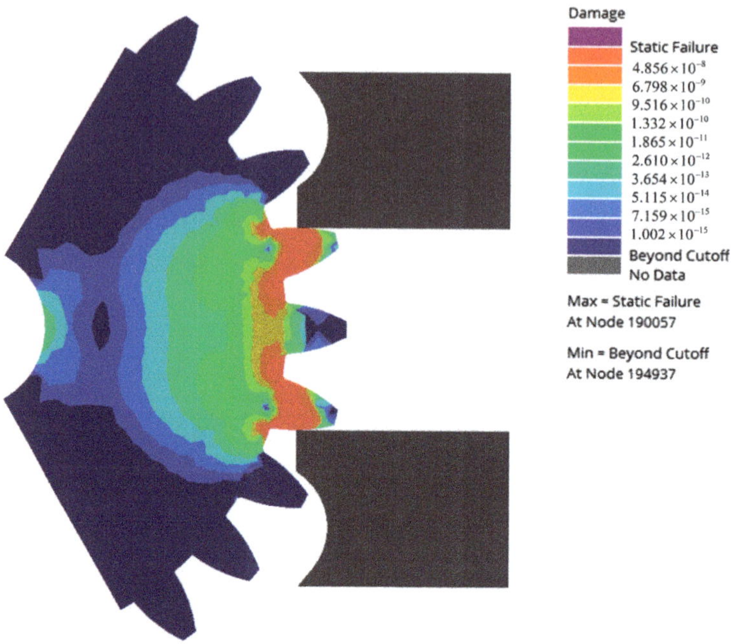

Figure 9. Life cloud map of gear.

Points are taken at the location of the maximum stress at the root bends under multi-stage load, and the stress and life value of each point are taken. Thus, the stress life curve of the gear can be drawn, as shown in Figure 10.

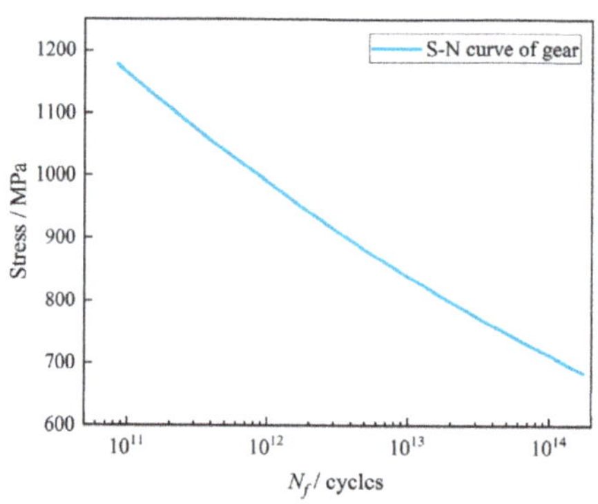

Figure 10. S-N curve of gear.

3.2. Bending Stress Distribution of Gear under Four-Season Loads

The strength degradation is closely related to the load level. It is very necessary to appreciate the bending stress of the gear when calculating the degradation path of the bending strength of the gear. In the natural environment, the wind load on the wind turbine is random, so the bending stress of the gear is also random. In this section, random stress is converted into regular stress that can be directly used for calculation. Taking a wind speed of 78 m as an example [41], the bending stress of the tooth root of the gear is calculated and the residual strength trajectory is analyzed.

3.2.1. The Bending Stress of Gear Is Calculated by Wind Speed

The force on the gear of the wind turbine is determined by the wind speed at the location of the wind turbine. The Weibull distribution is generally used to describe the wind speed [42]. The mean wind speed and variance of the four seasons are known. Then, the calculation formulas of the shape parameter f and scale parameter g of the Weibull distribution can be formulated as [43]

$$f = \left(\frac{\sqrt{H(v)}}{E(v)} \right)^{-1.086} \tag{15}$$

$$g = \frac{E(v)}{\Gamma\left(\frac{1}{f} + 1\right)} \tag{16}$$

where v is the random wind speed, $H(v)$ is the variance of the random wind speed, and $E(v)$ is the mean value of the random wind speed.

The shape and scale parameters of the Weibull distribution of the four seasons are calculated using Equations (15) and (16) based on the known mean and variance of wind speed in reference [36]. The estimated calculation results of the wind speed mean, variance, and distribution parameters are shown in Table 4.

Table 4. List of wind speed information.

Season	Average of Wind Speed/m·s^{-1}	Variance of Wind Speed/m^2·s^{-2}	Scale Parameter g	Shape Parameter f
Spring	5.48	18	5.95	1.32
Summer	6.92	11.6	7.70	1.56
Autumn	11.81	26.54	13.28	1.78
Winter	8.63	19.12	9.57	1.51

The torque of the gear can be obtained from the random wind speed [44]. According to the torque of the gear, the tangential load can be easily obtained. Then, the bending stress of the gear is calculated. The bending stress can be formulated as [40]

$$\sigma = \frac{K_A K_V K_\beta K_\alpha F_t}{bm} Y_F Y_S Y_\varepsilon Y_\beta \tag{17}$$

where K_A is the service coefficient, K_V is the dynamic load coefficient, K_β is the tooth load distribution coefficient, K_α is the tooth load distribution coefficient, F_t is the circumferential force on the pitch circle of the end face, b is the smaller tooth width in meshing gears, m is the normal modulus, Y_F is the tooth profile coefficient under the load and addendum, Y_S is the stress correction coefficient under the action of the load and tooth tip, Y_ε is the coefficient of the coincidence degree, and Y_β is the helix angle coefficient.

The tooth width of the sun gear is 170 mm, and its normal modulus is 16 [45]. The parameter values in the calculation formula of gear bending stress are shown in Table 5.

Table 5. Relevant parameters for calculating bending stress of tooth root.

Parameters	Mean Value	Standard Error	Parameters	Mean Value	Standard Error
K_A	1.1	0.036	Y_F	2.21	0.073
K_V	1.15	0.035	Y_F	1.64	0.066
K_β	1.32	0.02	Y_ε	0.78	0
K_α	1.01	0.003	Y_β	1	0

Thus, the gear bending stress of four seasons can be obtained, as shown in Figure 11.

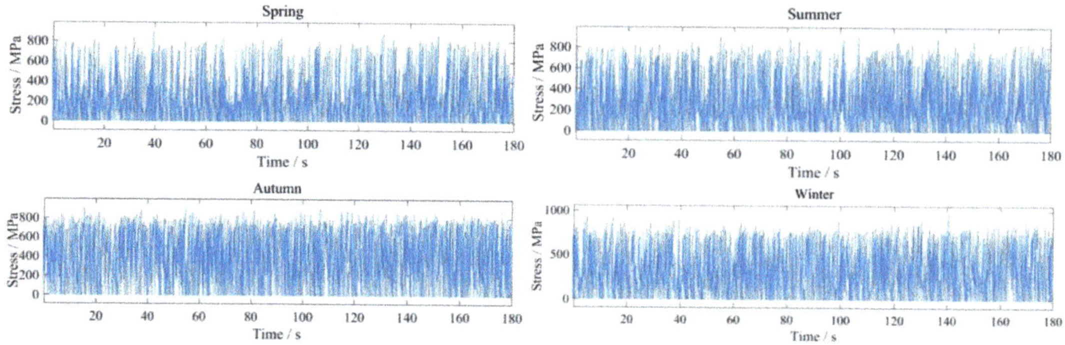

Figure 11. Root bending stress in 180 s in four seasons.

3.2.2. Random Stress Is Treated as Symmetrical Cyclic Stress

The stress calculated by the random wind load in each season is random stress, which is also known as variable amplitude stress. The proposal of the residual strength model is based on the concept of fatigue damage, which requires the stress life curve of gear for residual strength model calculation. The S-N curve of the gear is simulated and fitted under symmetric cyclic loading with a load stress ratio of −1. Therefore, it is necessary to convert the actual random load into a symmetric load, as shown in Figure 12.

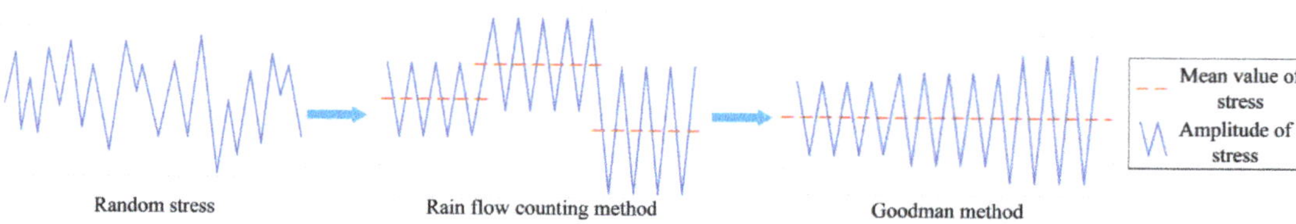

Figure 12. Flow chart of stress treatment.

First, the rain flow counting method is used to perform cyclic counting of stresses with the same mean and amplitude [46]. Then, the Goodman method is used to unify the stress ratios of each group, and the equivalent stresses for four seasons can be obtained. By fitting the distribution of equivalent force, it can be used to calculate residual strength.

After processing the four seasons' loads using the rain flow counting method, the following results can be obtained, as shown in Figure 13.

The mean stress of the load obtained by the rain flow counting method is usually not equal to 0, which means the stress ratio is not equal to −1. This problem can also be observed from the two-dimensional load spectrum, as shown in Figure 13. Therefore, in order to effectively estimate the fatigue life of gear using S-N curves, it is necessary to convert the mean and amplitude of each level of load in the two-dimensional load spectrum into equivalent loads corresponding to the S-N curve [47]. Further processing of seasonal loads was carried out according to Goodman's fatigue empirical formula

$$S = \frac{\sigma_d}{\sigma_d - S_m} \tag{18}$$

where S is the equivalent load, σ_d is the tensile strength, S_a is the amplitude of the load, and S_m is the mean load.

In general, the stress distribution of the gear can be fitted using the Weibull distribution [48]. Therefore, a two-parameter Weibull distribution fitting is performed on the equivalent stress of the four seasons, and the cumulative probability density function is used to represent the fitting effect. The fitting results of equivalent stress in four seasons are shown in Figure 14.

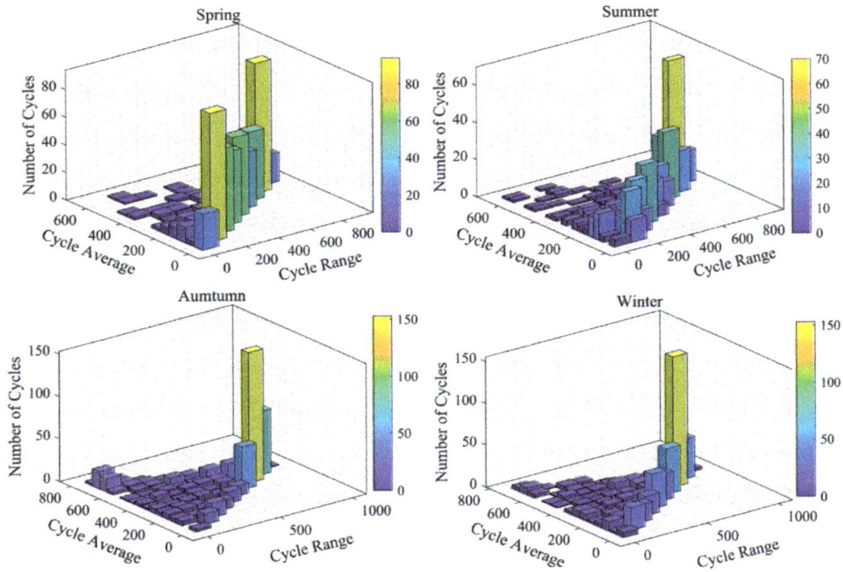

Figure 13. Resulting diagram of the rain flow counting method.

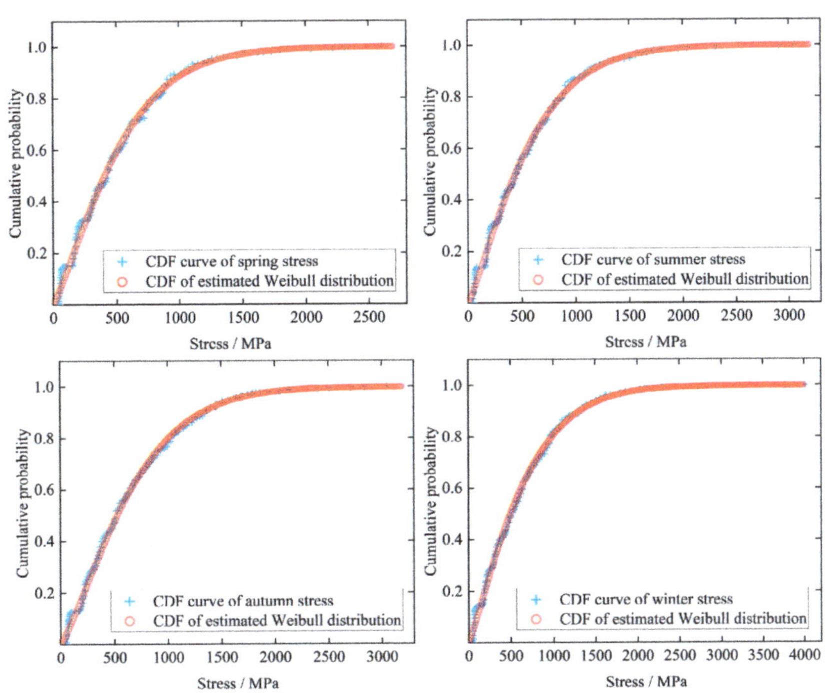

Figure 14. CDF fitting diagrams of equivalent stress for four seasons.

The results show that the CDF of the Weibull distribution almost coincides with the CDF of equivalent stress samples. The estimated values of Weibull distribution parameters for stress in each season are shown in Table 6.

Table 6. Weibull distribution fitting results of equivalent stress in four seasons.

Season	Scale Parameter h of Weibull Distribution	Shape Parameter j of Weibull Distribution
Spring	1.28	550.97
Summer	1.27	600.17
Autumn	1.32	704.99
Winter	1.25	679.85

In summary, by fitting the random stress with a mean of 0, the bending stress distribution of the gear in spring, summer, autumn, and winter is obtained.

4. Analysis of the Residual Strength and Dynamic Reliability of Gear

In general, the strength degradation of machine parts and materials is closely related to the properties of the materials and the loads to which they are subjected. The load on the wind turbine gear is random. The uncertainty of the load makes the strength degradation uncertain. The randomness of strength degradation makes the reliability analysis and prediction of mechanical structures more complex and difficult. Therefore, in order to better predict wind turbine gear bending failure, it is necessary to fully consider the randomness of strength degradation. In this section, the residual strength variation trend and dynamic reliability of gear under multistage random loads in spring, summer, autumn, and winter are calculated and analyzed.

4.1. Residual Strength Model for Tooth Root Bending Strength

If the equivalent stress of a season is considered a one-level load, then the gear will be subjected to four-level loads every year, in the order of spring, summer, autumn, and winter. After each level of load is applied, Equation (14) needs to be used for residual strength equivalence, and then the residual strength after the next level of load is calculated. The corresponding life after n times of bending stress is also the random variable that follows a certain distribution, so the residual strength has randomness at the determined time t. Next, we calculate the residual strength of the gear according to Equations (7) and (14) for residual strength. However, it is difficult to calculate the residual strength of the gear under such a multistage random load using conventional probability methods. Therefore, the Monte Carlo method is used to deal with such problems because of its good adaptability and randomness. It can be applied to address various problems and can simulate the relationship between a variety of complex probability distributions and random variables [49,50]. As the number of simulations increases, the simulation results are closer to the real situation and can provide more accurate estimates [51]. The flowchart for calculating the residual strength of gear using the Monte Carlo method is shown in Figure 15.

We calculate the residual strength at the end of each season and obtain the residual strength path of the gear within 15 years. The calculation results are shown in Figure 16.

In Figure 16, it can be seen that the residual strength of the gear shows the degradation trend over time. Due to the randomness of stress, the residual strength of the gear also represents randomness. At time t, the residual strength of the gear is not a fixed value but a random variable that follows a distribution. As the service life increases, the range of gear residual strengths gradually widens. In order to better describe the law of the residual strength of gear, the distribution of the residual strength is fitted for each season. In general, a two-parameter Weibull distribution can be used to describe the residual strength distribution after any given fatigue cycle [16]. The Q-Q and CDF tests show that the residual intensity at the end of each season follows a Weibull distribution. Taking the spring residual strength of the first year as an example, the shape parameter of the fitted

Weibull distribution is 34,678.07, and its scale parameter is 3746.73. The test results of the Q-Q chart are shown in Figure 17.

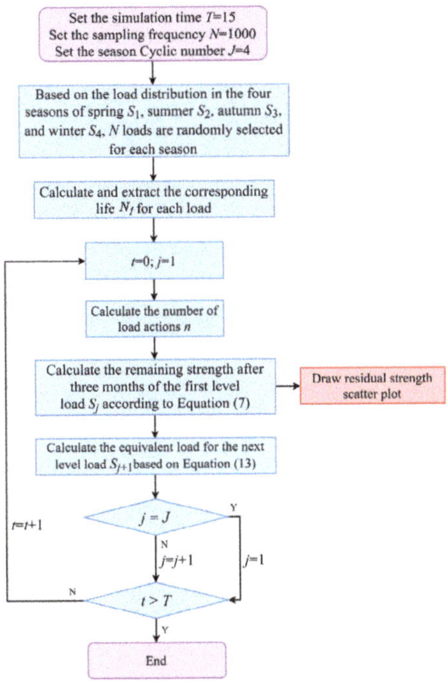

Figure 15. Flowchart for calculating residual strength.

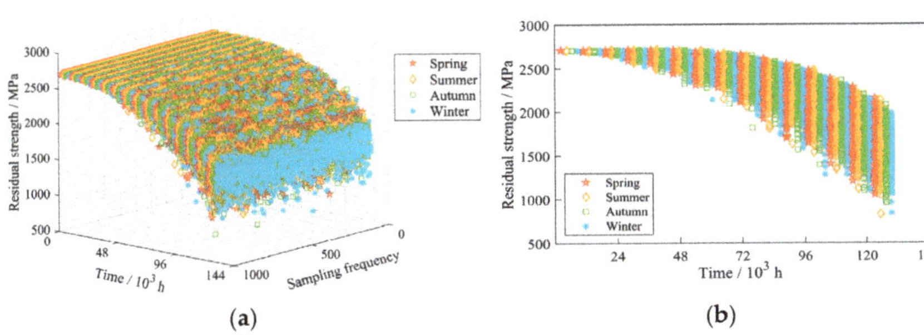

Figure 16. Residual strength path of gear with randomness. (**a**) Three-dimensional diagram of residual strength; (**b**) two-dimensional diagram of residual strength.

The fitted Weibull distribution is close to the actual residual strength quantile and the Q-Q plot is in a straight line, and R^2 between each quantile and the diagonal is 0.9938. From the non-parametric CDF test, it can be seen that the maximum vertical difference between the actual data and the fitted data is very small, and the two CDF curves almost coincide. Therefore, it can be considered that using the Weibull distribution to fit the residual strength at time t is reasonable.

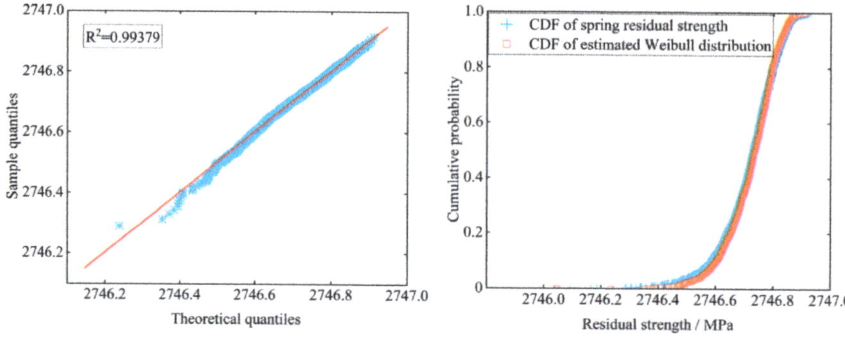

(a) **(b)**

Figure 17. Weibull distribution test of spring residual strength. (**a**) Q-Q diagram of distribution test; (**b**) test of cumulative distribution function.

Since the residual strength of time t can be described by the Weibull distribution, the distribution of residual strength changing with time can be described by the Weibull distribution of parameters changing with time. After obtaining the scale and shape parameters of the Weibull distribution fitted by residual strength at the end of each season, the variation of the parameters over time is analyzed. The fitting results of parameters over time are shown in Figure 18.

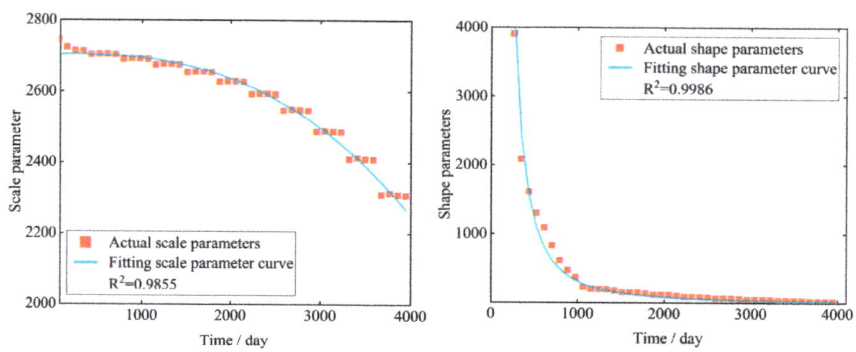

(a) **(b)**

Figure 18. Curve fitting of shape and scale parameters over time. (**a**) Fitting result of scale parameters; (**b**) fitting result of shape parameters.

The coefficient of determination of scale parameters is 0.9855 and the coefficient of determination of the shape parameter is 0.9986. Both values are very close to 1, indicating that the fitting result is relatively suitable. Therefore, the residual strength of gears follows a two-parameter Weibull distribution, and the scale parameter k and shape parameter w at time t can be formulated as

$$k = -6.901 \times 10^{-8} t^{2.725} + 2706 \tag{19}$$

$$w = 2.863 \times 10^{8} t^{-1.984} \tag{20}$$

4.2. Gear Reliability Analysis Considering the Failure of Tooth Root Bending

There are many methods for reliability analysis. For instance, Huang et al. [52] combined the chi-square approximation and numerical integration methodologies to calculate the reliability of positioning accuracy. Li et al. [53] used a Bayesian copula network based on a fuzzy rough set to evaluate and make decisions. Yazdi et al. [54] used an improved fault tree method to analyze reliability. Yan et al. [55] evaluated the reliability of multiple failure modes based on the method of failure modes and effects criticality analysis. The performance of mechanical components usually varies over time and there are multiple failure modes. Yu et al. [56–59] have studied the time-varying reliability calculation method for complex products. In this section, in addition to calculating the static reliability of gears for four seasons, the time-varying reliability of gears is also considered.

The stress level of gear varies in different seasons, and it can be assumed that the stress distribution of the four seasons does not change with the increase in gear operating years. In other words, within the prediction of 15 years, it can be assumed that the stress level remains constant throughout the four seasons of each year. Without taking into account the degradation in the strength of the gear, the stress–strength interference theory suggests that the reliability of the gear in the same season will remain the same regardless of the year. According to the calculation, the reliability of gears at the end of spring, summer, autumn, and winter is 0.9995, 0.9988, 0.9973, and 0.9964, respectively. It can be seen that the reliability of gear is the highest in spring.

When considering the strength degradation of a gear, the stress on the gear is a seasonal distribution, and the remaining strength of the gear is a temporal distribution. Based on the stress strength interference theory, the criterion for gear failure is that if the residual strength is less than the random load, the gear will fail. The reliability and failure rate results are calculated by the Monte Carlo method, as shown in Figures 19 and 20.

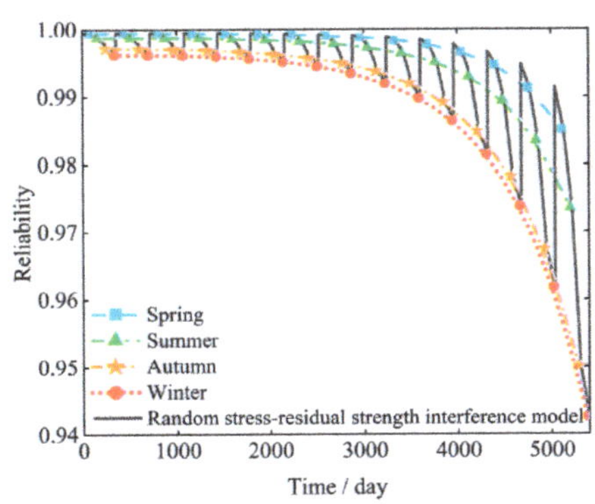

Figure 19. Reliability variation result of gear.

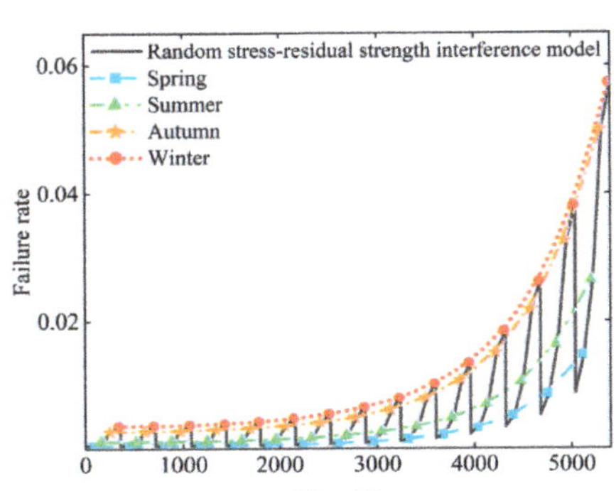

Figure 20. Failure rate variation result of gear.

In Figures 19 and 20, it can be seen that the reliability of gear does not monotonically decrease over time but rather has a significant span from the end of winter to the end of spring each year. Although the decreasing trend of residual strength is continuous, the load on the gear varies from season to season as a result of the influence of stress levels. The explanation diagram of the reliability jump is shown in Figure 21.

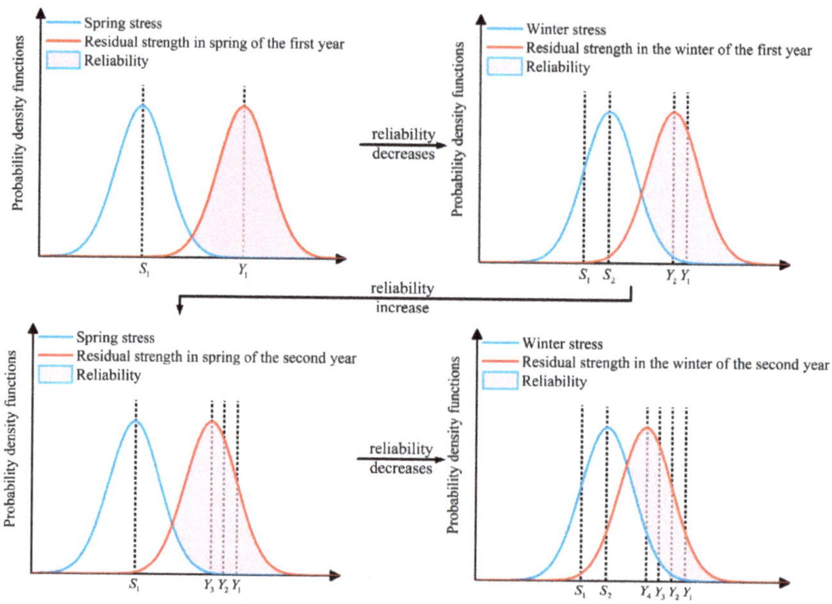

Figure 21. Explanation diagram of reliability jump.

The remaining strength of the gear gradually decreases over time. The strength of the gear at the end of spring in the first year is Y_1, and after one year of service, the strength of the gear at the end of winter in the second year is Y_4. The stress level S_1 of gear in spring is lower than the stress level S_2 in winter. The stress level is only related to the season and does not change with the increase in service life. The strength Y_1 at the end of spring in the first year is higher than the strength Y_2 at the end of winter in the first year. Under the influence of stress and strength, the reliability of spring in the first year is higher than that of winter. The residual strength Y_3 at the end of spring in the second year is lower than the strength Y_2 in winter in the first year, but the stress level S_1 in spring is much lower than the stress level S_2 in winter. The reliability at the end of spring in the second year will be higher than that at the end of winter in the first year.

As mentioned above, it can be concluded that the differences in stress levels among different seasons have a significant impact on gear reliability. The reliability trend over the four seasons is determined by both the stress level and residual strength of the gear concurrently. In the spring of each year, the reliability of the gear is the highest, since the load on the gear is the smallest, and the residual strength of the gear is the highest. This result is consistent with the reliability results of the gear without considering strength degradation. The changes in stress levels throughout the four seasons do not make the reliability of gear monotonically decrease over time, but rather experience a sudden increase in reliability.

By observing the variation pattern of reliability at the same stress level, the following three aspects can be determined:

- The overall decreasing trend of reliability is determined by the degradation trend of gear strength. The gear's reliability in each season decreases monotonically from year to year, which indicates that the reliability of the gear has decreased compared to the previous year in all seasons. Due to the sudden increase in the decay rate of the residual strength, the reliability of the gear suddenly decreases rapidly in the 15th year.

- By observing the distance between the four seasonal reliability curves, it can be found that the distance between the summer and autumn reliability curves is the largest, the distance between the spring and summer curves ranks second, and the distance between the autumn and winter curves is the smallest. It can be considered that the impact of load amplitudes in the four seasons causes a change in the distance between the reliability curves of adjacent seasons. In Table 4, it can be seen that there is a significant difference in load amplitudes between summer and autumn, resulting in a significant downward shift in the reliability curve from summer to autumn. The difference in amplitude between autumn and winter loads is the smallest, so the overall downward movement of the reliability curve from autumn to winter is relatively small.
- The difference in reliability between the four seasons is relatively small in the first few years. In the first nine years, the reliability of gears fluctuated between 1 and 0.99 per year. As the service life increases, the reliability difference of the gear in the four seasons of the same year becomes increasingly significant. In the 15th year, the reliability fluctuation range of the gear within one year is 0.99 to 0.94. This is affected by the randomness of decreasing residual gear strength. As time passes, the range of residual gear strength increases, resulting in a greater range of changes in gear reliability throughout the year.

5. Conclusions

In this study, from the perspective of fatigue damage accumulation, a residual strength model is established that considers the interaction of multistage loading and the influence of loading sequence. The load characteristics of wind turbine gears are focused, and the randomness and regularity of load level fluctuations throughout the four seasons are considered. Furthermore, the residual strength and dynamic reliability of wind turbine gears under multistage random load levels are calculated. Overall, the main conclusions can be summarized as follows:

(1) The proposed residual strength model is validated using experimental data from two materials, and the calculation results showed that the proposed model has good predictive performance. In addition, by comparing its predictive performance with the classical Schaff's model, it can be concluded that the proposed model can more accurately predict the residual strength of wind turbine gears.

(2) The residual strength of the gear at a determined time point is a random variable that follows the Weibull distribution and is affected by the randomness of the load. The overall residual strength of the gear shows a decreasing trend. Moreover, the randomness of the residual strength of the gear at a certain time becomes stronger, and the range of residual strength values becomes wider as the service time increases.

(3) Wind load amplitudes in each season influence the reliability of wind turbine gears. Initially, there is a small difference in reliability between seasons, but as the service time increases, the difference becomes more significant. Overall, the reliability of gears decreases monotonically over time in each season. However, there is a jump in reliability due to the effect of wind speed on the gears in different seasons.

Author Contributions: Methodology, software, investigation, writing—review and editing, funding acquisition, J.G.; formal analysis, software, original draft preparation, Y.L.; investigation, writing—review and editing, supervision, Y.Y.; data curation, writing—original draft preparation, F.H. All authors have read and agreed to the published version of the manuscript.

Funding: This work was supported by the National Natural Science Foundation of China (Grant No. 52065062), Fundamental Research Funds for Universities in Xinjiang Uygur Autonomous Region (Grant No. XJEDU2023P007), the Natural Science Foundation of Xinjiang Uygur Autonomous Region

(Grant No. 2020D01C056), and the Key Research and Development Program of Xinjiang Uygur Autonomous Region (Grant No. 2021B01003).

Institutional Review Board Statement: Not applicable.

Informed Consent Statement: Not applicable.

Data Availability Statement: Not applicable.

Conflicts of Interest: The authors declare no conflict of interest.

References

1. Pérez, J.M.P.; Márquez, F.P.G.; Tobias, A.; Papaelias, M. Wind turbine reliability analysis. *Renew. Sustain. Energy Rev.* **2013**, *23*, 463–472. [CrossRef]
2. Kusiak, A.; Li, W.Y. The prediction and diagnosis of wind turbine faults. *Renew. Energy* **2011**, *36*, 16–23. [CrossRef]
3. Chen, S.; Qiao, Z.J.; Xie, C.Y.; Zhu, R.H.; Lai, Z.H.; Xu, X.F.; Zhou, S.T. Transfer condition monitoring across wind turbines using feature alignment and parameter fine-tuning. *Meas. Sci. Technol.* **2023**, *34*, 125901. [CrossRef]
4. Dui, H.; Wang, X.; Zhou, H. Redundancy-based resilience optimization of multi-component systems. *Mathematics* **2023**, *11*, 3151. [CrossRef]
5. Su, H.; Zhao, Y.; Wang, X. Analysis of a state degradation model and preventive maintenance strategies for wind turbine generators based on stochastic differential equations. *Mathematics* **2023**, *11*, 2608. [CrossRef]
6. Costa, Á.M.; Orosa, J.A.; Vergara, D.; Fernández-Arias, P. New tendencies in wind energy operation and maintenance. *Appl. Sci.* **2021**, *11*, 1386. [CrossRef]
7. Meng, D.B.; Yang, S.Y.; De Jesus, A.M.P.; Zhu, S.P. A novel Kriging-model-assisted reliability-based multidisciplinary design optimization strategy and its application in the offshore wind turbine tower. *Renew. Energy* **2023**, *203*, 407–420. [CrossRef]
8. Meng, D.B.; Yang, S.Y.; Lin, T.; Wang, J.P.; Yang, H.F.; Lv, Z.Y. RBMDO using Gaussian mixture model-based second-order mean-value saddlepoint approximation. *CMES-Comp. Model. Eng. Sci.* **2022**, *132*, 553–568. [CrossRef]
9. Meng, D.B.; Yang, S.Y.; He, C.; Wang, H.T.; Lv, Z.Y.; Guo, Y.P.; Nie, P. Multidisciplinary design optimization of engineering systems under uncertainty: A review. *Int. J. Struct. Integr.* **2022**, *13*, 565–593. [CrossRef]
10. Mseddi, A.; Naifar, O.; Rhaima, M.; Mchiri, L.; Makhlouf, A.B. Robust Control for Torque Minimization in Wind Hybrid Generators: An H_∞ Approach. *Mathematics* **2023**, *11*, 3557. [CrossRef]
11. Yan, Y. Load characteristic analysis and fatigue reliability prediction of wind turbine gear transmission system. *Int. J. Fatigue* **2020**, *130*, 105259. [CrossRef]
12. Schaff, J.R.; Davidson, B.D. Life prediction methodology for composite structures. Part I—Constant amplitude and two-stress level fatigue. *J. Compos. Mater.* **1997**, *31*, 128–157. [CrossRef]
13. Hahn, H.T.; Kim, R.Y. Proof testing of composite materials. *J. Compos. Mater.* **1975**, *9*, 297–311. [CrossRef]
14. Chou, P.C.; Croman, R. Residual strength in fatigue based on the strength-life equal rank assumption. *J. Compos. Mater.* **1978**, *12*, 177–194. [CrossRef]
15. Ganesan, C.; Joanna, P.S. Fatigue life and residual strength prediction of GFRP composites: An experimental and theoretical approach. *Lat. Am. J. Solids Struct.* **2018**, *15*, e72. [CrossRef]
16. Cheng, H.C.; Hwu, F.S. Fatigue reliability analysis of composites based on residual strength. *Adv. Compos. Mater.* **2006**, *15*, 385–402. [CrossRef]
17. Li, L.; Xie, L.Y.; He, X.H.; Hao, G.B. Strength degradation law of metallic material under fatigue loading. *Chin. J. Mech. Eng.* **2010**, *32*, 967–971.
18. Gao, J.; An, Z. A new probability model of residual strength of material based on interference theory. *Int. J. Fatigue* **2019**, *118*, 202–208. [CrossRef]
19. Jiang, C.J.; Liu, X.T.; Wang, X.L.; Wang, X.; Su, S.C. Interval dynamic reliability analysis of mechanical components under multistage load based on strength degradation. *Qual. Reliab. Eng. Int.* **2021**, *37*, 567–582. [CrossRef]
20. Yang, B.; Fu, K.K.; Lee, J.; Li, Y. Artificial neural network (ANN)-based residual strength prediction of carbon fibre reinforced composites (CFRCs) after impact. *Appl. Compos. Mater.* **2021**, *28*, 809–833. [CrossRef]
21. Lu, H.F.; Xu, Z.D.; Iseley, T.; Matthews, J.C. Novel data-driven framework for predicting residual strength of corroded pipelines. *J. Pipeline Syst. Eng. Pract.* **2021**, *12*, 04021045. [CrossRef]
22. Miao, X.; Zhao, H. Novel method for residual strength prediction of defective pipelines based on HTLBO-DELM model. *Reliab. Eng. Syst. Saf.* **2023**, *237*, 109369. [CrossRef]
23. Meng, D.B.; Yang, S.Y.; De Jesus, A.M.P.; Ferradosaet, T.F.; Zhu, S.P. A novel hybrid adaptive Kriging and water cycle algorithm for reliability-based design and optimization strategy: Application in offshore wind turbine monopile. *Comput. Methods Appl. Mech. Eng.* **2023**, *412*, 116083. [CrossRef]
24. Yu, L.J.; Zhong, S.Y.; Bian, X.D.; Heilman, W.E. Climatology and trend of wind power resources in China and its surrounding regions: A revisit using Climate Forecast System Reanalysis data. *Int. J. Climatol.* **2016**, *36*, 2173–2188. [CrossRef]
25. Whitworth, H.A. Evaluation of the residual strength degradation in composite laminates under fatigue loading. *Compos. Struct.* **2000**, *48*, 261–264. [CrossRef]

26. Miner, M.A. Cumulative damage in fatigue. *J. Appl. Mech.* **1945**, *12*, A159–A164. [CrossRef]
27. Manson, S.S.; Halford, G.R. Practical implementation of the double linear damage rule and damage curve approach for treating cumulative fatigue damage. *Int. J. Fract.* **1981**, *17*, 169–192. [CrossRef]
28. Freudenthal, A.M.; Heller, R.A. On stress interaction in fatigue and a cumulative damage rule. *J. Aerosp. Sci.* **1959**, *26*, 431–442. [CrossRef]
29. Zhu, S.P.; Huang, H.Z. A generalized frequency separation–strain energy damage function model for low cycle fatigue–creep life prediction. *Fatigue Fract. Eng. Mater. Struct.* **2010**, *33*, 227–237. [CrossRef]
30. Zhu, S.P.; Huang, H.Z.; Ontiveros, V.; He, L.P.; Modarres, M. Probabilistic low cycle fatigue life prediction using an energy-based damage parameter and accounting for model uncertainty. *Int. J. Damage Mech.* **2012**, *21*, 1128–1153. [CrossRef]
31. Risitano, A.; Risitano, G. Cumulative damage evaluation of steel using infrared thermography. *Theor. Appl. Fract. Mech.* **2010**, *54*, 82–90. [CrossRef]
32. Peng, Z.C.; Huang, H.Z.; Wang, H.K.; Zhu, S.P.; Lv, Z.Q. A new approach to the investigation of load interaction effects and its application in residual fatigue life prediction. *Int. J. Damage Mech.* **2016**, *25*, 672–690. [CrossRef]
33. Huang, B.X.; Wang, S.C.; Geng, S.L.; Liu, X.T. Improved numerical model for fatigue cumulative damage of mechanical structure considering load sequence and interaction. *Adv. Mech. Eng.* **2021**, *13*, 1687814021995309. [CrossRef]
34. Gao, J.X.; Heng, F.; Yuan, Y.P.; Liu, Y.Y. Fatigue reliability analysis of composite material considering the growth of effective stress and critical stiffness. *Aerospace* **2023**, *10*, 785. [CrossRef]
35. Ganesan, C.; Joanna, P.S. Modeling the residual strength and fatigue life of carbon fiber composites under constant amplitude loading. *Mech. Adv. Mater. Struct.* **2020**, *27*, 1840–1848. [CrossRef]
36. Fu, Z.; Hu, X.; Zhang, J. A new fatigue life prediction method based on nonlinear fatigue cumulative damage generalized expression. *J. Mech. Sci. Technol.* **2022**, *36*, 205–212. [CrossRef]
37. Osman, T.; Velex, P. A model for the simulation of the interactions between dynamic tooth loads and contact fatigue in spur gears. *Tribol. Int.* **2012**, *46*, 84–96. [CrossRef]
38. Grbovic, A.; Rasuo, B. FEM based fatigue crack growth predictions for spar of light aircraft under variable amplitude loading. *Eng. Fail. Anal.* **2012**, *26*, 50–64. [CrossRef]
39. Khan, M.A.A.; Sheikh, A.K.; Gasem, Z.M.; Asad, M. Fatigue life and reliability of steel castings through integrated simulations and experiments. *Metals* **2022**, *12*, 339. [CrossRef]
40. Meng, D.B.; Lv, Z.Y.; Yang, S.Y.; Wang, H.T.; Xie, T.W.; Wang, Z.H. A time-varying mechanical structure reliability analysis method based on performance degradation. *Structures* **2021**, *34*, 3247–3256. [CrossRef]
41. Ouammi, A.; Dagdougui, H.; Sacile, R.; Mimet, A. Monthly and seasonal assessment of wind energy characteristics at four monitored locations in Liguria region (Italy). *Renew. Sustain. Energy Rev.* **2010**, *14*, 1959–1968. [CrossRef]
42. Wais, P. A review of Weibull functions in wind sector. *Renew. Sustain. Energy Rev.* **2017**, *70*, 1099–1107. [CrossRef]
43. Altunkaynak, A.; Erdik, T.; Dabanlı, İ.; Şen, Z. Theoretical derivation of wind power probability distribution function and applications. *Appl. Energy* **2012**, *92*, 809–814. [CrossRef]
44. Qian, B.Y.; Zhou, K.C.; Gao, X.X.; Liu, W. Torque transmission law of wind turbine drive system under the excitation of uneven wind load. *J. Phys. Conf. Ser.* **2022**, *2218*, 012057. [CrossRef]
45. Gao, J.X. Reliability Analysis of Wind Turbine Gearbox Considering Strength Degradation and Failure Dependence. Master's Thesis, Lanzhou University of Technology, Gansu, China, 2014. (In Chinese).
46. Kebir, T.; Correia, J.; Benguediab, M.; Jesus, A.M.D. Numerical study of fatigue damage under random loading using Rainflow cycle counting. *Int. J. Struct. Integr.* **2021**, *12*, 149–162. [CrossRef]
47. Jiang, S.; Li, W.; Xin, G.F.; Sheng, L.C.; Wang, Y.Q. Study on dynamic reliability of permanent magnet gear transmission system with wear and failure correlation. *Eng. Fail. Anal.* **2022**, *131*, 105802. [CrossRef]
48. Nejad, A.R.; Gao, Z.; Moan, T. On long-term fatigue damage and reliability analysis of gears under wind loads in offshore wind turbine drivetrains. *Int. J. Fatigue* **2014**, *61*, 116–128. [CrossRef]
49. Kroese, D.P.; Brereton, T.; Taimre, T.; Botev, Z.I. Why the Monte Carlo method is so important today. *Wiley Interdiscip. Rev.-Comput. Stat.* **2014**, *6*, 386–392. [CrossRef]
50. Papadopoulos, C.E.; Yeung, H. Uncertainty estimation and Monte Carlo simulation method. *Flow Meas. Instrum.* **2001**, *12*, 291–298. [CrossRef]
51. Nakazawa, M. Examining the Advantages and Disadvantages of Pilot Studies: Monte Carlo Simulations. Master's Thesis, The University of New Mexico, Albuquerque, NM, USA, 2011.
52. Huang, P.; Gu, Y.K.; Li, H.; Yazdi, M.; Qiu, G.Q. An optimal tolerance design approach of robot manipulators for positioning accuracy reliability. *Reliab. Eng. Syst. Saf.* **2023**, *237*, 109347. [CrossRef]
53. Li, H.; Yazdi, M.; Huang, H.Z.; Huang, C.G.; Peng, W.; Nedjati, A.; Adesina, K.A. A fuzzy rough copula Bayesian network model for solving complex hospital service quality assessment. *Complex Intell. Syst.* **2023**, 1–27. [CrossRef] [PubMed]
54. Yazdi, M.; Mohammadpour, J.; Li, H.; Huang, H.Z.; Zarei, E.; Pirbalouti, R.G.; Adumene, S. Fault tree analysis improvements: A bibliometric analysis and literature review. *Qual. Reliab. Eng. Int.* **2023**, *39*, 1639–1659. [CrossRef]
55. Yan, Y.T.; Luo, Z.Q.; Liu, Z.Y.; Liu, Z.B. Risk Assessment Analysis of Multiple Failure Modes Using the Fuzzy Rough FMECA Method: A Case of FACDG. *Mathematics* **2023**, *11*, 3459. [CrossRef]

56. Yu, S.; Wang, Z.L. A general decoupling approach for time-and space-variant system reliability-based design optimization. *Comput. Methods Appl. Mech. Eng.* **2019**, *357*, 112608. [CrossRef]
57. Yu, S.; Wang, Z.L.; Li, Y. Time and space-variant system reliability analysis through adaptive Kriging and weighted sampling. *Mech. Syst. Signal Process.* **2022**, *166*, 108443. [CrossRef]
58. Yu, S.; Zhang, Y.W.; Li, Y.; Wang, Z.L. Time-variant reliability analysis via approximation of the first-crossing PDF. *Struct. Multidiscip. Optim.* **2020**, *62*, 2653–2667. [CrossRef]
59. Yu, S.; Guo, P.; Wu, X. Adaptive first-crossing approach for life-cycle reliability analysis. *Chin. J. Mech. Eng.* **2023**, *145*, 091707. [CrossRef]

mathematics

MDPI

Article

Artificial Bee Colony Algorithm to Optimize the Safety Distance of Workers in Construction Projects

Eric Forcael [1,*], Ibzan Carriel [2], Alexander Opazo-Vega [2], Francisco Moreno [3,*], Francisco Orozco [3], Rubén Romo [3,*] and Duzgun Agdas [4]

1 College of Engineering, Architecture, and Design, Universidad San Sebastián, Concepción 4081339, Chile
2 Department of Civil and Environmental Engineering, College of Engineering, Universidad del Bío-Bío, Concepción 4051381, Chile
3 College of Engineering, Universidad Panamericana, Guadalajara 45010, Mexico
4 Engineering School of Sustainable Infrastructure and Environment, University of Florida, Gainesville, FL 32611, USA
* Correspondence: eric.forcael@uss.cl (E.F.); fmorenoa@up.edu.mx (F.M.); rromog@up.edu.mx (R.R.)

Abstract: This paper presents the results of a simulation model regarding the productivity and safety working space for construction workers through the floors of a building using swarm intelligence (SI), a field of artificial intelligence (AI), and specifically using artificial bee colony (ABC) optimization. After designing the algorithm used to build the simulation model, the simulation was used in an actual building project by comparing the travel times of workers conventionally transporting material with another group working on routes optimized by the algorithm. Thus, the proposed algorithm provides routes combining shorter travel times and correct distances between workers when transporting materials in a construction site, handling the interference between crews. After validating the algorithm on-site, no statistically significant differences were found between the travel times of workers and the times delivered by the algorithm. Additionally, the travel times using the routes obtained through the algorithm were significantly lower than those made by workers who moved freely without a predefined route. In summary, the algorithm proposed may help construction practitioners maintain safe movements that respond to hazard contexts imposed by any restriction that demands a safety distance.

Keywords: artificial bee colony; swarm intelligence; route optimization; safety distance; hazard analysis; buildings

MSC: 68T20

1. Introduction

The construction industry is one of the most dangerous, as people are susceptible to workplace accidents, injuries, and even fatalities [1]. Construction projects are becoming increasingly complex, which has led to intricate and dynamic relationships [2]. Working in the same area increases the potential for interferences or disruptions (like blocking the access of one crew by another crew) [3].

Site congestion and overcrowding are usually attributed to inappropriate construction site arrangements and the overcrowding of workers in some workplaces, which can cause obstructions to the desired productivity and quality [4]. Crews usually have to share the limited working space with other workers to perform their tasks during construction [3].

An unprecedented factor that has affected the construction industry has been the social distancing requirements for worker safety to reduce the transmission risk among those on-site [5]. Given this scenario, the objective of this study was to develop an artificial bee colony (ABC) algorithm to optimize the movement and distancing between workers in building projects [6,7]. The specific goals are to establish the variables that determine the safe distance between workers, obtain parameters of cost and safe travel for worker movements in a building project, implement the new optimization model based on the ABC algorithm, and validate the model by applying it to an actual construction project.

Thus, this research aims to reach these goals by optimizing worker movements with an ABC algorithm, thus increasing the on-site productivity. Significant downtimes, inefficient routes, and interferences between workers are among the usual issues in worker movements. These factors all lead to time wastage and decreased overall efficiency. In other words, the present research searched to optimize worker mobility and task execution using an ABC algorithm, which finds optimal solutions by emulating the foraging behavior of bees. Implementing this type of algorithm may increase worker productivity and safety on construction sites so that they may complete the work more quickly and without interruptions. Therefore, this research aims to show how effectively a swarm intelligence (SI) algorithm (ABC, in this case) can reduce inefficiencies, shorten waiting times, and enhance worker cooperation based on solid algorithm-driven solutions that maximize worker movements and significantly improve site management procedures on construction sites.

2. Literature Review

2.1. Health and Safety

Considering that the construction industry employs millions of workers who may experience accidents, it is essential to understand how these accidents and injuries are generated [8]. Correct management and planning are ways to avoid unplanned events like accidents, where an effective health and safety (H&S) plan can help prevent work-related injuries [9].

The contents of the H&S plan help discern the risk mitigation measures that need to be adopted, given that the work schedule of the site is known in advance [10]. Thus, on a construction site, it is possible to find interferences such as a situation where two or more teams share the same working area (e.g., workers walk through the same paths or share some equipment), but they are not compliant with the schedule considered in the H&S plan, which is usually included as a Gantt chart. This means that it is not expected to have an analyses of the risks generated by the concurrent presence of workers in the same area; hence, no mitigation measures are taken, and the involved workers are not aware of the potential risks.

On the other hand, in terms of avoiding congested work areas, it is essential to emphasize that crews have better efficiency and productivity (more than 30%) when they have similar scopes in the same working area [11,12]. In this sense, the ABC algorithm provides many benefits for global optimization problems based on local search, memory, and solution enhancement [13], where optimization may reduce the likelihood of worker overlap and collision, and consequently, the risk of accidents and the need for rework.

2.2. Pandemics and the Construction Industry

Pandemics such as COVID-19 and the corresponding limitations to physical activities have changed the professional landscape as most of the service jobs were moved entirely online, and telework has become the norm. The construction industry is one of the select few in which telework was not an option. This fact added a dimension to a complicated working environment due to supply chain issues and commodity price fluctuations [14].

The World Health Organization (WHO) recommended keeping, at least, a 1-m distance between people to reduce the airborne infection transmission risk due to typical daily activities of talking or simply breathing [15]. This measure was supplementary to using personal protective equipment (PPE), staggering work activities to reduce population density at workplaces, offering training on COVID-19, and administering temperature checks before entering the workplace [16].

2.3. Complexities in the Construction Industry

The construction industry is complex as its products are generally unique, substantial in resource requirements, and complicated in contractual agreements. Construction is risky for companies and workers as it ranks high in occupational health and hazards [17,18]. COVID-19 and related issues changed the workplace dynamics and increased the complexity that already existed during the execution phase of construction. The number of people allowed on sites, their productivity with the new crew compositions, and the management of these unusual constraints made planning and project management more challenging [19].

Different tools and management philosophies have long been proposed to address the complexity problem in construction. Some of these approaches and methods included lean construction, integrated project delivery (IPD), and building information modeling (BIM) [20]. These mainstream approaches are a precursor to a much greater set of modeling, simulation, and optimization approaches within each approach to address specific issues within the industry. An exciting case is optimization in construction. Due to the nature (e.g., discrete activities) and sheer size of tasks needed to complete projects, traditional exact solutions have scarcely been used in construction optimization research as their feasibility diminishes with an increase in the problem size. What has been expected, however, is the use of heuristics and metaheuristics in different construction engineering and management problems [21,22].

In this sense, the workers' movements within a construction zone can be treated as a route optimization problem. Routing optimization problems on networks consists of finding paths between the nodes of the networks efficiently, where their solutions have proven to be essential to solving many real-world decisions in applications as diverse as logistics, transportation, and computer networking, among others [23]. In construction, it is also possible to find research and applications related to routing optimization problems such as the optimization of construction and demolition waste transportation [24] and inventory routing problems for construction-related transport [25]. Similarly, other investigations have focused on optimizing workers' movements while dealing with construction inefficiencies and their impact on quality, scheduling, safety, and health [26]. Another example of complexities within construction is the site layout planning, where ABC-based algorithms have proposed optimal layout plans with low costs and safety facilities [7].

Thus, to solve complex problems, a way to reach efficient solutions is through the use of one of the branches of artificial intelligence (AI) called swarm intelligence (SI) [27], where techniques based on swarm optimization have been applied to solve optimization problems in civil engineering [28]. In this sense, recent swarm intelligence metaheuristics have been developed to help solve various complex optimization problems in construction projects [29].

2.4. Swarm Algorithms

The concept of swarm intelligence (SI) was first used by Beni and Wang [27] in their work on a cellular robotic system with stationary robots and its application to manufacturing lattices. SI corresponds to a group of techniques based on the study of collective behavior in self-organized and decentralized systems [30]. However, Bonabeau et al. [31] mentioned the limited scope of these techniques, later broadened by Martinoli [32] to include diverse efforts to design algorithms or problem-solving mechanisms based on the collective behavior of the social colonies of insects. Swarm behavior becomes collective intelligence when a group can use it to solve a problem collectively so that members of the group cannot do it individually [33]. These kinds of problems frequently have an endless number of possible answers. Finding a practical solution within the allotted time is crucial in these circumstances. In practically every science, engineering, and business field including data mining, optimization, computational intelligence, business planning, bioinformatics, and industrial applications, SI is useful for resolving nonlinear design problems with practical applications [34].

Two fundamental concepts—self-organization and division of labor—must be considered to understand the behavior of SI.

(a) Self-organization: Self-organization is defined as a set of dynamic mechanisms that result in the global-level structures of a system through interactions between its low-level components [35]. These mechanisms establish basic rules for the interactions between the system members and guarantee that the exchanges are executed based on purely local information without relation to global patterns. Four basic self-organization properties are characterized by positive feedback, negative feedback, variations, and multiple interactions [36].

(i) Positive feedback is a simple "general rule" of behavior that promotes the conformation of appropriate structures (i.e., recruitment and reinforcement such as establishing trails and monitoring some species of ants or the waggle dances of bees).
(ii) The negative feedback counteracts the positive feedback and helps stabilize the collective pattern to avoid saturation regarding available foragers, food source depletion, overcrowding, or competition in food sources.
(iii) Variations such as errors, random walks, and random task changes between individuals in the swarm are crucial for innovation and creativity. Moreover, randomness is often vital for emergent structures, allowing for the discovery of new solutions.
(iv) Generally, self-organization requires a minimum density of mutually tolerant individuals, enabling them to use the results of their activities, consequently generating multiple interactions.

(b) Division of labor: Specialized individuals perform different tasks concurrently within a swarm. The simultaneous execution of tasks through the cooperation of individuals specialized in some tasks is more efficient than the sequential execution of these by non-specialized individuals [37]. The division of labor also enables the swarm to respond to changing conditions in the search space [35].

In addition, according to Millonas [38], SI must satisfy the following principles:

(i) Proximity principle: The ability to make simple space and time calculations.
(ii) Quality principle: The ability to respond to environmental quality factors.
(iii) Diverse response principle: It must not conduct the swarm's activities along excessively narrow channels.
(iv) Stability principle: The ability to keep its mode of behavior the same with environmental fluctuations.
(v) Adaptability principle: The ability to change the mode of behavior when necessary.

Among the many SI algorithms that have been created, ant colony optimization (ACO) [39] and particle swarm optimization (PSO) [40] have been the most popular in construction engineering and management research. However, the characteristics of self-organization and division of labor [31] and satisfaction principles [38], which swarm intelligence requires, can be seen with greater force and clarity in honeybee colonies. Thus, artificial bee colony (ABC) optimization has recently gained popularity [41]. An ABC algorithm of particular interest and importance is the MOABC (multi-objective artificial bee colony), which enables the use of two or more functions [42–44] that correspond to the algorithm considered in this research.

2.5. Application of Bee Swarm Algorithms in Construction

The ACO, PSO, cuckoo optimization algorithm (COA), and ABC algorithms stand out mainly in solving problems associated with project management, transportation, design, and structural calculation, among others. Some of the ABC algorithms used in engineering have been developed for the optimized design of cooling towers [45] and heat exchangers [46], for leak detection in pipelines [47], the design of truss structures [48,49], the optimized design of construction sites [50], or to determine the logistics associated with the construction of precast elements [51], amongst others.

Other examples can be found in construction project management, where some researchers have evaluated the use of diverse machine learning algorithms such as PSO for cost optimization and predictive modeling [52], or in pavement engineering by combining image processing and salp swarm algorithm-optimized machine learning to detect pavement cracks and sealed cracks [53].

In summary, as the construction industry is known as one of the riskiest industries in the world with high rates of accidents and fatalities, models based on SI such as ABC programming approaches may help improve the safety performance within construction projects [54], and at the same time, solve daily problems such as cost optimization, constructive problem detection, and travel time optimization, which were the main objectives of the present research.

3. Methodology

3.1. Problem Formulation

It is proposed that the ABC algorithm can be used to address the issue of social distancing within construction zones to facilitate the safe movement of workers.

3.2. System Definition

3.2.1. Definition of the Species

This stage consisted of a preliminary background search and its contextualization based on the problem tackled. The species considered here was the European bee Apis mellifera, known as the domestic bee or honeybee, characterized by its social nature, turning its colony into a "superorganism" capable of creating synergy through the interaction between each of the individuals that compose it.

3.2.2. ABC Algorithms

Based on the theory that supports SI, an ABC algorithm was developed that considered as the primary criterion, a minimum physical distance of 1 m between workers who moved materials from one point to another within a building project to generate a safe distance that would keep workers without any interference between crews.

3.3. Modeling

3.3.1. Model Formulation

The model to be implemented must be able to accurately search for an optimal material collection point that guarantees a lower transfer cost (i.e., the shortest and safest route to the work front where the worker will deposit the transferred material). In the case of several alternatives, the model must select the optimal point based on input parameters representing the actual conditions of the terrain to be simulated.

3.3.2. Implementation and Verification of the Model

We used MATLAB^{TM} R2024a to implement the ABC algorithm to solve the worker movement problem, the details of which are further explained in Section 4.2. The corresponding debugging process was carried out once the algorithm was designed, coded, and compiled.

3.4. Validation

The ABC algorithm was validated through measurements of the safe movement times of workers throughout the floors of an apartment building in the middle of the construction stage. Specifically, the measurements were made in an actual building project, as will be detailed later in Section 5 (model validation).

4. Design of the Algorithm

4.1. Problem Statement and Model Development

The artificial bee colony in an ABC algorithm consists of three groups of bees: employed bees, onlooker bees, and scout bees [55]. Specific instructions for each are as follows:

Employed bees are associated with food sources.

Onlooker bees watch the waggle dance of the employed bees in the hive to select the food source.

Scout bees go in search of random food sources.

Both bees, onlookers and scouts, are also known as unemployed bees. In the beginning, all positions of food sources are found by scout bees [35]. The behavior of the bees described above is presented in Figure 1.

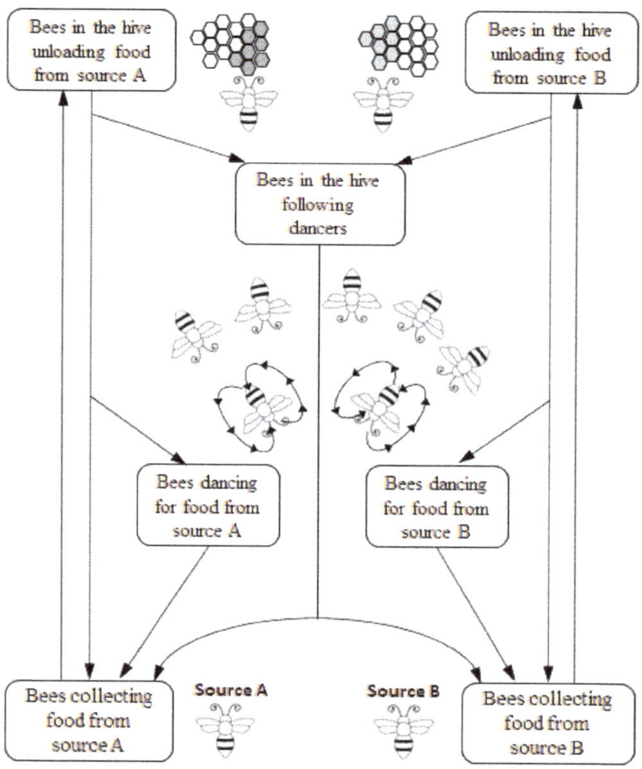

Figure 1. General scheme of bee behavior.

Once the food sources are discovered, employed bees and onlooker bees exploit the nectar from the food sources. This exploitation continues until food sources are depleted. At that point, the employee bee using the depleted food source becomes a scout bee searching for other food sources. In an ABC algorithm, the location of a food source means a potential solution to the problem, and the amount of food from a food source is equivalent to the quality (fitness) of the associated answer. Thus, the pseudocode of the algorithmic structure of the ABC optimization approach is shown below:

***Process** ABC*
Initialization Phase;
Variables;
Control parameters;
REPEAT
Scout Bees Phase;
REPEAT
Employed Bees Phase;
Onlooker Bees Phase;
Scout Bees Phase;
Memorize the best solution achieved so far;
TO(Cycle = Max num of cycles)
TO(Length = Max num of nodes)
End

Before proceeding to the mathematical formulation, Figure 2 shows a simplified flowchart of the proposed ABC algorithm adapted to optimize the safety distance of workers on construction projects, whose routines were later programmed in MATLAB^{TM}.

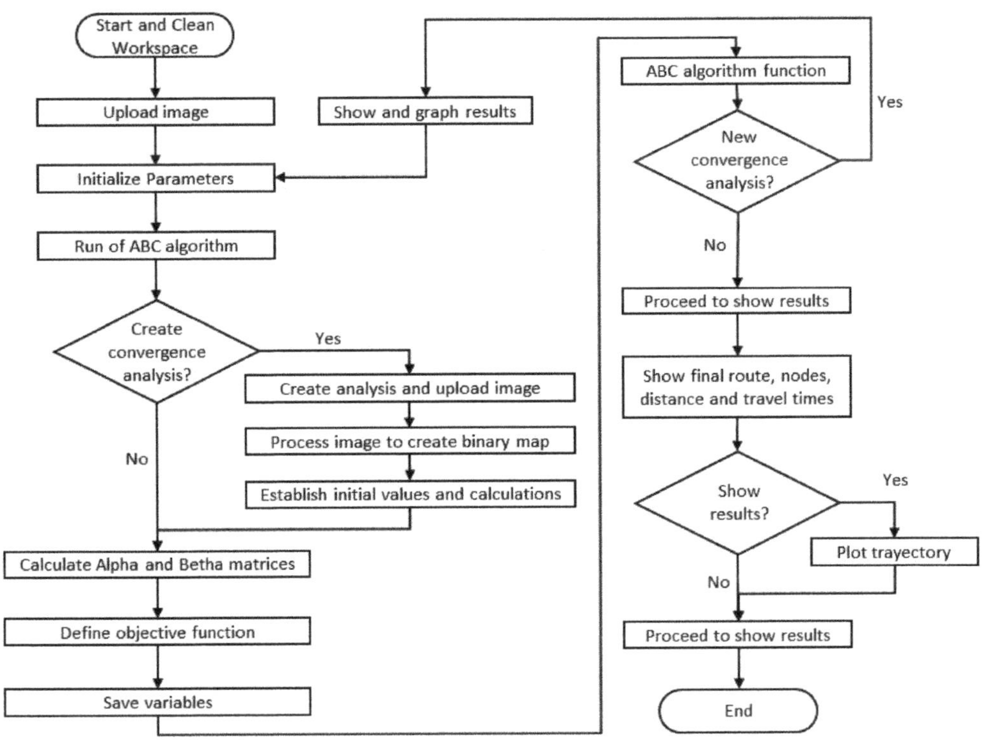

Figure 2. Flowchart of the proposed ABC algorithm adapted to optimize the safety distance of workers on construction projects.

Below is the general mathematical formulation of the proposed ABC algorithm, adapted from Karaboga [35], Karaboga and Akay [56], Akbari et al. [42], and Akay and Karaboga [41], where all of the variables are fully explained from Section 4.1.1. onward:

1. Initialization of Solutions

Each scout bee generates an initial solution randomly within the defined limits for each dimension of the problem:

$$x_{i,j} = x_{min,j} + rand(0,1) \times \left(x_{max,j} - x_{min,j}\right)$$

- $x_{i,j}$: Position of bee i in dimension j.
- $x_{min,j}$ and $x_{max,j}$: Minimum and maximum limits in dimension j.
- $rand(0,1)$: Uniform random number between 0 and 1.

2. Movements of Employed and Onlooker Bees

Employed and onlooker bees explore new positions in the solution space based on positions of other bees:

$$v_{i,j} = x_{i,j} + \phi_{i,j} \times (x_{i,j} - x_{k,j})$$

- $v_{i,j}$: New proposed position for bee i in dimension j.
- $\phi_{i,j}$: Random adjustment factor in range [−1, 1].
- $x_{k,j}$: Position of another bee k randomly selected in dimension j.

3. Probabilistic Selection of Onlooker Bees

Onlooker bees select food sources based on probability proportional to the solution quality:

$$P_i = \frac{f_i}{\sum_{i=1}^{n} f_i}$$

- P_i: Probability of selecting solution i.
- f_i: Quality of solution i, inversely proportional to the objective function value.

4. Update of Best Solutions

Best solutions are updated if a better position with higher quality is found:

$$if\ f(v_i) < f(x_i)\ then\ x_i = v_i$$

- $f(v_i)$: Objective function value at new position v_i.
- $f(x_i)$: Objective function value at current position x_i.

5. Objective Function

In this specific context, the objective function f_0 is defined as:

$$f_0 = 0.9 \times \alpha + 0.5 \times \beta$$

- α: represents the inverse of the security matrix.
- β: represents the costs of each node, using randomly generated values between 0 and 10.

6. Ending Conditions

The ABC algorithm ends after a maximum number of iterations or when a convergence criterion is met.

4.1.1. Initialization Phase

The control parameters such as iterations and area limits are established in the initialization phase. This phase begins with a search for food by a group of scout bees, flying to random points within the range of the parameters' limits based on what is established in Equation (1). The random choice scan phase is shown in Figure 3.

$$X_{ij} = X_{jmin} + rand(0,1)(X_{jmax} - X_{jmin}) \tag{1}$$

where:

$i = 1 \ldots SN$;

$j = 1 \ldots D$;

SN is the number of food sources;

D is the number of optimization parameters.

Additionally, the counters that store the number of solution trials are reset to 0 in this phase.

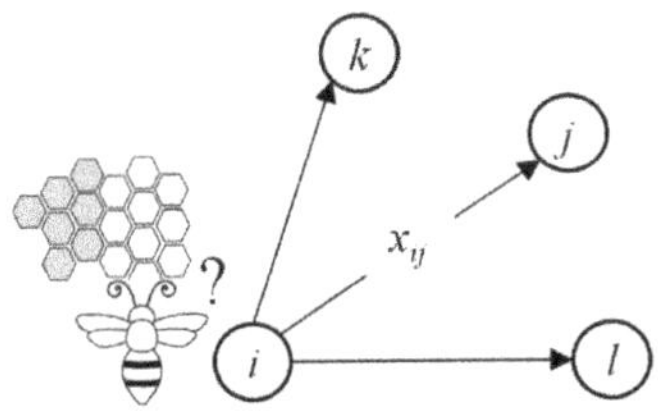

Figure 3. Random choice scan phase.

After the start, the population of food sources (solutions) is subjected to repeated cycles of the foraging processes of employed bees, onlooker bees, and scout bees. The termination criteria for the ABC algorithm can either reach a maximum cycle number (MCN) or meet an error tolerance (ε).

4.1.2. Employed Bee Phase

An employed bee changes the food source's location (solution) within its memory based on local data (visual information), thus finding a neighboring food source and then assessing its quality. In the ABC, finding an adjacent food source is defined by Equation (2).

$$v_{ij} = X_{ij} + \phi_{ij}\,(X_{ij} - X_{kj}) \tag{2}$$

Within the vicinity of each food source site represented by X_i, a food source v_i is determined by changing a parameter of X_i, where j is a random integer in the range [1, D], $k \in \{1,2, \ldots, SN\}$ is a randomly chosen index that has to be different from i, and ij is a uniformly distributed real random number in the range [1, 1]. The difference between the parameters of $X_{i,j}$ and $X_{k,j}$ decreases, and the disturbance at position $X_{i,j}$ decreases. Thus, the step length adaptively reduces as the search approaches the optimal solution within the search space.

On the other hand, if a parameter value coming from this operation surpasses its predetermined limits, the parameter may be set to a suitable value. For example, in the present investigation, the value of the parameter that exceeds its limit is set to its limits, so that if $X_i > X_{imax}$, then $X_i = X_{imax}$; y is $X_i < X_{imin}$, then $X_i = X_{imin}$. After producing v_i within the bounds, a fitness value for a minimization problem can be assigned to the solution v_i using Equation (3).

$$fitness_i = \begin{cases} \frac{1}{1+fi}, \ if\ fi \geq 0 \\ \frac{1}{abs(fi)}, \ if\ fi < 0 \end{cases} \tag{3}$$

where according to Sarkar et al. [57], *fi* is the cost value of the solution v_i, and for maximization problems, the cost function can be utilized directly as a fitness function, and a greedy choice is used between x_i and v_i to pick the best one based on the fitness values representing the amount of food from the food sources in x_i and v_i. If the source in v_i is larger than in x_i, in terms of efficiency, the employed bee keeps in mind the new position and forgets the old one [58]. The previous position is saved in the bee's memory if this scenario does not occur. If x_i cannot be upgraded, its counter containing the number of attempts is increased by 1; if it can be improved, the counter is reset to 0 [57].

Following this, the employed bees share their food source data with the onlooker bees waiting in the hive by dancing on the dance floor.

4.1.3. Onlooker Bee Phase

As a multiple interaction feature of the ABC artificial bees, once all the employed bees finish their search, they share data about the available food and its location with the onlooker bees in the dance sector [58]. An onlooker bee analyzes the food information from all employed bees and selects a food source site considering the probability associated with its amount of food, where this probabilistic choice is based on the fitness values of the population's solutions. The picking method can be stochastic universal sampling, spinner, or other choice mechanisms. The basic ABC uses a spinner-picking method, where each spinner portion is correlated to the fitness value, as shown in Equation (4).

$$P_i = \frac{fitness_i}{\sum_{i=1}^{SN} fitness} \tag{4}$$

As the amount of nectar in food sources (the fitness of solutions) increases, the number of onlooker bees that visit them also increases. This medium is the ABC positive feedback function.

Selection of Food Site

The ABC algorithm generates a random real number within the range [0, 1] for each source. Suppose the probability value (P_i in Equation (4)) associated with that source is more significant than this random number; then, the onlooker bee changes the position of this food source site using Equation (2), as in the case of the employed bee. After evaluating the source, a greedy choice is applied, and the onlooker bee memorizes the new position by forgetting the old one or keeping the old one. If solution x_i cannot be upgraded, its counter hold trials are increased by 1; otherwise, the counter is reset to 0. This process repeats until all viewers are distributed to the feed source sites.

4.1.4. Scout Bees Phase

Bees whose solutions cannot be enhanced by a preestablished number of attempts—called the "limit"—become scout bees, and their solutions are abandoned. The explorers then begin searching for new answers at random. Therefore, sources that are at first poor—or have become impoverished by exploitation—are abandoned, and negative feedback behavior stands up to balance the positive feedback.

These three steps are repeated until a completion criterion, cycle number, or maximum processing time is met.

4.2. *Implementation*

4.2.1. Construction of the Route

In the previous section, it was explained how bees explore between their nest and the food source and then exploit the most convenient food sources. This mechanism is similar to finding an optimal and safe point and its different iterations to achieve a route, which allows for an adaptation of the algorithm proposed by Karaboga [35]. Their natural environment determines the behavior of bees, and they travel up to a certain limited distance in search of food, avoid obstacles, and teach the routes to their companions. Then, if there are more alternatives, they look for the best option as a food source.

For our optimization problem, each optimal food source represents a place to reach, so by distributing different optimal food sources, a specific location can be compared with the safest conditions and at a lower cost. We constructed this network by carrying out multiple iterations to find each source (i.e., the worker moves from the place of the collection of materials to the work front) (Figure 4).

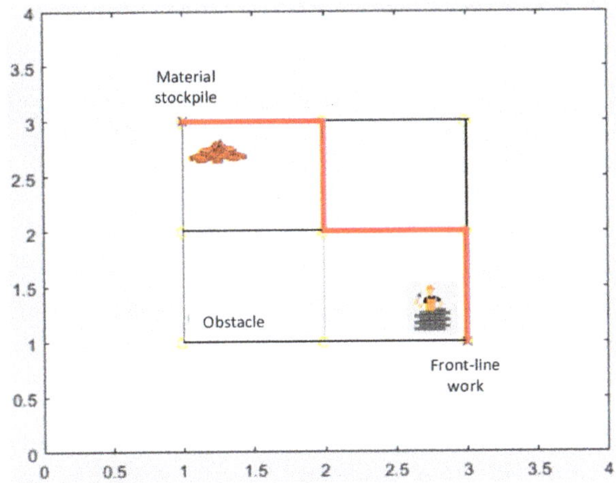

Figure 4. Construction of the route for the worker.

4.2.2. Optimization Method

Step 1: The convergence analysis counter *contconv* is initialized to import the plan's image from the *pdf* to *jpg* format, then converted into a matrix of black-and-white points, represented in terms of 1 and 0, respectively. The value of each parameter is assigned as upper limits x_{max} and lower limits x_{min}. The minimum cost found is defined as *globest.cost*, the position matrix as *bee.loc*, and the cost vector as *bee.cost* of the food sources found.

```
Process ABC
Contconv=1 ← Convergence Analysis Initialization;
  //Import drawing image
Import map;
Image to B&W transformation;
  //Variables
xmax ← Upper boundary;
xmin ← Lower boundary;
npop ← Bee population;
itermax ← Maximum iterations (MCN);
alph← Alpha matrix;
Beth← Beta matrix;
ssteps← Maximum Node Length;
Node_fin← End node (frontwork);
Node_ini← Start node (Acope);
Globest.cost= inf← Infinite global cost to start;
bee← Position structure and costs of food sources;
```

Step 2: The initialization process of random exploration of the scout bees *i* is started by searching for the location of a food source *bee(i).loc* to store the cost in a vector *bee(i).cost*. The rand variable is included to assign the visited node randomly.

```
//Each bee i randomly searches for a food source
For i ← 1 To npop With Step by step Do

        Generate solution xi;
        bee(i).loc=xmin+rand(0,1)(xmax-xmin)    ← Save the source position;
        bee(i).cost=func(bee(i).loc) ← Save the cost of the source found;

    If bee(i).cost < Globest Then
            Bee value is saved as new source position with minimal cost;
        globest←bee(i)
    EndIf
EndFor
```

Step 3: The cycle of the bees begins up to the maximum iteration *itermax*, and the employed bees' phase *i* begins searching for the location of a food source *newbee.loc*, to later save the cost in a vector *newbee.cost*, which is compared with the position of a randomly chosen source *k*, where $k \in \{1, \ldots \text{npop}\}$, and ∅ is the uniformly distributed random real number in the range $[-1, 1]$. If the cost of the new source is less than the previously saved *bee(i).cost*, then the latter is replaced by the new one.

```
//Employed Bee phase
For iter ← 1 To itermax With Step by step Do
For i ← 1 To npop With Step by step Do
        Generate solution ki;
        newbee.loc=xij+∅ ij(xij-xkj)    ← Save the source position;
        newbee.cost=func(newbee.loc) ← Save the cost of the source found;
    If newbee.cost < bee(i).cost Then
            Newbee value is saved as new source position with minimal cost;
        bee(i)←newbee;
    Else
        C(i)=c(i)+1;            1 is added to the attempt counter
    EndIf
EndFor
```

Step 4: The onlooker bees' phase *i* is started where the fitness function for each $fitness_i$ node is generated, and then the probability P_i is calculated for each food source.

```
//Onlooker bee phase - probability calculation
F← Fitness vector of npop size;
For i ← 1 To npop With Step by step Do
        Generate fitness function for each node
```

$$\text{fitness}_i = \begin{cases} \frac{1}{1+bee(i).cost}, If\, bee(i).cost \geq 0; \\ \frac{1}{abs(bee(i).cost)}, If\, bee(i).cost < 0; \end{cases}$$

```
EndFor

For i ← 1 To npop With Step by step Do
        Calculate solution Pi for each node
```

$$P_i = \begin{cases} 0.5 + \frac{fitness_i}{\sum_{j=1}^{SN} fitness_j} * x0{,}5, \boldsymbol{If}\, solution\ is\ feasible; \\ 1 - \frac{Violation_i}{\sum_{j=1}^{SN} Violation_j} x0{,}5, \boldsymbol{If}\, solution\ isn't\, feasible; \end{cases}$$

```
EndFor
```

Step 5: In the onlooker bees' phase *i*, using the probabilities calculated in the previous step, they decide if it is convenient for them to go to the previously created source or to one generated by a randomly chosen probability using the same equations from Step 3.

```
//Onlooker bee phase - visit food sources
For j ← 1 To npop With Step by step Do
    If rand <Pi Then
        Generate solution ki;
        (The same process as in Step 3)

    If newbee.cost < bee(j).cost Then
        (The same process as in Step 3)
    Else
        C(j) = c(j)+1;              1 is added to the attempt counter
    EndIf
    EndIf
EndFor
```

Step 6: The final stage of the ABC algorithm is the scout bee phase, where bees go to random nodes in search of food sources as long as the attempt counter *C(i)* is equal to or less than the number of allowed mistakes *lim*. The exact process is used as in Step 2 to generate the solution x_i.

```
//Scout Bees Phase
For i ← 1 To npop With Step by step Do
        If C(i) <= lim Then
           Generate solution xi;
           (The same process as in Step 2)
        C(i) = 0;              The attempt counter returns to 0
        EndIf
EndFor
EndFor // End of the bee stage iteration cycle
```

Step 7: The routes created with their respective nodes and costs are taken, to which a total travel cost is calculated, and the route with the lowest cost is selected.

```
//Convergence analysis phase, final part
For i ← 1 To (contconv) With Step by step Do
           Anmax(i) = sum(play(i). p).
EndFor
           Anmin = min(Anmax);
           posmin← find position of anmin in play structure;

        Plot convergence analysis;
           Plot route;
        Show results table;
FinScript//End script
```

4.3. Application of the Algorithm to the Case Study

4.3.1. The Case Study: A Residential Building

Since the experiments focused on applying the ABC algorithm within the construction industry, several construction projects in southern Chile were analyzed to conduct the tests. Depending on the construction degree of progress (buildings in the excavation stages were discarded, and buildings close to being finished were also unconsidered), four buildings were considered to implement the ABC solution found before finally selecting the case study based on an appropriate number of walls as obstacles to test the algorithm and the permissions provided to the workers to be part of the study. The residential building under study has seven floors, an underground, and a constructed area of approximately 6500 m^2. The experiments were run on floor 3, which presented a sufficient degree of advance (appropriate number of walls, constant movement of materials to test the algorithm, etc.). Figure 5 (general view) and Figure 8 (detailed views) show the building's plan views.

Eight participants were randomly selected from volunteers among the workers to perform the routes with and without the guidance of the ABC algorithm. Each participant completed five laps of carrying the material from the stockpile node to the work node. The time and route were recorded by timing the start and end points under discreet supervision to ensure that the participants were not influenced by external observers, minimizing the Hawthorne effect, as explained in Section 5.1.

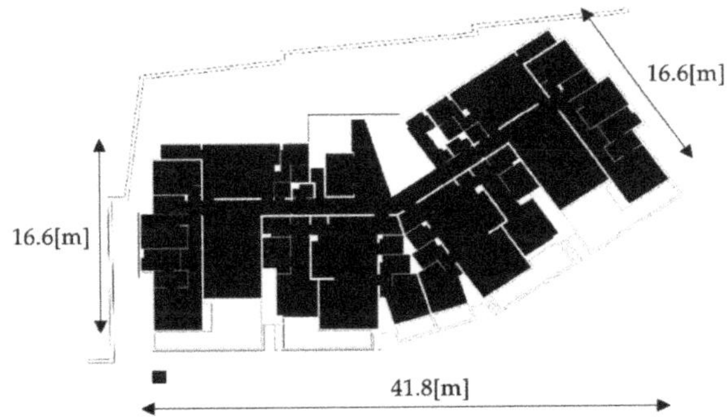

Figure 5. Example of a floor plan of the building under study in JPG format.

To establish the starting and ending nodes, the on-site construction professionals were asked about the stockpile points within the floor under study and the points where the workers would be required to deliver the materials. With this information, the site plans were converted into a format readable by MATLAB^{TM}, where the starting and ending nodes were located, as explained below.

4.3.2. Map and Distance between Nodes

First, a map matrix was elaborated from the floor plans obtained from the building work considered as the case study. To produce this, maps of the floors in PDF format were converted to JPG images, as shown in the example in Figure 5. This process is necessary because MATLAB^{TM} requires at least one primary color (the contrast between black and white) to read the images.

4.3.3. Factors α and β to Establish the Safe Distances between Workers

To establish the safe distances between workers and their proximity to various objects on the site (walls, for example), the factors α and β were created as objective functions. The original ABC code allows for the implementation of only one objective function, so we decided to use a variant of the ABC algorithm called MOABC (multi-objective artificial bee colony), which enables using two or more functions. In this investigation, they were established by matrices of the values that would make up the factors α and β, as shown in Figure 6. The size of both matrices was based on the size of the image of the building plan to be studied and its number of pixels, which were reduced to a tenth of them, but without losing the details of the walls and circulation areas.

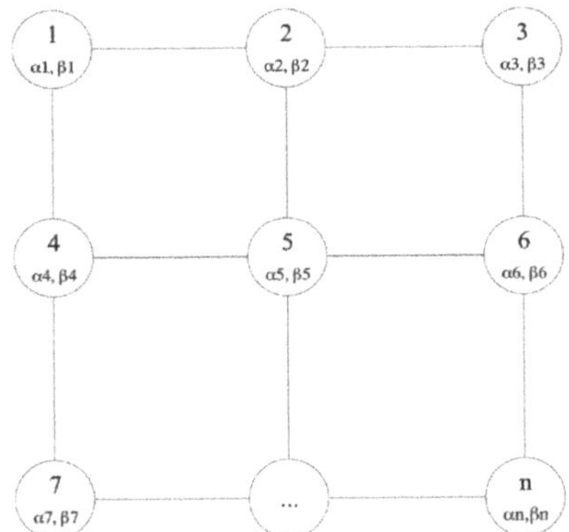

Figure 6. Graphical representation of the factors α and β.

The alpha and beta matrices were created for n nodes to represent the factors α and β, as shown in Equations (5) and (6), respectively.

$$\text{Alpha} = \begin{pmatrix} \alpha 11 & \cdots & \alpha 1n \\ \vdots & \ddots & \vdots \\ \alpha n1 & \cdots & \alpha nn \end{pmatrix} \quad (5)$$

$$\text{Beta} = \begin{pmatrix} \beta 11 & \cdots & \beta 1n \\ \vdots & \ddots & \vdots \\ \beta n1 & \cdots & \beta nn \end{pmatrix} \quad (6)$$

The alpha matrix represents the inverse of the safety matrix, with values inversely proportional to the distances to an object. A value of infinity was used for the nodes that were part of a wall or some obstacle of the building to prevent the algorithm of this study from taking impossible routes as an alternative. The values of α that were incorporated into the equations are as follows:

$$\alpha = \begin{cases} 0.5 & \text{7 or more distance nodes from the wall} \\ 0.7 & \text{5 to 6 distance nodes from the wall} \\ 0.8 & \text{3 to 4 distance nodes from the wall} \\ 0.9 & \text{0 to 2 distance nodes from the wall} \end{cases}$$

The beta matrix represents the costs of each node, and, in this case, the cost associated with the unloading of materials by the workers and must meet the condition of having the necessary space for unloading, using randomly generated values between 0 and 10, simulating some momentary obstruction in the path and decision randomness but considering the distance from the node to the final objective.

The objective function results from a sum between the alpha and beta matrices with the Euclidean distance between the node being evaluated $x_{i,j}$, and the objective node $x_{m,n}$, as shown in Equation (7).

$$F(x_{i,j}) = \alpha(x_{i,j}) + \beta(x_{i,j}) * \sqrt{(x_{i,j})^2 + (x_{m,n})^2} \quad (7)$$

4.3.4. Travel Times

Travel time was applied in the convergence analyses after having the complete route between the materials collection node and the work front, using an average speed of passage of 2.53 km/h (42 m/min), which was obtained by measuring the time it takes a group of workers to travel a certain distance, as shown in Equation (8).

$$T[min] = \frac{d(m)}{42\left(\frac{m}{min}\right)} \quad (8)$$

4.4. Model Verification

4.4.1. Model Convergence

The behavior of the model was verified by employing the matrix of map points, which, as indicated, represents the floors of the building under study, with a size of 367 × 367; however, 10 × 10 sub-matrices were also used to find each node of the path, for which 100 iterations were used for each sub-matrix with a population of four bees. This number of iterations (100) was used despite the ABC algorithm already beginning to converge toward minimum values between iterations 25 and 30, as shown in Figure 7.

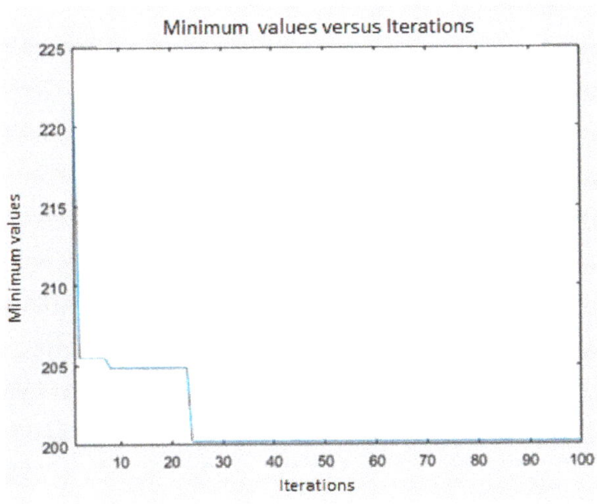

Figure 7. Convergence graph for the calculation of minimum values.

4.4.2. Optimization Results

Once the ABC algorithm was developed to address the problem of safe distancing between workers who moved along the floor of a building, different outputs were generated, of which two sample routes are presented in Figure 8.

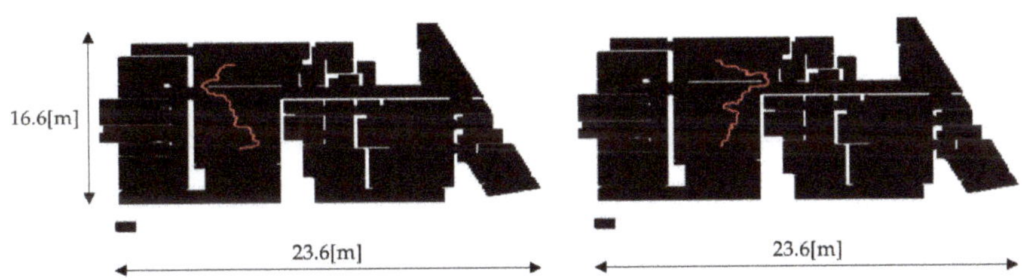

Figure 8. Two alternative routes produced by the algorithm.

5. Model Validation

The previous sections presented a model based on ABC algorithms to find circulation routes for workers transporting loads while maintaining a safe physical distance during a pandemic. These routes were appropriate considering the existing conditions in a building (walls, pillars, etc.) and the safety of the workers, so we proceeded to validate the developed model through accurate measurements made in an apartment building.

To verify the functionality of the routes obtained through the ABC algorithm developed in this research, two experiments were carried out with two groups of volunteer workers who moved to transport materials along one of the floors of the apartment building under study (structure of seven stories high and departments with an average surface area of 100 m^2 each). The participants were randomly selected from a volunteer worker pool after requesting their participation as volunteers.

5.1. Evaluation of the Results Produced by the Model

Two test exercises were considered based on the time needed to transport materials between the two previously established nodes. The first test consisted of positioning the participants in a starting node, where they had to take a load and take it to the final node, for which their location was indicated but not the route to follow to reach the said node, so this exercise was called **No Guidance**. In the case of the second exercise, the participants were given the route information provided by the ABC model through boundaries on the floor that went from the initial node to the final node, where this event was called **With Guidance**.

On the other hand, there is a phenomenon known as the Hawthorne effect, which is inherently associated with the enthusiasm and greater attention paid by people who know they will be part of a study [59]. In this sense, to obtain a solid argument about the differences between two populations, it is crucial to assume their independence, which has been analyzed through the Hawthorne effect in studying humans [60]. In other words, the Hawthorne effect occurs when subjects are stimulated to make more significant efforts merely because of a study's novelty [61]. To minimize the adverse consequences of this effect, participants in this research were informed that they would be part of a study; nevertheless, neither the group with guidance nor the group without guidance were informed about who would be the control group or the study group. Thus, both groups showed the same interest and disposition to participate, avoiding possible biases associated with this effect.

Finally, because of the relevance of randomizing subjects in comparative studies [62], the researchers selected the participating workers from the whole pool of workers of the project under study (randomly picking one worker per crew) without any previous knowledge about their professional background or experience (at no time did the researchers talk to the workers' supervisors to obtain information about their working profiles).

5.1.1. No Guidance Group

Participants were taken to the floor, where the measurements were taken. They were positioned at the starting point (collection of material) and asked to transfer a 20 kg load from there to a certain point. During the entire transportation process of this first exercise, the participants followed different routes randomly based only on their perception of the area, for example, avoiding constructive elements (walls, columns). The times were timed from the moment the participants started walking from the starting point until they arrived at the unloading zone.

5.1.2. With Guidance Group

The participants restricted the route they should use on the floor to join the departure and arrival nodes, which was built based on the results of the ABC algorithm developed in this research. The times were recorded when the volunteers began moving from the initial node to the final unloading point.

5.2. Statistical Analysis

The Wilcoxon statistical test was used, with a significance level of 5%, to compare the movement times of workers. The Wilcoxon test is a nonparametric test that was selected because of its robustness, as parametric tests require several assumptions that this dataset would like to violate [63].

Table 1 shows the times obtained in seconds from left to right for the exercises without a route (**No guidance**) and with a route (**With Guidance**), in addition to the times provided by the model based on the ABC algorithm.

The respective hypotheses, according to the experiments carried out and the model, are as follows:

(a) Hypothesis for the comparison of times with and without guidance

H_0 = The travel times for the test participants without any previously known route are equal to those who participated in the experiment knowing a previously defined route.

Ha = The travel times for the test participants without any previously known route differ from those who participated in the experiment knowing a previously defined route.

(b) Hypothesis for the comparison of the times of the model versus those with no guidance

H_0 = The worker movement times given by the model are the same as those produced by the first movement exercise, that is, without a known route.

Ha = The worker movement times given by the model are different from those produced by the first movement exercise, that is, without a known route.

(c) Hypothesis for the comparison of the times of the model versus those with Guidance

H_0 = The worker movement times given by the model are the same as those produced by the second movement exercise, with a known route.

Ha = The worker movement times given by the model are different from those produced by the second movement exercise, with a known route.

Table 1. Measured times in the experiments.

Measurement	No Guidance	With Guidance	Model
	t (s)	t (s)	t (s)
1	11.81	12.45	13.10
2	10.23	10.56	13.50
3	30.27	13.47	14.30
4	13.08	13.10	12.90
5	13.40	14.25	12.90
6	19.90	12.24	12.90
7	20.35	14.53	11.30
8	21.70	13.27	13.50
9	25.27	13.67	13.00
10	22.45	11.56	12.90
11	25.41	13.09	13.20
12	17.82	12.96	12.60
13	21.68	10.23	11.90
14	18.39	11.99	13.00
15	13.83	11.94	12.90
16	13.28	13.16	13.50
17	15.38	11.64	12.10
18	17.46	12.39	13.00
19	16.73	11.80	12.90
20	13.58	13.27	12.60
Averages	18.10	12.58	12.90

As seen in Table 2, first, it can be concluded that the hypothesis of equality between the travel times of workers without a route (No Guidance) and with a route (With Guidance) is rejected (p-value < 0.0001), as there was a statistically significant difference that showed that the workers who followed the route provided by the model took less time than those who traveled without a previously defined route. In other words, the p-value < 0.0001 shows the significance of the differences between the workers who followed the path provided by the ABC algorithm (less travel time) in comparison with the workers who did not use the path (longer travel time).

Table 2. Results of the Wilcoxon test for differences in travel times.

Obs (1)	Obs (2)	N	Average (1)	Average (2)	Difference	SD	p-Value
No Guidance	With Guidance	20	18.10	12.58	5.52	5.16	<0.0001
No Guidance	Model	20	18.10	12.90	5.20	140.55	<0.0001
With Guidance	Model	20	12.58	12.90	−0.32	1.26	0.1482

Note: We did not correct for the Type I error inflation as significant p-values were an order of magnitude smaller than 0.05. While details were beyond the scope of this article, Type I error inflation occurs when multiple tests are conducted within a dataset that should be independently conducted [64].

Similarly, the hypothesis of equality between the travel times of workers without a designated route concerning the times given by the model was also rejected (p-value < 0.0001), with a statistically significant difference in favor of the travel times given by the model (ABC algorithm). This finding shows that workers who moved without a defined path took longer than the travel times provided by the model.

Finally, the last comparison corresponded to the times measured in the field for the workers who followed the route provided by the model in comparison with the times computed by the ABC algorithm, where there was no statistically significant difference between the times measured in the field and equality hypothesis was not rejected (p-value = 0.1482). Therefore, this no statistically significant difference allowed us to confirm the model's accuracy.

Thus, the proposed model made it possible to safely deliver routes for transporting material from one place to another, avoiding obstacles and abiding by social distancing rules, but at the same time, significantly reducing the travel times by following a defined route and maintaining order and organization in work areas. This finding is because the routes generated by the ABC algorithm developed in this study delivered more accurate travel information to the workers, thus decreasing the decisions to be made during the journey.

6. Conclusions and Recommendations

This research proposed a model for safe movement between different points within a construction site based on the behavior of a colony of artificial bees, whose algorithm is known as the ABC. The model was also validated in the field, finding no statistically significant differences between the times measured in the workers' movements in an actual project, and the times the developed model produced. The travel times using the routes obtained through the ABC algorithm proved significantly lower than those made by workers who moved freely without a predefined route. This finding is significant, as social distancing between workers in the ABC algorithm development was used as a restriction. This approach can be expanded to multiple source nodes associated with different types of materials to be moved on-site, combined with varying nodes of arrival (work fronts) whose trips are made simultaneously.

Pandemics such as COVID-19 have been a global disgrace, from which it must be learned how to improve the interaction between all human beings. This research contributes to the knowledge of how to work more effectively, comply with safety regulations, and, at the same time, generate advanced productivity in construction processes, specifically by increasing productivity while reducing and guaranteeing minimal interference between crews. This objective can only be reached if communication between work fronts or contractors is fluid, and the management of the H&S plan is more accessible to follow for its correct application and supervision.

In terms of limitations of the simulation approach presented in this research, despite being shown that the model studied was appropriate to provide routes combining shorter travel times and safety distances between workers when transporting materials in construction sites, some real-world uncertainties were not captured and could potentially influence results such as delays related to the occasional crowding of workers in the material stockpile area, or potential brief pauses of workers along the route to check their cellphones (usual practice in young workers). Finally, regarding future research, we recommend considering more simultaneous material stockpiles but maintaining the same simulation principles of this research, along with running the same problem presented in this study, but based on other swarm intelligence algorithms such as particle swarm optimization or ant colony optimization.

Author Contributions: Conceptualization, E.F., F.M., F.O. and D.A.; Methodology, E.F., I.C., A.O.-V. and F.M.; Software, I.C. and F.M.; Validation, E.F., F.O., A.O.-V. and D.A.; Formal analysis, I.C., F.M. and R.R.; Investigation, E.F., I.C., F.M. and R.R.; Resources, E.F., A.O.-V., F.M. and R.R.; Data curation, I.C., F.M. and R.R.; Writing—original draft preparation, E.F. and I.C.; Writing—review and editing, E.F., F.M., F.O. and D.A.; Visualization, I.C. and F.M.; Supervision, E.F., A.O.-V., F.O. and D.A.; Project administration, E.F. and A.O.-V.; Funding acquisition, E.F., F.M., R.R. and A.O.-V. All authors have read and agreed to the published version of the manuscript.

Funding: This research received no external funding.

Data Availability Statement: The original contributions presented in the study are included in the article, further inquiries can be directed to the corresponding authors.

Acknowledgments: The authors would like to acknowledge the support provided by the following universities: Universidad San Sebastián and Universidad del Bío-Bío, Chile; Universidad Panamericana, Mexico; and the University of Florida, USA.

Conflicts of Interest: The authors declare no conflicts of interest.

References

1. Fang, W.; Ding, L.; Love, P.E.D.; Luo, H.; Li, H.; Peña-Mora, F.; Zhong, B.; Zhou, C. Computer Vision Applications in Construction Safety Assurance. *Autom. Constr.* **2020**, *110*, 103013. [CrossRef]
2. Wang, Y.; Thangasamy, V.K.; Hou, Z.; Tiong, R.L.K.; Zhang, L. Collaborative Relationship Discovery in BIM Project Delivery: A Social Network Analysis Approach. *Autom. Constr.* **2020**, *114*, 103147. [CrossRef]
3. Abbsaian-Hosseini, S.A.; Liu, M.; Hsiang, S.M. Social Network Analysis for Construction Crews. *Int. J. Constr. Manag.* **2019**, *19*, 113–127. [CrossRef]
4. Naoum, S.G. Factors Influencing Labor Productivity on Construction Sites: A State-of-the-Art Literature Review and a Survey. *Int. J. Product. Perform. Manag.* **2016**, *65*, 401–421. [CrossRef]
5. Chu, D.K.; Akl, E.A.; Duda, S.; Solo, K.; Yaacoub, S.; Schünemann, H.J.; Chu, D.K.; Akl, E.A.; El-harakeh, A.; Bognanni, A.; et al. Physical Distancing, Face Masks, and Eye Protection to Prevent Person-to-Person Transmission of SARS-CoV-2 and COVID-19: A Systematic Review and Meta-Analysis. *Lancet* **2020**, *395*, 1973–1987. [CrossRef]
6. Pan, Y.; Zhang, L. Roles of Artificial Intelligence in Construction Engineering and Management: A Critical Review and Future Trends. *Autom. Constr.* **2021**, *122*, 103517. [CrossRef]
7. Nguyen, P.T. Construction Site Layout Planning and Safety Management Using Fuzzy-Based Bee Colony Optimization Model. *Neural Comput. Appl.* **2021**, *33*, 5821–5842. [CrossRef]
8. Chi, S.; Han, S. Analyses of Systems Theory for Construction Accident Prevention with Specific Reference to OSHA Accident Reports. *Int. J. Proj. Manag.* **2013**, *31*, 1027–1041. [CrossRef]
9. Bhole, S.A. Safety Problems and Injuries on Construction Site: A Review. *Int. J. Eng. Tech.* **2016**, *2*, 24–35.
10. Naticchia, B.; Vaccarini, M.; Carbonari, A. A Monitoring System for Real-Time Interference Control on Large Construction Sites. *Autom. Constr.* **2013**, *29*, 148–160. [CrossRef]
11. Thomas, H.R.; Riley, D.R.; Sinha, S.K. Fundamental Principles for Avoiding Congested Work Areas—A Case Study. *Pract. Period. Struct. Des. Constr.* **2006**, *11*, 197–205. [CrossRef]
12. Seppänen, O. *Empirical Research on the Success of Production Control in Building Construction Projects*; Helsinki University of Technology: Helsinki, Finland, 2009.
13. Seidgar, H.; Kiani, M.; Fazlollahtabar, H. Genetic and Artificial Bee Colony Algorithms for Scheduling of Multi-Skilled Manpower in Combined Manpower-Vehicle Routing Problem. *Prod. Manuf. Res.* **2016**, *4*, 133–151. [CrossRef]
14. Gamil, Y.; Alhagar, A. The Impact of Pandemic Crisis on the Survival of Construction Industry: A Case of COVID-19. *Mediterr. J. Soc. Sci.* **2020**, *11*, 122–128. [CrossRef]
15. WHO. *World Health Organisation Advice for the Public: Coronavirus Disease (COVID-19)*; WHO: Geneva, Switzerland, 2023.
16. Alsharef, A.; Banerjee, S.; Uddin, S.M.J.; Albert, A.; Jaselskis, E. Early Impacts of the COVID-19 Pandemic on the United States Construction Industry. *Int. J. Environ. Res. Public Health* **2021**, *18*, 1559. [CrossRef] [PubMed]
17. Alwasel, A.; Abdel-Rahman, E.M.; Haas, C.T.; Lee, S. Experience, Productivity, and Musculoskeletal Injury among Masonry Workers. *J. Constr. Eng. Manag.* **2017**, *143*, 05017003. [CrossRef]
18. Forcael, E.; Morales, H.; Agdas, D.; Rodríguez, C.; León, C. Risk Identification in the Chilean Tunneling Industry. *Eng. Manag. J.* **2018**, *30*, 203–215. [CrossRef]
19. Araya, F. Modeling the Spread of COVID-19 on Construction Workers: An Agent-Based Approach. *Saf. Sci.* **2021**, *133*, 105022. [CrossRef]
20. Xue, K.; Hossain, M.U.; Liu, M.; Ma, M.; Zhang, Y.; Hu, M.; Chen, X.; Cao, G. BIM Integrated LCA for Promoting Circular Economy towards Sustainable Construction: An Analytical Review. *Sustainability* **2021**, *13*, 1310. [CrossRef]
21. Agdas, D.; Warne, D.J.; Osio-Norgaard, J.; Masters, F.J. Utility of Genetic Algorithms for Solving Large-Scale Construction Time-Cost Trade-Off Problems. *J. Comput. Civ. Eng.* **2018**, *32*, 04017072. [CrossRef]
22. Sonmez, R.; Aminbakhsh, S.; Atan, T. Activity Uncrashing Heuristic with Noncritical Activity Rescheduling Method for the Discrete Time-Cost Trade-Off Problem. *J. Constr. Eng. Manag.* **2020**, *146*, 04020084. [CrossRef]
23. Jaillet, P.; Qi, J.; Sim, M. Routing Optimization Under Uncertainty. *Oper. Res.* **2016**, *64*, 186–200. [CrossRef]
24. Elshaboury, N.; Marzouk, M. Optimizing Construction and Demolition Waste Transportation for Sustainable Construction Projects. *Eng. Constr. Archit. Manag.* **2021**, *28*, 2411–2425. [CrossRef]

25. Nolz, P.C. Optimizing Construction Schedules and Material Deliveries in City Logistics: A Case Study from the Building Industry. *Flex. Serv. Manuf. J.* **2021**, *33*, 846–878. [CrossRef]
26. Zhang, S.Z.; Lee, C.K.M. An Improved Artificial Bee Colony Algorithm for the Capacitated Vehicle Routing Problem. In Proceedings of the 2015 IEEE International Conference on Systems, Man, and Cybernetics, Hong Kong, China, 9–12 October 2015; IEEE: New York, NY, USA, 2015; pp. 2124–2128.
27. Beni, G.; Wang, J. Swarm Intelligence in Cellular Robotic Systems. In Robots and Biological Systems: Towards a New Bionics? Springer: Berlin/Heidelberg, Germany, 1993; pp. 703–712.
28. Lhee, S.C.; Issa, R.R.A.; Flood, I. Using Particle Swarm Optimization to Predict Cost Contingency on Transportation Construction Projects. *J. Inf. Technol. Constr.* **2016**, *21*, 504–516.
29. Hussein, M.; Eltoukhy, A.E.E.; Darko, A.; Eltawil, A. Simulation-Optimization for the Planning of Off-Site Construction Projects: A Comparative Study of Recent Swarm Intelligence Metaheuristics. *Sustainability* **2021**, *13*, 13551. [CrossRef]
30. Muñoz, M.A.; López, J.A.; Caicedo, E.F. Swarm Intelligence: Problem-Solving Societies (a Review). *Rev. Ing. E Investig.* **2008**, *28*, 119–130. [CrossRef]
31. Bonabeau, E.; Dorigo, M.; Theraulaz, G. *Swarm Intelligence: From Natural to Artificial Systems*, 1st ed.; Oxford University Press Inc.: New York, NY, USA, 1999; ISBN 978-0-19-513158-1.
32. Martinoli, A. Collective Complexity out of Individual Simplicity. *Artif. Life* **2001**, *7*, 315–319. [CrossRef]
33. Fisher, L. *The Perfect Swarm: The Science of Complexity in Everyday Life*; Basic Books: New York, NY, USA, 2009.
34. Yang, S.; Wang, H.; Xu, Y.; Guo, Y.; Pan, L.; Zhang, J.; Guo, X.; Meng, D.; Wang, J. A Coupled Simulated Annealing and Particle Swarm Optimization Reliability-Based Design Optimization Strategy under Hybrid Uncertainties. *Mathematics* **2023**, *11*, 4790. [CrossRef]
35. Karaboga, D. *An Idea Based on Honey Bee Swarm for Numerical Optimization*; Erciyes University, Engineering Faculty, Computer Engineering Department: Kayseri, Turkey, 2005.
36. Anderson, C. Swarm Intelligence: From Natural to Artificial Systems. Eric Bonabeau, Marco Dorigo, Guy Theraulaz. *Q. Rev. Biol.* **2001**, *76*, 268–269. [CrossRef]
37. Jeanne, R.L. The Evolution of the Organization of Work in Social Insects. *Monit. Zool. Ital.* **1986**, *20*, 119–133.
38. Millonas, M.M. Swarms, Phase Transitions, and Collective Intelligence. *Artif. Life III* **1994**, *17*, 417–445.
39. Dorigo, M.; Birattari, M.; Stützle, T. Ant Colony Optimization Artificial Ants as a Computational Intelligence Technique. *IEEE Comput. Intell. Mag.* **2006**, *1*, 28–39. [CrossRef]
40. Kennedy, J.; Eberhart, R. Particle Swarm Optimization. In Proceedings of the ICNN'95—International Conference on Neural Networks, Perth, WA, Australia, 27 November–1 December 1995; IEEE: New York, NY, USA, 1995; Volume 4, pp. 1942–1948.
41. Akay, B.; Karaboga, D. A Modified Artificial Bee Colony Algorithm for Real-Parameter Optimization. *Inf. Sci.* **2012**, *192*, 120–142. [CrossRef]
42. Akbari, R.; Hedayatzadeh, R.; Ziarati, K.; Hassanizadeh, B. A Multi-Objective Artificial Bee Colony Algorithm. *Swarm Evol. Comput.* **2012**, *2*, 39–52. [CrossRef]
43. Mahmoodabadi, M.J.; Shahangian, M.M. A New Multi-Objective Artificial Bee Colony Algorithm for Optimal Adaptive Robust Controller Design. *IETE J. Res.* **2022**, *68*, 1251–1264. [CrossRef]
44. Zou, W.; Zhu, Y.; Chen, H.; Zhang, B. Solving Multi-objective Optimization Problems Using Artificial Bee Colony Algorithm. *Discret. Dyn. Nat. Soc.* **2011**, *2011*, 569784. [CrossRef]
45. Rao, R.V.; Patel, V.K. Optimization of Mechanical Draft Counter Flow Wet-Cooling Tower Using Artificial Bee Colony Algorithm. *Energy Convers. Manag.* **2011**, *52*, 2611–2622. [CrossRef]
46. Şencan Şahin, A.; Kiliç, B.; Kiliç, U. Design and Economic Optimization of Shell and Tube Heat Exchangers Using Artificial Bee Colony (ABC) Algorithm. *Energy Convers. Manag.* **2011**, *52*, 3356–3362. [CrossRef]
47. Mandal, S.K.; Chan, F.T.S.; Tiwari, M.K. Leak Detection of Pipeline: An Integrated Approach of Rough Set Theory and Artificial Bee Colony Trained SVM. *Expert. Syst. Appl.* **2012**, *39*, 3071–3080. [CrossRef]
48. Sonmez, M. Artificial Bee Colony Algorithm for Optimization of Truss Structures. *Appl. Soft Comput.* **2011**, *11*, 2406–2418. [CrossRef]
49. Sonmez, M. Discrete Optimum Design of Truss Structures Using Artificial Bee Colony Algorithm. *Struct. Multidiscip. Optim.* **2011**, *43*, 85–97. [CrossRef]
50. Prayogo, D.; Cheng, M.-Y.; Wu, Y.-W.; Redi, A.A.N.P.; Yu, V.F.; Persada, S.F.; Nadlifatin, R. A Novel Hybrid Metaheuristic Algorithm for Optimization of Construction Management Site Layout Planning. *Algorithms* **2020**, *13*, 117. [CrossRef]
51. Fang, Y.; Ng, S.T. Genetic Algorithm for Determining the Construction Logistics of Precast Components. *Eng. Constr. Archit. Manag.* **2019**, *26*, 2289–2306. [CrossRef]
52. Almahameed, B.; Bisharah, M. Applying Machine Learning and Particle Swarm Optimization for Predictive Modeling and Cost Optimization in Construction Project Management. *Asian J. Civ. Eng.* **2024**, *25*, 1281–1294. [CrossRef]
53. Hoang, N.-D.; Huynh, T.-C.; Tran, X.-L.; Tran, V.-D. A Novel Approach for Detection of Pavement Crack and Sealed Crack Using Image Processing and Salp Swarm Algorithm Optimized Machine Learning. *Adv. Civ. Eng.* **2022**, *2022*, 9193511. [CrossRef]
54. Abbasianjahromi, H.; Mohammadi Golafshani, E.; Aghakarimi, M. A Prediction Model for Safety Performance of Construction Sites Using a Linear Artificial Bee Colony Programming Approach. *Int. J. Occup. Saf. Ergon.* **2022**, *28*, 1265–1280. [CrossRef] [PubMed]

55. Abu-Mouti, F.S.; El-Hawary, M.E. Optimal Distributed Generation Allocation and Sizing in Distribution Systems via Artificial Bee Colony Algorithm. *IEEE Trans. Power Deliv.* **2011**, *26*, 2090–2101. [CrossRef]
56. Karaboga, D.; Akay, B. A Modified Artificial Bee Colony (ABC) Algorithm for Constrained Optimization Problems. *Appl. Soft Comput.* **2011**, *11*, 3021–3031. [CrossRef]
57. Sarkar, M.; Julai, S.; Wen Tong, C.; Toha, S. Effectiveness of Nature-Inspired Algorithms Using ANFIS for Blade Design Optimization and Wind Turbine Efficiency. *Symmetry* **2019**, *11*, 456. [CrossRef]
58. Karaboga, D.; Basturk, B. A Powerful and Efficient Algorithm for Numerical Function Optimization: Artificial Bee Colony (ABC) Algorithm. *J. Glob. Optim.* **2007**, *39*, 459–471. [CrossRef]
59. Forcael, E.; Glagola, C.; González, V. Incorporation of Computer Simulations into Teaching Linear Scheduling Techniques. *J. Prof. Issues Eng. Educ. Pract.* **2012**, *138*, 21–30. [CrossRef]
60. Hjalmarson, M.A.; Herman, G.L.; Douglas, K.A. Considerations for Engineering Education Research Using Quantitative Methods. In *International Handbook of Engineering Education Research*; Johri, A., Ed.; Routledge: New York, NY, USA, 2023; pp. 638–659, ISBN 9781003287483.
61. Tamur, M.; Kusumah, Y.S.; Juandi, D.; Wijaya, T.T.; Nurjaman, A.; Samura, A.O. Hawthorne Effect and Mathematical Software Based Learning: A Meta-Analysis Study. *J. Phys. Conf. Ser.* **2021**, *1806*, 012072. [CrossRef]
62. McCarney, R.; Warner, J.; Iliffe, S.; van Haselen, R.; Griffin, M.; Fisher, P. The Hawthorne Effect: A Randomised, Controlled Trial. *BMC Med. Res. Methodol.* **2007**, *7*, 30. [CrossRef]
63. Devore, J.L. Probability and Statistics for Engineering and the Sciences. *Biometrics* **1991**, *47*, 1638. [CrossRef]
64. Good, P.I.; Hardin, J.W. *Common Errors in Statistics (and How to Avoid Them)*, 3rd ed.; John Wiley & Sons: Hoboken, NJ, USA, 2008.

MDPI AG
Grosspeteranlage 5
4052 Basel
Switzerland
Tel.: +41 61 683 77 34

Mathematics Editorial Office
E-mail: mathematics@mdpi.com
www.mdpi.com/journal/mathematics

www.ingramcontent.com/pod-product-compliance
Lightning Source LLC
Chambersburg PA
CBHW061601210926
51850CB00009B/2181
9783725871469